MW01434626

BYTE's DOS Programmer's Cookbook

Craig Menefee, Lenny Bailes, Nick Anis

Osborne **McGraw-Hill**

Berkeley • New York • St. Louis • San Francisco
Auckland • Bogotá • Hamburg • London • Madrid • Mexico City • Milan
Montreal • New Delhi • Panama City • Paris • São Paulo
Singapore • Sydney • Tokyo • Toronto

Osborne **McGraw-Hill**
2600 Tenth Street
Berkeley, California 94710
U.S.A.

For information on translations or book distributors outside of the U.S.A., please write to Osborne McGraw-Hill at the above address.

BYTE's DOS Programmer's Cookbook

1234567890 DOC 9987654

ISBN 0-07-882048-0

Publisher
Lawrence Levitsky

Acquisitions Editor
Jeffrey M. Pepper

Project Editor
Nancy McLaughlin

Technical Editor
John Heilborn

Copy Editor
Kathryn Hashimoto

Proofreader
Stefany Otis

Indexer
Sami Menefee

Computer Designer
Lance Ravella

Series Design
Ruffin Prevost

Cover Design
Davison Design

This book is for Jeremy Selden and Ethan Craig Menefee—names that span four generations.

—Craig Menefee

To all the shareware hackers who have made this book possible.

—Lenny Bailes

My dedication goes to Craig Menefee, who deserves every consideration for having survived this ordeal.

—Nick Anis

Contents at a Glance

Contents

Part 3: Do Not Disturb: Gone Hacking

Acknowledgments

Like any book, *BYTE's DOS Programmer's Cookbook* has benefited from many people's willingness to pitch in and help. This one in particular came under its hardest deadline early on, when several people who had planned to participate in the effort full-time found themselves unable to, for a variety of reasons. Even then, they helped the authors find the mix of best-selling and lesser-known, but interesting or exemplary, software and code that wound up on the CD-ROM includedwith this book. Under the deadline, many people put aside other commitments to jump in late and fill gaps in the project, providing expertise in a wide variety of areas.

First, we'd like to thank Sami Menefee for her painstaking review of all the authors' proofs, and for putting up with the long, deadline grind of 4 A.M. work sessions that her husband Craig slides into when a book comes due. Sami is always game for any adventure, and always contributes more than her fair share.

We'd also like to thank Keith Graham, longtime DOS utility hackmeister and programmer extraordinaire from Lockheed, for his insights into where DOS fits into the overall programming universe, and for reviewing dozens of programs in various parts of the book. Thanks also to Rob Rosenberger, keeper of the Association of Shareware Professionals (ASP) software catalog, who let us tap into his many years of experience as a shareware professional for the important insights and information on that topic in the first three chapters.

Steve Hudgik, president of HomeCraft Software, helped us put together the programs and much of the body of text dealing with data compression and encryption (Chapter 5). John Heilborn, known to millions of readers as "Dr. John" of the popular "Ask Dr. John" column, took time off from starting an important new computer newsletter to help out with material on printer utilities (Chapter 9). John Ribar, author of the Windows volume in this Cookbook series, also pitched in on the *DOS Cookbook* with programs and notes on video (Chapter 11) and on DOS interrupts (Chapter 12). Steve Nameroff did the lion's share of testing programs and writing descriptions for a truly fine collection of assemblers, disassemblers, and associated programs (Chapter 13), and provided a thoughtful discussion of applying the finishing touches to a program and taking it to market (Chapter 14).

Walnut Creek Software (of Concord, not Walnut Creek, California) earned our gratitude for their professional competence and their willingness to work late, under deadline, mastering the rather complex CD-ROM that you'll find at the back of this book. They also provided a front-end, adapted from their own CD-ROM of the Internet SIMTEL software collection, that makes it a breeze to select any software you want, specify a directory for it, and unpack it automatically. This program does *nothing* strange or unnecessary to your boot files, makes no arrogant assumptions about your target disk, and in no way violates the bounds of polite computer behavior.

While many of the files on the CD-ROM came from places around the Internet or from small BBSes, most were gathered from more organized venues. One of the biggest and best-maintained collections we know of is on Channel 1 in Cambridge, Massachusetts. For good reason, Channel 1 is widely considered the best large subscription BBS/small information service in the U.S. We particularly want to mention Tess Heder, who co-manages this incredibly rich motherlode of electronic access, for providing us with sample QIC tapes of various file areas of interest to this book. Her sole restriction was that she wanted the tapes back when we were finished. (Tapes are not cheap.) Thanks, Tess, and we trust UPS brought your tapes safely back to you!

We also owe huge thanks to the more "traditional" (does that word apply to PCs?) information services: CompuServe, America Online, Delphi, and GEnie. All maintain large, well-organized, intelligent collections of shareware programs, public domain ware, demos, and other files. They also are gold mines of expert advice in just about any field, and they made their resources freely available for this book and for several other projects. Delphi in particular provided a structured and expertly guided access to the heaving, ill-differentiated virtual organic mass that is the Internet.

"I-Netonauts" occasionally excoriate Delphi and the other information services for letting unwashed, non-UNIX PC users onto the Net, but such criticism seems to us elitist and ill-considered. Delphi and, increasingly, the others (AOL in particular) provide a genuine service to their users, and if in the process they add useful structure to Internet access, so much the better. Providing organized portals and useful contexts is at least as worthwhile as further broadening the Internet's indiscriminate bandwidth.

We deeply appreciate copy editor Kathryn Hashimoto's successful efforts to smooth the many rough edges in the manuscript without hampering the flow. The same for Nancy McLaughlin, known on the net as "McLaugh," who made serene (mostly) this book's hectic production endgame. She accomplished this unlikely task by taking unto herself, and managing, all the chaos we worked so hard to inject into Osborne's butter-smooth processes. Nancy also kept the beacon of Political Correctness and Decency burning bright, no mean feat for a book so steeped in hackish irreverence. By unplugging some of the manuscript's excess "attitude" (despite harumphs, growls, snarls and yowls from us) she earned all the credit for making this work almost acceptable in polite society.

Finally, how can we describe our debt to Osborne's Editor-in-Chief, Jeff Pepper? His ability to create islands of calm in the midst of havoc defies imagination and, probably, the laws of science. He's too nice to have made a deal with the devil, so we can only assume this magical ability was heaven-sent. Thanks, Jeff.

Introduction

MS-DOS is probably the perfect operating system for a hacker. Many programmers we know love programming in Windows or OS/2, and we consider UNIX a great environment too. Even the Mac has been made amenable to the ministrations of problem-oriented individuals who program. Either we or the people who contributed to putting this book together (see the Acknowledgements) have used VMS, TSO, CMS, CP/M, and a few others as well. Each has its advantages and disadvantages, but when it comes to serious hacking, we'll take simple old DOS every time.

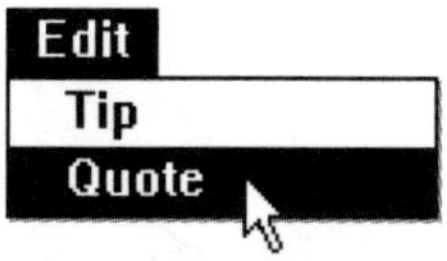
Edit
Tip
Quote

My younger sister hated computers until I taught her to play Commander Keen. Now I can't get her off it long enough for me to do my homework.
—Danny B., a 16-year-old programmer

There are good reasons to object to MS-DOS, but hating it (as some profess to do) strikes us is an awful waste of energy. How can you spend time hating an operating system that does practically nothing? We love MS-DOS not for what it does, but for what it doesn't do. DOS is a program loader with disk services. Period. It does practically nothing but give you a command line for loading programs and a simple way to manage disk space and files. When you get down to how DOS interacts with the silicon, there's hardly anything there to hate. Might as well love it.

We know we are not alone in feeling this way. Some 70-to-110 million DOS users (depending upon whom you listen to) must agree with us. The power of 386+ machines with fast processors may have taken many of the major applications out of DOS and into Windows or OS/2, and there is much to be said for both GUI systems. But some things are simply done best at the command line—like hacking out elegant, original solutions to low-level problems, managing files and directories, and in other ways working close to a system's silicon logic or to a hard drive's magnetic metal oxides.

Of course, some of us just prefer the speed and efficiency of DOS, no matter how fast our machines may be or how huge our memory resources. The spare, minimalist approach that DOS takes has its own appeal.

A minimalist approach is also the main virtue of UNIX. A DOS hacker can feel right at home programming in UNIX because, again, there is so little to it. UNIX is rich in utility programs, or so we often hear, but then so is MS-DOS. That DOS is a single-user system simplifies a programmer's life. If you want to lock the system or trash the disk, it's your privilege to do so. There is no Big Brother operating system to keep you from hurting yourself. Instead, DOS pretty much leaves you alone to do whatever you want. As far as we're concerned, that makes MS-DOS the operating system of choice.

To be fair, leaving you alone is a privilege UNIX doesn't give you, because it can't. As a multi-user system, UNIX must protect users from each other as well as from wayward programs. To do that, it must act like Big Brother, watching over your shoulder, stepping in when you screw up. Since so much hacking involves finding new and clever ways around and through problems, the UNIX hacker often gets a virtual ruler across the hacking knuckles for not respecting conventions.

The Hackish Nature

Hackers are by nature not very good at respecting conventions, whether of 0-Ring origin or the well-meant warnings of family, teachers, or peers. Conformity to other people's notions of what is "correct" is not usually a hacker's strong point. Mrs. Grundy—Thomas Morton's 19th Century character who tsk-tsked at anything fun, unconventional, or slightly gonzo in life—would have sternly disapproved of the average hacker, whose attitudes would not typically be buttoned up and constipated enough to suit her.

This book is not nearly as gonzo as much of the hackish literature out there in places like the Internet, but we do hope it is not buttoned up and constipated enough to make Mrs. Grundy comfortable, either. Where we express opinions in the text, we hope you'll bear in mind that's all they are—opinions. Strong opinions seem to go with the territory when you deal with DOS, DOS programmers, and anyone of hackish frame of mind. We are not what we'd consider accomplished hackers ourselves, except in many of our attitudes, but we appreciate what hackers—and all manner of other accomplished programmers—do.

For this book, we did our best to maintain the hackish attitude and ignore the gray-toned conventions of Mrs. Grundy. We hope you will find the result free-wheeling, informative, and easy to read. But the primary focus is on elegant, original, unusual, or exemplary programs, utilities and code—mostly in C and ASM—that we hope programmers of all stripes, not just anarchistic hackers, will enjoy.

How This Book Works

This Cookbook is organized into three parts, in roughly increasing order of technical depth. We say "roughly" because there's another undercurrent to the book: We like shareware and public domain programming, and we like the programmers who work there. So a lot of this cookbook has to do not with how to create good programs (we learn from hackers, not the other way 'round), but with how to create programs that can succeed in the shareware marketplace. We start, in Part I, with a discussion of the marketplace, including tips on which programs will succeed and which will probably have difficulty. In Chapter 3, "Walking the Wires," we offer tools to make it easier to access "cyberspace," the electronic virtual market where more than half of all registered shareware users hang out. Chapter 3 is also where the first programs on the CD-ROM are described. (See "Quotes, Tips, and Hack Facts" in the next section for pointers on finding the descriptions).

Part II, "Tools for the Hackmeister," offers some great tools for working programmers. These include a rich selection of superior editors, compresson tools needed by any shareware program author, and a series of tools for managing your system's disk storage, memory, and I/O ports. Part II finishes with some interesting printer utilities and a large grab-bag of assorted goodies for the programming connoisseur.

In Part III, "Do Not Disturb: Gone Hacking," we cover working with video and using DOS interrupts, and we finally wind out the book with a selection of tools designed to help you take a finished product to market effectively.

The programs on the CD-ROM are described in detail, with instructions on how to access them, in the Appendices.

Quotes, Tips and Hack Facts

Throughout the book, you'll find boxed information and other supplemental material scattered through the text and in the margins. These items are variously labeled Quotes, Tips, or Hack Facts. The quotes are often there just for fun, or because they are pertinent somehow to what the text covers at the point where they appear. The tips are just that—little juicy bits of info on a current topic or program that didn't quite fit into the text, or that we wanted to emphasise so you wouldn't miss it.

The "Hack Facts" boxes are what to look for when you need to find a particular program. They appear next to each main program where it is introduced, and serve double duty as the not-quite-a-headline that introduces the program itself. Each "Hack Facts" box gives the crucial information about a file, including in order:

- The program name and version
- The author's name, company (if any) and address
- Contact information that may include voice phone, BBS, electronic information service or Internet address, telephone order number, and more
- The size of the pertinent file as it is stored on the CD-ROM
- The price of registering your copy (if it's shareware and you decide to keep using it)
- The name of the file or files on the CD-ROM

With all this information at your fingertips, we're betting you won't have a great deal of trouble finding the program on the CD-ROM and then either contacting the author or registering the program.

So read on, try the programs (all public domain, shareware, or functional demos), play with the sample code, and then get out there and hack. DOS is a great place to do it.

011010 11000110 0011010 11001001 100010001

11010 11000110 0011010 11001001 100010001

0011010 11001001 100010001

part 1

At the Front End...

1

Hackers: Artists of the Good Stuff

Hacking's alive! Long live the hacker!

In the popular mind, a "hacker" is a pimply-faced, post-adolescent male who has graduated from school at least one year ahead of his peers, hasn't kissed a girl, and still lives with his parents. He holds down two part-time jobs, one at Radio Shack and the other at Taco Bell or McDonald's. He writes computer viruses for a hobby and consumes mass quantities of pizza and Coke™. If he reads anything other than computer technical journals, it's comic books and science fiction. He's about a half bubble off true, with an unfocused and slightly shifty look about him.

But we prefer to regard hackers under the *original* definition: A person who loves computers and wants to push them to the limit. Hackers want to know everything about their computers and they want to develop software they can call their own. A good hacker is a creative artist in his or (let us not forget) her own right.

Hacking is a bit like cooking. The more you know, the better you are, but to some extent you're always improvising. Many people who like to prepare food buy cookbooks to help them, but they know the book can't do the cooking. If you're a hacker, you like to prepare programs and tweak your system. This book is like a cookbook for hackers: It will point the way toward better code and a faster, leaner system to run it on, but it won't substitute for the hacking that makes a program or a system *right*. But then, if you didn't enjoy doing that part of it yourself, you never would have bought, borrowed, or stolen this book.

Now, some food preparers will learn enough to get jobs as chefs, if they have the knack and the determination. Others will only go on to jobs as short-order cooks, but they'll get PAID to do something they really like to do. And some will continue cooking for the pure fun of doing it—they may never even consider taking jobs as cooks, turning their hobby into (eek!) work.

Hackers have the same choices. Some learn enough to start up their own companies. (Bill Gates did, for instance, and he hasn't done badly.) Others may go on to make a few grand—sometimes quite a few grand—each year at their hacking. They'll work out of their basements or maybe at some software house, getting PAID to do something they really like to do. And some others may just keep hacking away for the sport of it.

Shareware and the Hacker

This brings us to the world of shareware, which is a kind of utopia for hackers.

Shareware is programs or code to which someone holds a copyright; it may or may not require that you pay a fee to the author if you keep using it. When no fee is required, it's still called shareware, because the term "freeware" is copyrighted. (We'll call it NoFeeWare just to honor the copyright.) The point is that hackers often copyright their work to keep it from being changed or, sometimes, just to put their name on it, like a "Kilroy Was Here" sign. Then they put it "out there" for anyone to use, usually with some "no fair charging for this" provisions attached.

Public domain or *PD* material, on the other hand, is just that—uncopyrighted, in the public domain, and free for anyone to use, improve, or meddle with. No one owns it and everyone owns it. Lots of very good and innovative hacks, such as the Xmodem file transfer protocol by Ward Christiansen, have been dedicated by their authors to the public domain. PD material represents the untrammeled attitudes of a true hacker (in the *best* sense of the term, Ward!).

Hackers love both PD ware and shareware. It gives them an affordable place to begin their art. Even the concept of shareware was more or less hacked together. Back in 1982, three ordinary guys started a software marketing revolution by giving copies of their programs to anyone who would try them out (see "When Shareware Was New," just ahead). They couldn't afford massive advertising campaigns, so they figured they'd just *give* their work to people and ask for a donation if it proved useful. That way they could keep their focus where they liked it, on the hacking itself.

People loved the idea, and the "small donations" quickly added up. Other hackers liked the concept and joined the fray, and the computer software market hasn't been the same since. Not a bad outcome for some guys working out of dens and basements.

When Shareware Was New

The term "shareware" was coined by Bob Wallace, author of PC-Write and one of the genre's early successes. Wallace's company QuickSoft is, alas, no longer with us. It fell by the wayside when faster, more powerful processors made ASCII-based word processors obsolete. But many hackers still use PC-Write to prepare their documentation, and the last non-menued version, v. 3.02, is a recognized classic.

Wallace's term *shareware* meant that he shared a portion of the registration fees with PC-Write users who recruited others. The term quickly became generic for all "try before you buy" software when Wallace dedicated the term to the public domain. Several attempts have been made since then to copyright the term, but Wallace ensured it would stay generic when he made it a PD term.

The two other "guys in basements" were Jim Button, founder of ButtonWare and author of PC-File, and Andrew Fluegelman, author of PC-Talk. Fluegelman used the term *freeware,* meaning freely distributed, but then he trademarked the term for his publishing company, *The Headlands Press,* which meant that no one else could use it. That's fine, since "freeware" is a misleading term anyway for software that people are expected to pay for.

Shareware is now a multimillion dollar institution that has spread around the world, to the continuing surprise of retailers and to the delight of hackers and other incipient anarchists.

Shareware, This Book, and You

This is a shareware book, because everything we cover in these pages and everything you'll find on the CD-ROM that comes with it is either shareware or in the public domain. You're invited to try it all and keep what you like. Heck of a deal.

but just for anyone who hasn't run into the concept before, let's get something straight: Shareware is *commercial software.* If there is a registration fee, the people behind these programs hope to earn money for their efforts, just as if their products sat on store shelves. The shareware concept is simply another way to market programs, so we'll often use the word "retail" rather than "commercial" to describe software of the sort that is sold at computer stores.

Shareware is "try before you buy" software, not "try after you buy and hope you like it" software. You usually get 30 to 90 days to test-drive a program before you have to pay for it. No salesman hangs over your shoulder giving bad advice. Documentation comes in text files included with the application. If a program doesn't meet your needs, you don't have to pay for it; you just stop using it.

Advertising of shareware happens largely by "word of disk." As part of their software copyrights, shareware authors encourage you to give copies to others for evaluation purposes. Whenever you pass a program along to friends and colleagues, you help to advertise it. By passing it around, you help the author make a living and you help to keep advertising and marketing costs down—and that's the crux of the savings that shareware represents. When an author doesn't spend thousands of dollars advertising a product in the national magazines or sending sales reps around to the big software stores, that cost doesn't get passed on to the user. That's how authors manage to sell programs worth hundreds of dollars for the low prices that shareware registration usually costs.

When you decide to keep a program, you register it by sending a payment to the author. Sometimes the author will then issue a "license" to continue using the software, but it comes to the same thing. By paying a small fee, you have helped keep superb software available to everyone at bargain basement prices.

To Sweeten the Deal

When you register a program, you often receive added benefits. Most registrations come with some combination of telephone, fax, and computer bulletin board support. Many authors send professionally printed manuals to registered users. You may also receive additional programs or utilities to enhance a program's power or a serial number to unlock additional features that enhance, but are not critical to, using the program. The documentation included with a program will describe the benefits of registering. Here are some common examples.

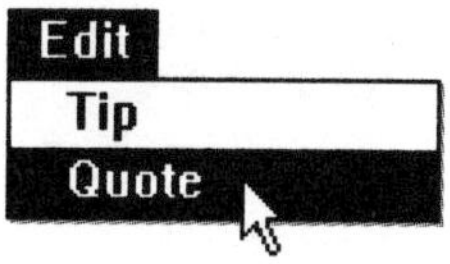
Edit
Tip
Quote

Shareware authors are more responsive to their customers. Try calling Bill Gates on a dark and stormy night when your program won't run.

—Steve Manes, author, Magpie BBS

Free Upgrades or Shared Fees

Many (but not all) shareware authors offer free upgrades with a registration. It's like getting a new car just by trading in last year's model. A few authors let you use all future versions of their programs. Others set a limit on how many times the customer may upgrade for free.

It's not common, but some shareware authors pay commissions to registered users who get others to register. This was the original meaning of shareware, but few authors do this anymore. The user tracking, tax reporting, and other problems can be hard to deal with.

Money Back Guarantees

Some shareware authors confidently offer a money back guarantee on their software. They will refund your registration fee, no questions asked, if you return everything in good condition within 30 days (some give you as much as 90 days). This lets you try a version, register for the extra benefits or capabilities if you like it, and then get a refund if, say, a fully registered version doesn't come up to your expectations.

Program Source Code and Customizing

Some benefits are absolute gold to hackers. For example, an author may provide a program's source code on registration. Sometimes you'll have to pay extra for this, but as a learning aid or just to produce a grow-your-own privately customized version, you can't beat a deal like that.

Customizing
An author may offer custom programming options in lieu of releasing a program's source code. This can be a blessing if a company needs a customized application.

Good Guy Status
Finally, sometimes a program's documentation will mention a *clear conscience* as one registration benefit. This is for people who weren't paying attention in kindergarten and whose mothers never mentioned that one can tell right from wrong. These people probably don't mean any harm; they're just, well, *social oafs* (for want of a better term). If you know someone like this, please help them by mentioning the benefits of registering their shareware.

Benefits for the Authors

As we've seen, shareware has enormous benefits for users. But what about program authors? Why would they want to go the shareware route, assuming their programs are even worth looking at? When you consider the schlock that some companies manage to sell for hundreds of dollars, you might wonder if the average shareware author's elevator goes all the way to the top.

Program authors like shareware for a variety of good reasons. They get to avoid the worst headaches of retail marketing. They can keep a regular job and sell their shareware products on the side. They don't have to be overly concerned with marketing, packaging, and advertising. Best of all, their work is their own. When they give birth to a software baby, no one can force them to raise it a certain way. Hackers are creative people, and keeping control over their work can be a powerful incentive. The "suits" (the corporate control freaks and bean counters) are not much admired among the hackish set. Shareware authors don't have to deal with them.

Shareware is also an inexpensive way to start a software business. An author can operate from home instead of from an expensive office building. A good shareware program tends to market itself, with just a little help from its author. There's no need to pay and pay and pay, so there's no need to overcharge the customer. These lower registration fees give shareware authors a competitive edge against the retailers. Everyone wins except professional marketers and people who don't know about, or who have been misled about, the incredible bargains that result.

How Good Is Shareware?

> *If you don't do it excellently, don't do it at all. Because if it's not excellent, it won't be profitable or fun, and if you're not in business for fun or profit, what the hell are you doing there?*
> —Robert Townsend

Shareware products must be good if they hope to compete against retail programs. As any movie maker can tell you, a marketer can buy anything for a price except "the buzz." Shareware depends upon good word of mouth, so the buzz had better be good. As a result, successful shareware programs tend to be—

- A little less powerful, but hundreds of dollars cheaper
- A little *more* powerful, but still hundreds of dollars cheaper
- Better targeted to the expert, the novice, or the specialist
- Different from the herd, offering a new approach or a different solution

Shareware authors go to great lengths to attract customers, but you'll still see a few idiots sneer when the subject of shareware comes up. The sneers often come from those with their own axes to grind—computer store owners who make no money from shareware, for example, or magazine editors with expensive ads to sell.

You may also hear a former shareware author complain about failing to make any money. That can happen when someone tries to sell a mediocre program or enters a market already saturated with similar products. When you hear such tales of woe, bear in mind that people on the other side of the fence—those who fail at commercial retail marketing—likewise tend to blame bigger companies, shareware competition, or anyone but themselves. It's human nature.

Correcting False Ideas

As a hacker, you may be thinking about taking a shareware marketing approach. Or if you're a software user, you may be wondering if you should rely on shareware products to further your hackish pursuits. Either way, we'd like to encourage you. So here are some misconceptions about shareware along with our attempts to promote a more accurate view.

"Shareware is second-rate software."

Okay, plenty of trashy shareware does exist. It's in the same league as the schlock sitting on store shelves next to the good stuff. You lose money if you buy schlock in a retail store. When you discard bad shareware you don't lose money, you gain disk space. But a ton of very good shareware exists that costs much less than its retail counterpart. Shareware also tends to be more bug-free than newly released retail software, especially the "point-zero" versions (1.0, 2.0, etc.). Shareware has a huge group of enthusiasts to do the equivalent of large-scale beta testing on every new shareware release. The real second-raters are the retail houses that put out programs with known bugs in order to stay in budget and keep the commercial bucks flowing in. You won't find many shareware authors pulling that kind of stunt; it would be too damaging to the buzz. But it's common among the shrink-wrap retailer set.

"Shareware authors just can't make it in the retail business."

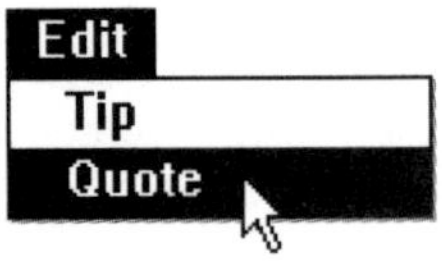
Edit
Tip
Quote

To strive with difficulties, and to conquer them, is the highest human felicity.
—Dr. Samuel Johnson

ButtonWare first made it onto the *SoftLetter-100* list in 1987, beating out hundreds of retail companies. Over two dozen shareware companies report $1 million or more in sales each year. Dozens more report yearly sales above $100,000, and hundreds of shareware authors are successfully self-employed. If you have a good product, you can make money.

"You can't rely on shareware authors to support their products."

Magee Enterprises, like many shareware companies, offers support even to non-registered users (we call them "potential customers" in the shareware industry). Shareware authors can, and do, provide support over the phone, by fax, on computer bulletin boards, on national bulletin board networks, and on national information services like CompuServe, AOL, Delphi, and GEnie. If you request a new feature, you'll often find it gracing the shareware channels as a mini-upgrade within days. Why? Because the authors aren't commercial drones who get paid by the week. They're *hackers* who find a good idea irresistible. Many authors accept credit cards, provide toll-free support lines, or both. Some even list their home phone numbers, in case you need support during evening hours. You won't find many who force you to call a by-the-minute 900-number voice mail system to get technical support, the way so many retail houses do. (People who call 900 numbers should be doing something more entertaining than talking about software bugs.)

"Retail software is more user friendly."
Shareware authors were among the first to offer popup windows, pulldown menus, context-sensitive help, custom programming, fast updates, and much more. They did this because they listened to their users, who asked for such features. Large companies experience delays in trying to upgrade software because they get bogged down by bureaucracies, advertising priorities, overhead, and production costs. You can take miles to change course on a tanker, but you can turn a hackish speed boat on a dime.

"Shareware hasn't won any awards for being great."
ButtonWare's PC-File program was the champion of a 1988 *Consumer Reports* reader survey—as a write-in candidate! The classic Procomm telecomm program captured its first *InfoWorld* Readers Choice award back in 1986. 4DOS was a finalist in the *PC Magazine* Technical Excellence Awards for 1989. Programs such as Newkey, Flu_Shot+, and InstaCalc have been named Editor's Choice in many computer magazines through the years. Magna Software was #151 in *Inc.* magazine's 1988 list of America's fastest growing private companies. These accolades continue up through 1993 and beyond.

"Shareware is cheap because you get what you pay for."
Shareware doesn't pay the salaries of lawyers, advertising agents, or the store clerks who ring up your purchase. You don't often pay for a colorful box designed to catch your eye while it sits on the shelf. You don't pay for the marketers who developed and tested its consumer appeal. These savings can be passed on to users as lower registration fees. So it's true—you get what you pay for. It's just that so much of what you pay for in a retail store has nothing to do with the program you thought you were buying.

"Shareware spreads computer viruses."
This is a popular statement in the non-computer mainstream press, though most of the PC magazines know better by now. Some "Chicken Little" computer virus books written to cash in on the recent virus hysteria also make this claim, *despite overwhelming evidence to the contrary.* Unfortunately, the same misinformation sources don't mention the scores of retail companies that have transmitted hundreds of thousands of infections via software sold off the shelf *in its original shrinkwrap.* Such infections can be planted by disgruntled employees and competitors, not just by refugees from the psycho ward. But you sure won't hear about them from the retailers! For more on this subject, see Chapter 5, "Data Compression and Encryption."

A Word About the ASP

The Association of Shareware Professionals (ASP) was formed in 1987 to strengthen the future of shareware as an alternative to traditional retail software marketing. ASP also serves as an information clearinghouse both for its members and for the public at large.

ASP members subscribe to a code of ethics and are committed to the shareware concept. The ASP demands professional conduct. Authors must acknowledge every registration (you get more than just a canceled check), and they must provide at least three months of support for their products. ASP members must also live up to any other benefits they offer.

you can turn to an ombudsman for help in resolving any problems with an ASP member. Members must explain this option in every shareware program, disk vendor catalog, or bulletin board service they offer. Few people ever ask the ombudsman for help, but it's nice to know you can turn to someone if you think you got a raw deal.

The term "shareware" is not trademarked, so authors can call any ware by that name even if it's not really "try before you buy" software. ASP authors have agreed to follow a set of guidelines, assuring you that any shareware program from an ASP member truly will let you "kick all the tires." All features in the registered version must be fully documented

Jim Button on the ASP

Jim Button, author of PC-File and a host of other programs, has turned his company, ButtonWare, into one of the largest shareware companies. In the mid-1980s he helped set up the ASP. According to Jim:

"In those early days, many programmers caught the vision of what shareware was all about and were eager to bring their own products to the shareware market. These were fun times, because we were all experimenting with different approaches to see what worked best.

"What price should I charge for my program? What incentives should I provide to those who send in a payment? What should I withhold? How does one advertise a shareware disk? How do I do press releases, and to whom should I send them? These questions, and many others, dominated the lives of budding shareware authors.

"I always regretted that I didn't have time to personally correspond with every potential shareware author who approached me with questions. There was definitely a need for some kind of coordination or information exchange.

"In 1986, I was contacted by several other shareware leaders to attend a meeting in Dallas. I leaped at the opportunity. The purpose of the meeting was to discuss the possibility of a coordinated approach to shareware. I viewed this as an opportunity to help provide information and assistance to thousands of potential shareware programmers.

"The outcome of the conference was an agreement to form a shareware association. The ASP was born."

in the shareware version, though you may have to register to activate some of them. ASP shareware can have beg screens that remind you to register (these usually pop up when you start a program). But they're not supposed to nag you with long delays or frequent interruptions with popup screens.

The ASP watches out for shareware authors and users in other ways, too. It keeps an eye out in Congress for potentially damaging legislation and has sent people to Washington, D.C. to testify. It has filed motions in countries as far away as England and South Africa to stop people who attempt to claim the word "shareware" as a trademark word.

ASP members "meet" online in a public forum of the CompuServe network to keep in touch with each other and exchange views on a daily basis. Once a year the ASP holds a face-to-face physical meeting, and it also sends people to the big shows like COMDEX and PC EXPO. If you have a user group, panel, or other forum, the ASP can supply speakers.

To learn more about the ASP, write to American Society of Shareware Professionals, 545 Grover Road, Muskegon, MI 49442. Or, if you have a modem and a CompuServe account, you can log on and use the GO CIS:SHAREWARE command to find more information.

The "Sooners" and the "Laters"

Most shareware authors give you a 30- to 90-day trial period in which to decide whether to continue using a program. But users tend to fall into two diametrically opposed groups: (1) those who register the same day they try out the product, and (2) those who register after a long stretch of use, sometimes a year or more.

This presents a thorny problem to authors. How can you get the "year or more" users to pay without upsetting them in the process? If you annoy them, they may withhold payment out of spite, even though that action is illegal. If you upset them too much or make your program too annoying to use, they'll throw out your program and buy a competitor's product!

Rob Rosenberger, sysop of CompuServe's SHAREWARE forum, has pondered this question for years. "I don't have an answer yet," he says candidly. A shareware author himself, he admits to having a large unpaid user base for each of his products.

But Rosenberger doesn't let this fact bother him much—he has a few tricks up his sleeve. He happily supports any unpaid user who calls for technical assistance, for example, and then quietly tells the caller: "I ain't supposed to say this, but we accept *anything* as a $5 coupon if you write the words '$5 coupon' on it." Rosenberger loses a few bucks each time, but he firmly believes the additional sales more than make up for it. He says that people like to think they got the best of a trade, even if it's a bargain to begin with.

"I think people just like an unadvertised bargain," he shrugs. "They must be right—they're the customers."

How Many People Actually Register?

Edit
Tip
Quote

I just bought my second house two blocks from the Florida beach with $70,000 in cash as a down payment. Got a pool in the backyard and everything. Not bad for a part-time shareware author.
—Paul Mayer, author, GRAB Plus

How many users actually register the shareware they use? Hey, take your pick of the statistics! We've seen the figure put at 63%, 60%, 50%, 45%, 33%, 30%, 27%, 25%, 20%, 15%, 13%, 12%, 10%, 8%, 6%, 5%, 4%, 3.14159%, 3%, 2%, 1%, 0.5%, 0.1%, 0.01% —or the popular and ever-reliable 0.0007241%.

Until recently, people who claimed to have a handle on shareware statistics actually had no idea at all. They just came up with a number and rationalized why it sounded plausible. But this trend is changing. Of two shareware surveys now considered valid enough to cite in debate, each showed about a 60% shareware registration rate.

Many somewhat paranoid shareware authors claim a "1%" registration rate, a figure derived from egotistical beliefs about the widespread use of their programs. CompuServe and GEnie tend to create some paranoia among authors who track how many people download their programs. Suppose you'd seen 300 downloads in the last two weeks, but only three customers had registered during that time—you might honestly but quite incorrectly claim a 1% pay-up rate. This logic is incorrect, because it assumes that everyone who's registered your program has downloaded it from the service, and that the 297 others who have downloaded it have continued to use it.

In many such cases, the authors have created "yet another" checkbook program or spreadsheet application or Rolodex database or virus scanning utility or file/directory sorter or whatever else you can think of. Shareware authors for the most part compete in markets already saturated by other products. Why should someone switch to a new file-viewing utility when two others are available for free, or when they can use three different ones included with retail packages purchased over the years?

These authors get frustrated because a product hasn't taken off like PC-File, Automenu, or PKZIP. Even a clearly superior new product often takes a nosedive because people just don't feel they need to upgrade the software they've used for years. If it satisfies all their needs, why should they switch to a new program? This has been the bane of retailers through the years as well. Users have this strange attitude that if their system ain't broke, why fix it?

Even worse for the authors, many of them not only compete in a saturated market, but their programs are simply inferior to the ones already out there. You could choke a moose with poorly designed Rolodex applications, yet more Rolodex duds debut each month as shareware. For one thing, it's a popular term project in programming classes. For another, just about any database engine nowadays can generate simple Rolodex-style "applications" as separate executables, making any adept user seem like a "real" programmer.

Finally, many smart shareware authors don't really worry about how many people will use their software without registering. They don't like piracy anymore than the next guy—but man, if people intend to pirate, those authors want them to pirate *their* products. The user gets hooked on their software, so now they just have to wait for him/her to pay up. At some upgrade or other, a nonregistered user will come across it right after church or after getting a check from their rich uncle's estate. Then nearly two out of three of them will register. The author's competitors, on the other hand, need to entice the user to switch from one product that works to another before they even have a shot at making a sale. Think about it.

Next Up

In the next chapter, we'll give you some great tips for designing a program that will succeed (i.e., make you some money!) in the ever-mutating shareware market. You'll learn how to add a marketeer's extra sparkle to your unpolished gem of a program. If you're thinking about putting a program "out there" in the shareware channels for users to try before they buy, Chapter 2 is must-read material.

2

The Art of the Gem

People who come to the shareware marketplace are on the hunt for gems, those bright offerings that stand out from the rest. It doesn't matter if you're a user or developer, a buyer or a seller; if the product in your hot little hands is conspicuously better than its competition, you'll do well. The trick lies in finding the gems—ideas for the developer, code for the programmer, tools for the hacker, and fast, tight programs for the user.

In this chapter, we'll discuss how to find, develop, create, and market the gems as shareware. If you're hacking for a boss somewhere, or you're just not interested in the shareware market, you might want to skip to the next chapter.

If you are interested in shareware channels, this chapter is for you. You may be a user who wants to trick out your system with mag wheels, tinted windows, and the works; we'll show you how to look in the places where the best shareware authors publish their work. If you're into developing or programming, you'll find valuable pointers culled from years of experience (both ours and others') on how and where to supply your gems to the discerning user. In either case, you'll wind up with a program that users will show to their friends: "Hey, look what I found!"

We'll start with the simplest—and hardest—part of a hacker's progress toward success: being systematic.

So You Wanna Be a Hacker

There's an investment technique in the stock market called the "Drunkard's Walk," where you lurch from side to side, picking stocks at random. As it turns out, this approach to the market works as well as any and better than most. It's similar to a system used by many horse bettors (unless you're one who believes that, say, a compliment from your mother on your new haircut is a cosmic portent that Mother's Pleasure will win in the seventh).

When you're marketing computer programs, however, aimlessness usually misses the target. A haphazard approach simply won't make you filthy rich or even financially comfortable. The first step in writing successful shareware is to decide what types of gems to find or produce. This first step is where beginners in the programming racket usually start to fail. Don't fret about them, though; when these beginners drop out, you'll still be in there hacking, and that by itself will draw attention to your products. Here are some longevity tips.

Don't Code for Yourself

People often write software for personal or business use. Then, *as an afterthought,* they try to make some pin money by dropping it into the shareware arena. This is not serious marketing. It crowds the channels with junk and will almost always annoy potential customers. For one thing, such ad hoc programs are almost always too limited. Having been designed to do one thing in one environment, they don't work for general use. And they usually come with little or no documentation. To cap the matter, they often have serious bugs when run on different hardware or under a different version of DOS.

Consider something as simple as an envelope addressing program. There are dozens of these programs on the shareware market. Product A works with Hewlett-Packard LaserJets. Product B can handle Epson dot matrix printers. Look for product C if you own a PostScript printer. Product D really makes a LaserProp Fax/Printer Beta 2B shine—**If** you remember to load it before SMARTDrive.

Edit
Tip
Quote

We received 34 new menuing programs in the last three months. That's not including file managers—just menu programs. I've got 10 checkbook managers, too. A lot of people are wasting their talent.
—Bob Ostrander, Public Brand Software

While these specialized programs rust on the neighborhood BBS hard drive, what envelope program gets the registrations? Product E. It works with nearly all printers, has a great user interface, plucks addresses right off the screen from any word processor, maintains a database of addresses, and has enjoyed continual development and enhancement for the past 10 years. It's the one most people recommend to their friends, the one that shareware newsletters review and love.

It's a *generic* program. It does the job for as many people as possible, as simply as possible, and with as wide a variety of popular hardware as possible. It uses a popular file format and a popular, standardized user interface. It may work with and enhance other popular programs.

Note that *popular* is a key word here. Note also that a program like Product E is planned. It's not something cobbled together at random and then dropped casually into the shareware stream.

Not Everything Sells

Shareware is a great way to sell software but it doesn't work well for everything. You need to target your market. You wouldn't sell Harleys in Retirement Village, and you shouldn't try to sell, say, DOS utilities to the under-21 arcade game set. Here are some general program types to avoid:

- **Games** don't usually do well as shareware, despite sometimes unbelievable numbers on the download counters. Two main kinds of users try games: kids who love your product but have no money, and adults who lose interest before they reach for the checkbook. Write programs that will help adults be more, not less, productive, and they'll register.
- **Educational software** is another poor shareware venture. Many typing instructors and DOS tutorials complete their teaching mission during the trial period. If you aim for the school or college market, you're dealing with tight budgets and, usually, a need to get bureaucrats to sign approvals. You might as well become a bureaucrat yourself and draw a paycheck.

- **Minor utilities** usually don't draw registrations. Tiny programs are considered trivial, especially if they have no upgrade potential. You stand a better chance if you bundle several useful utilities into a single product, but that puts you in direct competition with PC Tools, Norton Utilities, and other big-time retail products. Tough market.
- **One-shot applications** have problems as shareware. Source code translators and hard disk interleave analyzers, for example, are used once and put on the shelf. This does not encourage people to register. If you have a one-shot product, either go retail or include it in a larger set of related utilities.

Why Some Programs Don't Work as Shareware

Some terrific programs will fail as shareware no matter what you do, for all sorts of reasons. For example, you may release a slick little utility, only to discover that a public domain utility beat you to the punch in 1987. Sorry, Charlie.

Other programs suffocate in an oversaturated market. Would you really expect to make money with yet another DOS shell or checkbook manager? Areas like that have had dozens or even hundreds of software solutions for years now, often including some killer public domain programs that people use for free. There are simply too many authors in too small a pool.

Other programs die for lack of an audience. Years ago, Saturday Night Live did a skit about a "Scotch Boutique" that only sold Scotch Tape™. The store did not thrive. If you program something for the linoleum industry, you'd better either sell it in a retail niche or open a Linoleum Shareware Boutique on Saturday Night Live.

What? Someone Already Invented the Wheel?

Some shareware authors complain of no registrations, though their program is as basic and necessary as the wheel. They forget that wheels have been out there for years, and most everyone who wants one already has one and is satisfied.

This problem is most common among new shareware authors. Somebody looks at various database applications and discovers not one of them can put away socks or scrape bugs off a windshield. This calls for Database Applications Man! Off he goes, expecting riches and fame, or at least enough registrations to buy groceries. Then he starves to death in his basement.

The YADS Syndrome

Quote

Our policy is to not add a new program that performs the same functions as programs already in the library.... So someone writing yet another checkbook program, DOS menu, file manager, sorted directory utility, etc., is going to have a VERY tough time getting into P(s)L.

—Nelson Ford, Public (software) Library

Product oversaturation has grown so common in the shareware industry that it even has a name: the YADS syndrome, for Yet Another DOS Shell. Here's a list of YADS programs guaranteed to be a tough sell for new entries:

- Spreadsheets, accounting packages, income tax software, payroll programs, financial calculators, lotto software, and home/office finance or amortization programs
- DOS shells, hard disk managers, directory sorters, directory viewers, calendars, calendar keepers, and desktop organizers

- Communication programs, phone dialers, BBS software, and file transfer protocols
- Text editors, file viewers, and word processors
- Flat file databases, inventory systems, church membership rosters, bible search programs, genealogy applications, and softball/bowling/golf statistics software
- File compression software and front-end utilities to run them
- Envelope addressing programs and label-making applications
- Computer virus prevention/detection/eradication software

Wheels of a Different Color

Okay, then, what areas *haven't* been saturated? Here are a few of the many programs people still look for on the shareware market:

- Network-based applications (a.k.a. "groupware")
- Truly relational databases
- Transparent, fast MNP support for non-MNP modems
- More CAD/CAM and CASE software
- Point of Sale (POS) applications (but beware the Linoleum Boutique hazard)
- More graphics "slide show" software
- Fax board applications and utilities
- PostScript interpreters for non-PostScript printers (the faster the better)
- More phone bill analysis software with more options
- Products designed specifically for the Windows, WinNT or OS/2 platforms
- Good PostIt™ type note programs in DOS or, better, in DOS-and-Windows

There are many other types of programs itching for a debut as shareware. The problem is to come up with new ideas. Everything else is a cinch.

Get a Hackish Tool Kit

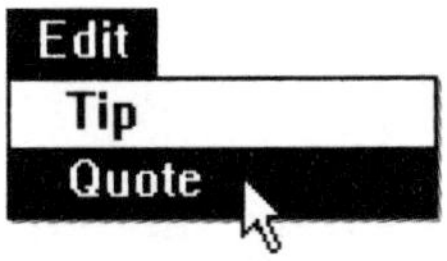
Edit
Tip
Quote

You wouldn't believe how many customers want new manuals whenever I upgrade my program.
—Dennis Lozen, author of FastBucks

Many aspiring shareware authors—especially new students of the programming art—write programs completely from scratch. The result is usually a dozen pegs down in quality from other programs in the same class. Why? Experienced programmers use toolkits. Throughout this book we'll discuss various tools you can use, like specialized editors and program function libraries, to save work, time, effort, and mistakes. Use them.

A wealth of code is available in programmer toolkits. A few are PD, some are shareware, and some are retail. The best toolkits come with at least 50,000 lines of royalty-free source code you can plug right into your software. Why spend weeks or months locked in debug struggles when you can buy the code (with manuals) for $25 to $150? You can get them for all the popular languages, including Pascal, BASIC, assembler, and C. It'd be silly not to use 'em.

Manuals Are Important

Shareware programs die a pauper's death if they come with poor documentation. You can easily get lost in the thrills and chills of program writing and leave the boring old manual for last, but that's a bad mistake. A programmer who has worked on a complex program for months may assume that all those familiar menu commands and hot key assignments should be obvious to anyone smart enough to remember to eat. Such programmers probably forget to eat.

Quote

The program is totally self explanatory to the professional user. Consequently, no operational manual is necessary.

—from a shareware medical program's READ.ME file

Only the most trivial utility is so obvious that potential users won't appreciate some tips and pointers. It's an axiom:

Mediocre programs with great docs outsell terrific programs with poor docs. Smart users know manuals save time, and they expect a programmer to know it too. No manual? They mark it down to carelessness and avoid the program. Most magazine reviewers and big-time corporate buyers won't even look at a program with no documentation.

Manuals That Sell Software

So you're resigned to writing a manual. What will you say? How will you arrange it? What should you leave out? There is no best way to document a program, but do follow these guidelines—especially if you're going to print your manual professionally:

- Use a professional word processor. There are several on the shareware market.
- Avoid "screen dumps" that don't show useful information. They waste trees.
- List every status or error message in your program. Don't waste space explaining the obvious ones, but do include them in the list.
- Don't bother to explain why you didn't include a minor function. But do tell about any major program limitations.
- Include an overview chapter describing your program. What are the important selling points? What makes it better than the competition? Why should a user trouble to learn to use it?
- Put the legal stuff at the front where it's hard to miss, but keep it brief. Let the lawyers make their livings off someone else. Use standard "boilerplate" legal statements (the ASP can help).
- Keep a positive tone—don't scold people or shake your finger at them. You have to trust the users if you hope to get their money.
- Put the installation instructions right after the legal stuff. Make it a separate chapter if there's more than a page or two. Don't skip installation, even if all you say is "copy [*filename*] to drive C and invoke over pizza and Coke™."

More aggressive Aquarians have put messages into their programs that threaten bad karma, ill luck, and lifelong guilt if you don't pay...Rather than spurring people to pay, they alienated their audience.

—Bill Machrone, Publisher, PC Magazine

Edit
Tip
Quote

A good manual sells programs. Many good writers are starving; don't be afraid to hire one.
—Rob Rosenberger, ASP catalog librarian

- Use correct spelling and good grammar. Spell checkers don't beep at grammatical errors, and magazines love to catch and quote properly spelled silly mistakes. You don't need the kind of publicity that makes people laugh at you.
- If writing isn't your shtick, hire a writer. That's what the big shareware successes do. Technical writing is an acquired skill and not everyone can do it well.
- Put a table of contents in front and an index in back. Smart users appreciate them.
- Don't document your program's antivirus or antitampering qualities. Some users will consider it an unconditional warranty; others will take it as a challenge.
- Always read the manuscript out loud. You wrote it. If your tongue stumbles, what chance will your poor readers have?

How About On-Disk Manuals?

Many authors distribute their manuals as text files and make printed copies an optional extra with registration. Some people like to have a book at their fingertips, but others prefer to keep the docs on a disk and use a browser when they need it. By making the printed book an option, you let the user choose, you save money on printing, and you can pass on the savings (or part of them anyway) to the users who prefer on-disk manuals.

2

Register Your Copyright

You must copyright your shareware program if you expect to have a legal foundation for charging people to use it.

Quote

Shareware, from a legal perspective, is nothing more than a selective waiver of copyright protections.

—Lance Rose, copyright attorney

These days it's easy to claim a copyright. You just flash "Copyright 19*xx* by John Doe" on the screen and include the same statement in your user manual. It's binding. But it's also smart to register the copyright with the Copyright

Office. Registration only costs $20, and it's irrefutable proof of your copyright date.

To contact the Copyright Office, call 202-707-9100 and leave a message on the Copyright Office answering machine. Speak slowly and clearly: "I would like five copies of Form TX, one copy of Circular R61, and one copy of Circular R1. My address is...." The Copyright Office will mail them to you free of charge.

In the completed package, be sure to include:

- One completed Form TX
- A check for $20 made out to "Register of Copyrights"
- One printed copy of the *first 25 pages* of the program's source code listing
- One printed copy of the *last 25 pages* of the program's source code listing
- One printed copy of the user manual

Put your package in a sturdy envelope and mail it to:

Register of Copyrights
Library Of Congress
Washington, DC 20559

The registered copyright date is the day they receive your package. You'll get a certificate approximately three months later. If a problem comes up, they'll give you 120 days to fix it (don't worry, you won't need to submit a new package).

Does (c) Equal ©? Not on Your Copyright!

The IBM PC can display 255 different text characters, but "©" isn't one of them. Most software companies (retail and shareware) substitute "(c)" in its place. If everyone uses it then it must be legally acceptable...right?

Wrong. The symbol (c) has no legal value. To be binding, a copyright notice must use the © symbol, the "Copr." abbreviation, or the word "Copyright." Congress and the rest of the world may someday recognize (c) as a valid designator, but they haven't gotten around to it yet.

The Perfect Copyright Notice

Use the following copyright notice as a model for your program and documents:

Copr. 1991,94 by John Smith; all rights reserved.

Here's what it tells the lawyers. The 1989 Berne Convention recognizes "Copr." as a valid abbreviation and it takes only two more characters than the non-valid "(c)." "1991,94" means you claimed an original copyright in 1991; then in 1994 you amended the product enough to consider it substantially different. Use a comma to separate the original copyright year from the latest substantial copyright year.

The U.S. and other major countries assume you reserve all copyrights unless you specifically give them up—but other (generally smaller) countries don't pay that courtesy. The phrase "all rights reserved" solves this potential problem. And notice we used a semicolon to separate the name from the "all rights reserved" clause. Never use a period! Never never never never never! A period ends both a sentence and a copyright notice. If you put in a period before the "all rights reserved" clause, you might as well leave it out. It means nothing.

Finally, pay attention: the copyright notice on this book probably differs from what we just told you. It probably differs from the one printed on the CD-ROM. It probably differs from all of the copyrights on all of the stuff stored on the CD-ROM. You know lawyers!

But the version we just showed you will suffice, and if you register at the copyright office, it's as good as bulletproof...or at least it is according to one lawyer we talked to.

2

"Copyrighted" Public Domain

A great oddity in shareware is the famous copyrighted-public-domain clause. It goes something like: "This software is copyright 19*xx* and released to the public domain so you can copy it."

What the author *meant* to say was: "I claim a copyright but you're free to use or pass this program along, provided you don't change it or claim it for yourself." What the author *legally* said was: "I hereby claim a copyright, but now I hereby relinquish it with a slip of the tongue."

If you're a user, please respect the author's intentions. Shareware authors trust people to pay. Hiding behind technicalities is for lawyers, not for people.

This problem has its roots in the days before shareware, when bulletin boards could legally carry only public domain programs. "Public domain" became a slang phrase (but *not* a legal phrase) for any software you could legally download from a BBS. Some authors still use it to let you distribute a program on bulletin boards, but they're shooting themselves in the legal foot. If an author labels a program as PD, it belongs to everyone and no one—most especially, not to the author who labeled it PD without understanding the implications.

Of course, that's not to say you shouldn't place your work in the public domain. Many great hackers do just that. Just understand that by doing so, you forfeit all control over how it is used or marketed afterward.

Open the Gates and Flood the Market

Okay, so you're ready to start pushing the product. Great! But don't expect to succeed if you just upload your program to a few local BBSs. You have to get your product out there, where people can try it and pass it along.

You'll find yourself running into some vexing questions. How many disks should you create? Which disk vendors can you trust to push your product ethically, and which should you avoid? Where can you find addresses for large computer clubs? Can you expect registrations if you send disks out to small computer clubs? Should you issue a press release, and if so, to whom—editors of national magazines? Editors of computer club newsletters? And what information should it contain if it is to succeed at garnering publicity?

Are you dizzy yet?

ASP members (see Chapter 1) can help answer such questions and provide other valuable tips. For example, many ASP authors recommend using a disk duplicator service for fifty or more disks. They can tell you where to buy a duplicator machine of your own, if you can afford one. They can tell you what to do if you decide to raise the price of your disks later on. If you join the ASP, you can use its trademark logo. A lot of users trust the logo because it says you stand behind your product and will offer more than

One File or Two?

For a long time, authors limited their shareware files to a size that would fit on a 360K diskette, at least when posting on BBSs or the major information services. This made sense back when many people had no hard drive and high density diskettes were not yet standard. But the "360K Upload Barrier" has long been a dead demon. If shareware authors have a size barrier now, it sits at 1.44MB—the capacity of a 3 1/2-inch HD floppy—but even that is really obsolete, since most users now have a hard drive. Do people a favor and keep your program files together in a single compressed downloadable file. If it's a huge program, consider posting a separate descriptive text file, but keep the actual program files together.

their canceled check for registration. It also gives users a place to call besides your home phone if, at 2:00 A.M., they decide they don't like your program after all.

How Much Is Enough?

The more you charge, the more you'll make, right? Or is it the more you charge, the fewer users will register? What's the happy medium?

it's not easy to decide on a registration fee. The first major hurdle is to decide what users might consider legit. Don't base the price on the weeks or months you spent programming. Most users only care if your program is good, well documented, and competitively priced.

Underpricing to lure customers from competitors doesn't always work. Smart users may dismiss your program on the theory that "you don't get what you don't pay for," and users with no idea of what such a program should cost won't know they're getting a bargain anyway.

A good marketing approach is to describe your program accurately (don't call an editor a word processor) and then charge about the same as others do. You won't go too far wrong, and you'll be targeting the right audience.

Rosenberger's Law of Shareware Pricing

Rob Rosenberger, who maintains the software library listings for the ASP, offers the following guidelines for aspiring shareware authors. They take into account the savings that shareware customers have come to consider fair in light of your reduced marketing costs:

- If your product performs *better than* the retail competition, consider charging two-thirds of the general retail street price for such a product.
- If it performs *as well as* its retail rivals, offer it for about half the going retail rate.
- If it is *slightly less powerful* than the retail versions, keep the charge down to a third or less of the retail street price for similar programs.

"John Smith, DBA Excellent Software and Pizza Co."

Many people will trust a company before they trust a person, because they figure a company has more to lose. Little do they know! But to counter such prejudices, you can adopt a more commercial image by using a company name instead of a personal one.

it's easy to "do business as" (DBA) a company in most places. In some states you file a form at a local courthouse and apply for a sales tax ID. You may also have to advertise in a local "newspaper of record," however your state defines that term. Then again, if you use your own name (John Smith Enterprises) or initials (JS & Co.) you may not have to notify anyone. The best approach is to call the local county courthouse and ask how to proceed. They'll know the details.

The Tax Man Cometh

Filing an income tax form as a DBA usually involves using the IRS 1040 Schedule C and doing some other minor paperwork. You might consider paying someone to prepare your taxes, at least during your first year of business. This practice doesn't cost much, it is deductible, and it saves mistakes.

Should You Incorporate?

Nah. Not at first, anyway. Consult a tax lawyer for professional advice before you attach an "Inc." and all its attached tax liabilities to your startup company.

Free Registered Copies

If your product is business-oriented, send some free registered copies to any big companies you think might use it. When a big outfit buys a program, they tend to buy big. If you have a fantastic new ZIP code lookup program, for example, you'd want to send "freebies" to the headquarters of Federal Express and UPS. Send a copy to their local

Impress Your Mom—Accept Credit Cards

Shareware registration services offer the benefits of credit card merchant status plus the proven lure of toll free 800-number order lines manned by real people. It only takes a few signatures to advertise a registration service as a place to register. For example, the Public (software) Library, or PsL, accepts American Express, Discover, MasterCard, and Visa, and charges only a very small transaction fee. Call PsL at 713-524-6394 for more details, and tell 'em we sent you.

CompuServe can also take shareware registrations. The service was designed for overseas users who don't have a credit card accepted in America, but business customers and individual CompuServe subscribers also consider it a major convenience.

To have CompuServe handle registrations for your program, you first need a CompuServe account. Then GO SWREG for more details or to sign up for the service.

offices, too. You can do marketing wonders by hitting a major corporation from both the top and the bottom.

You may want to send copies to major computer magazines too—but don't bother with the editors or publishers. They're above all that. Look instead for the names of "contributing editors" or "staff writers." Those people generally get little mail by comparison, and they make part of their living by reviewing interesting new or upgraded established programs.

Voice and BBS Support

Voice phone support is critical to attracting business customers. If you can't man the phone on weekdays, say so in the manual and then get a phone answering machine. You don't necessarily have to return calls at your own expense, though it will make customers think highly of you.

Also offer BBS support even if your program doesn't deal directly with modems. The shareware industry has built itself around people who use modems, and these people remain a majority of the users who register programs. Some will have sent checks to an obsolete address given in program documentation only to have it returned as undeliverable or cashed without a thank-you or go-to-hell. This is annoying, so many users who would otherwise register a program will put it off indefinitely if they think they might not be able to contact you.

If you don't have your own BBS, many BBS sysops will provide user support on a contract basis, and you can deduct the typically minor cost as a business expense.

To Have a Friend, Be a Friend

Quote

I'll share with you the BIGGEST reason that people register shareware. They LIKE the author. Think about it. It's so simple. Other incentives, like a [printed] manual and support and upgrades pale in comparison. What are you going to do to create a feeling of friendship so that they'll voluntarily send you money?

—Jim Button, CEO, ButtonWare, Inc.

Paul Mayer, onetime president of the ASP, offered a list of the most common complaints heard by the ASP ombudsman:

- The author failed to respond to letters.
- The shareware program is crippled; the registered version has more features.
- The dealer I bought these from never said I had to pay the author more money.
- My check was cashed six months ago and I never received the registered version.
- The registration encouragement screens go out of their way to annoy me when I try to evaluate the program.

For some great software to help turn your product from one that shrivels and dies of user indifference into the latest gotta-have-it hot program, see Chapter 14, "Hacker Graduation."

To an extent, these complaints reflect the fact that "Begware" and "Annoyware" do what they're supposed to do—nag the user to register. Everyone hates a nag. But do your best to walk that fine line between what's reasonable and what's hostile and counterproductive. When shareware is done right, everybody wins.

Next Up

The next chapter covers the ins and outs of using modems, BBSs and telecomm services to find or distribute shareware.

3

Walking the Wires

To find programming tool kits, to hook up with people in the computer industry, to distribute your own software as a shareware product—to do all of these things you simply have to go cyber. The so-called *cyberspace* defined by computers and modems includes tens of millions of people in dozens of countries around the world. They walk "The Wires"—the telephone wires—so that's where you must go to meet them. These people are the ones who send in registrations, so they're the ones you need to be in touch with.

Edit
Tip
Quote

I am a happy nerd in cyberspace, where no one can see my haircut.
—Dave Barry

If information is power, cyberspace represents raw power. You can make a local telephone call and "speak" (actually, type) to people in California, New York, Illinois, England, Switzerland, Russia, China, Japan—any of more than 200 nations worldwide. You can ask questions about *anything* and get back so many answers you may wish you hadn't asked. You'll find people from all walks of life with opinions and solutions for any problem you can think of. If a community is a place where people meet, talk and argue, buy and sell things, even fall in love and marry, then cyberspace is a real community. It's the first genuine global village.

Okay, okay, this book isn't supposed to be a rhapsody. But if you think of cyberspace as an arcade game peopled by computer nerds and distorts of the *he was so quiet until he bought the Uzi* type—you're missing a worldwide marketing opportunity.

Getting Started

To venture into cyberspace, all you need is a phone line, a modem, and some telecommunications (also called *comm* or *telecomm*) software. In the latter department, we recommend Qmodem, a powerhouse product now published by Mustang Software. This book's CD-ROM contains a fully functional "test-drive" version of Qmodem; it's no-fee shareware by another name.

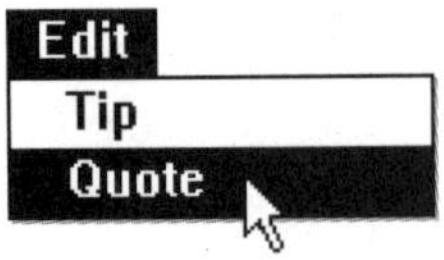
Edit
Tip
Quote

Replacing all of the 9600-baud modems with bicycle couriers would be a Bad Thing.

—*from "The Jargon File"*

The 1992 test-drive version of Qmodem effortlessly competes with the best telecomm programs on the market, and costs nothing to use. Mustang Software bets you'll love it enough to buy the even more powerful Qmodem Pro version. It's working for them—they get a *lot* of new business this way.

If Qmodem isn't your cup of tea, there are plenty of terrific comm programs on BBSs and information services. Some of the best are Boyan, GT Power Comm, pre-retail Telix and pre-retail Procomm. If you have system limitations, or if you need a tiny comm-to-host program suite or have other special needs, check out the alternative comm programs on this book's CD-ROM. They're described in the next few pages.

Hack Facts

Qmodem Test Drive

Version 4.52
Mustang Software, Inc.
P.O. Box 2264
Bakersfield, CA 93303
Sales: 800-999-9619
Office: 805-873-2500
BBS: 805-873-2400
CIS: 75236,3312 or PCVENA,
689,458 bytes
No fee for personal use.
QM452TD.ZIP

Qmodem is a powerhouse communications program, one of the best on the market for accessing computer bulletin boards even in its "test drive" version. In its fully registered and upgraded (but retail) "Pro" versions, it is one of the best general comm programs anywhere. It also comes in a Windows version.

Among its other features, Qmodem has an incredibly easy setup. Figure 3-1 shows the Test Drive configuration screen activated. You just pick your modem from a fairly comprehensive list and let Qmodem optimize the initialization strings and other modem-specific options. Most of the default configuration values won't require changing, though

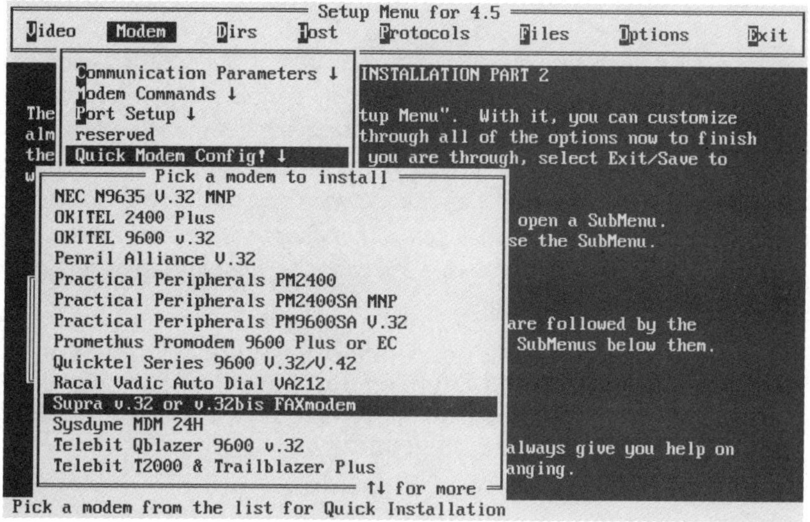
Setup Menu for 4.5
Video Modem Dirs Host Protocols Files Options Exit
Communication Parameters ↓
Modem Commands ↓
Port Setup ↓
reserved
Quick Modem Config! ↓
INSTALLATION PART 2
tup Menu". With it, you can customize
through all of the options now to finish
you are through, select Exit/Save to
Pick a modem to install
NEC N9635 V.32 MNP
OKITEL 2400 Plus
OKITEL 9600 v.32
Penril Alliance V.32
Practical Peripherals PM2400
Practical Peripherals PM2400SA MNP
Practical Peripherals PM9600SA V.32
Promethus Promodem 9600 Plus or EC
Quicktel Series 9600 V.32/V.42
Racal Vadic Auto Dial VA212
Supra v.32 or v.32bis FAXmodem
Sysdyne MDM 24H
Telebit Qblazer 9600 v.32
Telebit T2000 & Trailblazer Plus
↑↓ for more
open a SubMenu.
se the SubMenu.
are followed by the
SubMenus below them.
always give you help on
anging.
Pick a modem from the list for Quick Installation

Figure 3-1. *Let Qmodem set up your modem automatically.*

there's plenty of room for a hacker to experiment and optimize.

Once you've selected a modem or entered your own initialization string, choose Exit/Save and start making calls by manually typing in the destination phone number. It's *that* simple.

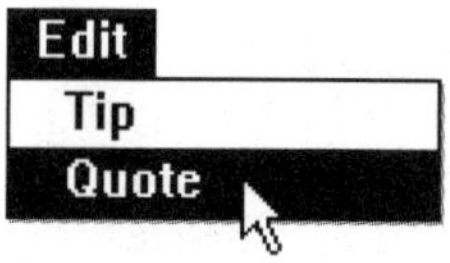
Edit
Tip
Quote

...A hacker might say that buying a smaller car to reduce pollution only solves a microproblem; the macroproblem of getting to work might be better solved by using mass transit, moving to within walking distance, or (best of all) telecommuting.

—from "The Jargon File"

Aside from its near-PD "test drive" status, we like Qmodem for its ease of use and flexibility. Its host mode can act as a mini-BBS complete with messaging, upload/download, and doorway capability when you're away. It supports most of the popular file transfer programs internally, but it also lets you substitute external protocols if that's what you want. It has a strong, easy to compile script language, but if you prefer a simpler approach, a QuickLearn feature will record any BBS log-on or other standard command sequence; go through the procedure once, and you're fully automated. If some of this telecomm jargon doesn't seem familiar, the docs do a very good job of explaining all this impressive power and showing how to use it.

Note

Opening a doorway lets you control the host machine from a remote keyboard. Some highly successful (and expensive) retail software does nothing more than that. If remote access is your primary reason for installing what might be a second comm program on your system, take a look at DOORWAY a bit later in this chapter. It comes with its own little comm program designed to interact seamlessly with remote machines.

If you don't like ordering by phone, you can find Qmodem Pro at Egghead Software Discount stores, Walden Software, Comp USA, Software Etc., and most other major retail outlets across the country.

Other Telecomm Choices

Telecommunications was one of the "basic four" applications that everyone knew about in the Golden Age of personal computing, currently figured as the early 1980s. (Computer "ages" last about one dog year and the one considered "golden" is likely to change without notice.) The other three were database management, spreadsheets, and word processing. The poor, benighted sods back then had never heard of sound boards, CD-ROM drives, cellular modems, palm-top computers, S&L rip-offs or carjackings. A Golden Age, indeed.

Nowadays we choose our applications from a much larger selection than four, but that just adds to the fun. In that spirit, here are a few more communication programs, just in case you want something starker, or smaller, or just...different. If you don't find exactly what you like in this CD-ROM collection, well, use one of these programs to range around the local BBSs or the information services and download some more choices. There's an almost unending supply.

Hack Facts

{COMMO}
Version 5.52
Fred P. Brucker
New Standard Software
P.O. Box 141537
Columbus, OH 43214
Voice: 614-326-1309
CIS: 71021,356
174,080 bytes
License only, $35
Shareware: $25-$35
COMMO.ZIP

When {COMMO} first appeared—and yes, the brackets are part of the name—its small size and its uncomplicated approach caused some users to dismiss it as a program that couldn't possibly be full-featured. After all, telecomm programs have to do a huge amount of computing to control all those functions at once—incoming data, disk saves, flow control, and on and on. When you got right down to it, {COMMO} was nothing much more than a collection of macros, right?

Well, almost right. There are macros, and then there are *by God MACROS*, and Fred Brucker's creation uses an almost unlimited number of *by God MACROS* to get the relatively small core program to do just about anything you could want of a comm package. The docs modestly call it a "small, fast reliable program" with an "unusually complete and flexible" macro language. Complete? Flexible? You bet. And if you're a starving student or a basement hacker running out of pizza money, you can register for as little as $25, $10 off the regular registration price.

It's hard to believe how much power this little program packs. Its main executable, COMMO.COM, is only 41,900 bytes in size, yet it easily handles macros to provide features many programs costing hundreds of dollars would choke on. The real evidence of how much thought has gone into this program is in the details. For example, you can tell {COMMO} to display modem activity indicators on the status line—a terrific feature if you have an internal modem and cannot see any activity lights.

the {COMMO} emphasis on macros makes this a true hack-your-own comm program, too. You can make this little program really flashdance, with hot-key menu bars to start any macro or built-in function. You can edit macros without leaving the program. You can edit text files up to 64K with an internal editor or bigger files with an external editor you stipulate.

{COMMO} packs built-in, non-macro surprises too, such as a host mode that supports doorway operations. It has the Xmodem and Ymodem file transfer protocols built in, but handles external protocols like DSZ and HS/Link (both on the CD-ROM and described later in this chapter) quite gracefully. It's aware of (and gets along with) every major multitasker, including DESQview, Windows, OS/2, OmniView, and DoubleDOS. {COMMO} is a fleet-footed, clean little comm program that lets you put in only the features you want and leave the rest behind, out of sight and off your cluttered hard disk.

Hack Facts

Lync
Version 3.0
Jason R. Alward
1607 Claymor Avenue
Ottawa, Ontario
Canada K2C1T4
613-224-3539 (voice)
Lync host mode BBS:
613-224-1368
69,760 bytes
Shareware: $26 (includes upgrade)
LYNC30.EXE

Lync keeps a very nice balance between flexibility and ease of use. It also packs unexpectedly powerful capabilities in its small frame, such as built-in file transfer protocols and a ready-to-go host mode. It's not as ultimately flexible as {COMMO}, but for use on limited iron, it will do anything most users could want. Some of its more advanced features, like Zmodem crash recovery and autostart, have no right to exist in a comm program so small. As Figure 3-2 shows, you can configure this little workhorse to fit just about any standard system that doesn't require some of the fine tuning features of, say, Qmodem.

For example, if you're using nonstandard port addresses or other strange iron, you might have a bit of trouble using Lync right out of the shareware file. But the author has a BBS for users (it runs Lync in host mode) where you can ask questions and get help with any

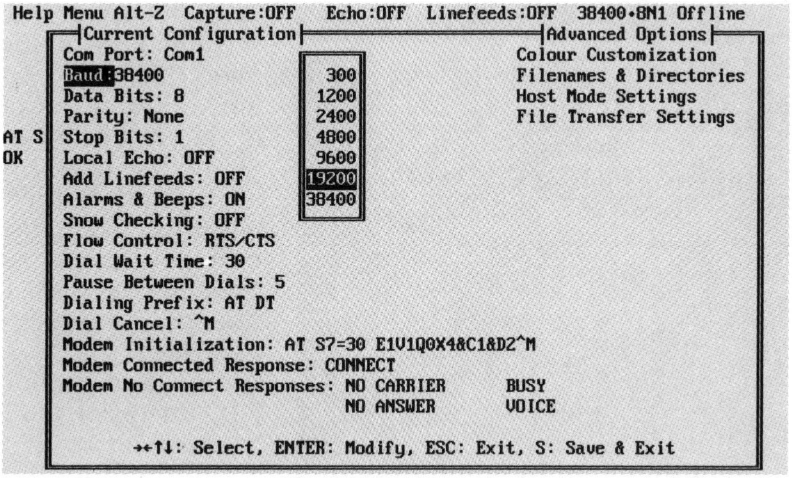
Help Menu Alt-Z Capture:OFF Echo:OFF Linefeeds:OFF 38400•8N1 Offline
Current Configuration
Advanced Options
Com Port: Com1
Baud: 38400
Data Bits: 8
Parity: None
Stop Bits: 1
Local Echo: OFF
Add Linefeeds: OFF
Alarms & Beeps: ON
Snow Checking: OFF
Flow Control: RTS/CTS
Dial Wait Time: 30
Pause Between Dials: 5
Dialing Prefix: AT DT
Dial Cancel: ^M
Modem Initialization: AT S7=30 E1V1Q0X4&C1&D2^M
Modem Connected Response: CONNECT
Modem No Connect Responses: NO CARRIER BUSY
NO ANSWER VOICE
300
1200
2400
4800
9600
19200
38400
Colour Customization
Filenames & Directories
Host Mode Settings
File Transfer Settings
AT S
OK
→←↑↓: Select, ENTER: Modify, ESC: Exit, S: Save & Exit

Figure 3-2. *The Lync configuration screen*

problems. The more likely case is that you'll run this trouble-free little program on your laptop or, if your old XT is gathering dust, take advantage of Lync's conservative memory requirements to run a private mini-BBS in your home or office. If you like a trouble-free comm program in this power range, and you don't have the time or inclination to macro up a roll-your-own system, Lync is probably just what you're looking for.

Tip

You'll get a free upgrade to a more recent version, currently 3.2, when you register. The upgrade supports up to 57.6 K, supports the 16550A UART FIFO mode, has a bigger dialing directory, supports more protocols, and so forth. Despite the added features, the executable has stayed under 40K, partly because it was programmed in a combination of C and assembly language. The author is willing to talk about making the source code available to interested users; contact him at his home number, given in the "Hack Facts" for Lync.

Hack Facts

TinyTerm
Version 1.0
Robert Woeger
Kinsman-Redeemer Software
P.O. Box 60369
Colorado Springs, CO
80960-0369
22,900 bytes
Shareware: $10 ($14 on disk with optional fee-sharing)
TINYTERM.ZIP

At 23,406 bytes, the TinyTerm (for Tiny Terminal) executable file is smaller than {COMMO} or Lync. It's a minimal but very capable comm program, great for laptops or other hardware with limited memory or disk resources. It has no built-in file transfer protocols but it works great with external protocols like Zmodem or HS/Link. More to the point, TinyTerm is a fully ANSI-compatible program that handles data speeds up to 38,400 bps (bits per second) and supports the 16550A UART FIFO operating mode. (If you're not up to speed on 16550 UARTs, see Chapter 8, "Ports of Call.")

This is a fine hack for a specific purpose, especially when working with limited resources. It will get you to a remote site so you can log on, do what you need to do, and log off. The author uses a share-the-registrations shareware policy similar to the one made famous by Bob Wallace of PC-Write—he'll pay you 75 cents whenever someone registers a copy of the program that's branded with your serial number. It's not a lot of money, but as the author points out, if you hand out copies to ten people at work, and they each hand it out to seven acquaintances, and everybody registers, your commission would come to $60. If that doesn't excite you, well, load TinyTerm onto your laptop and give it a spin anyway. It's a good, basic, *small* but capable comm program. Then, if you decide to use it, register it (remember what oatmeal spokesman Wilford Brimley said about doing the right thing) and let the author keep the 75 cents.

Tip

TinyTerm and its companion program TinyHost (described later in this chapter) make an effective team. Use them to call your main office or desktop PC from your laptop when you're on the road.

JaxTalk: Gnat-Sized

Never trust a computer you can't throw out a window.
—Steve Wozniak

JaxTalk is the ultimate minimalist telecomm program. {COMMO} is small, as such applications go, and Lync is even smaller. TinyTerm is, well, tiny...for a comm program. All are very good hacks. Such programs must handle an awful lot of resources at once, under very unforgiving conditions. They have every right to be larger than the average directory sorter. So when we came across JaxTalk, we thought it was a gag. It's only—ready for this?—*469 bytes long.* (Okay, 512 bytes in its distribution form.) This *paragraph* is bigger than that. So we won't bother with a Hack Facts box here; it would violate the whole spirit of JaxTalk. Just look for JT.ZIP on the CD-ROM and understand that JaxTalk is about as minimal as a program can get and still be graced with the label. (At one time JT was a bit larger, but author Jack Kilday shaved off a final 13 bytes by doing away with the DSR test, leaving only a CTS test.)

Note

JaxTalk is hard-coded to COM1 at N-8-1 and 1200 bps, but Kilday includes instructions for using DEBUG to switch to 300 or to a hotrod 2400 baud, the latter being the practical speed limit when Kilday put JT out on the wires in 1985. There's no copyright notice, so feel free to hack this little toy into a 469-byte, v.32bis telecomm powerhouse if you can. Hackers, you may consider this a challenge.

BBS Systems: Hosting All Callers

The incredibly large array of BBS software available just for IBM PCs makes it impossible for us to cover even one BBS in detail. If you need to call in digitally from time to time, or want to set up an e-mail system, your telecomm program's host mode may not be enough. In that case, you can choose between PC Board, RBBS, Opus, and a host of other great shareware BBS programs. All are designed to answer modem call-ins and provide an easy-to-use host/caller interface.

Edit
Tip
Quote

Out-of-band: ...(3) In personal communication, using methods other than email, such as telephones or {snail-mail}.
—from "The Jargon File"

There also are some fine retail BBS systems, such as Wildcat! (by the Qmodem people). A huge proportion of all retail BBSes have their roots in shareware. Maybe it's because by the time anyone outside a corporate e-mail room wants to run a BBS, they're already shareware converts.

Most BBS packages use similar keystroke commands: B to read new bulletins, C to chat with the sysop or another user, D to download files, F to access the file area, G to say good-bye, M to enter the message area, U to upload a file, and so forth. BBS packages have minor variations from one system to the next, but it's like the differences between cars. They look different, act different, can be harder or easier to master, but on the whole, you'll never confuse the brake pedal with the accelerator. Figure 3-3 shows a simple but well-designed BBS main menu. Notice that it gives a good idea of the options available on that board. (We called the Azusa Pacific College BBS in California to get the shot).

Some BBSes accept keystroke commands instantly; others demand that you press ENTER to execute the command. Some display commands or selections which you lack authority to

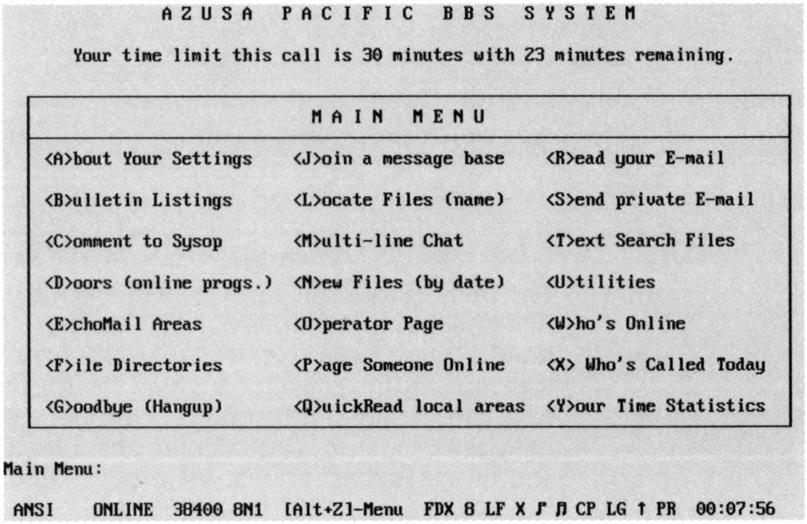
A Z U S A   P A C I F I C   B B S   S Y S T E M
Your time limit this call is 30 minutes with 23 minutes remaining.
M A I N   M E N U
<A>bout Your Settings
<J>oin a message base
<R>ead your E-mail
<B>ulletin Listings
<L>ocate Files (name)
<S>end private E-mail
<C>omment to Sysop
<M>ulti-line Chat
<T>ext Search Files
<D>oors (online progs.)
<N>ew Files (by date)
<U>tilities
<E>choMail Areas
<O>perator Page
<W>ho's Online
<F>ile Directories
<P>age Someone Online
<X> Who's Called Today
<G>oodbye (Hangup)
<Q>uickRead local areas
<Y>our Time Statistics
Main Menu:
ANSI ONLINE 38400 8N1 [Alt+Z]-Menu FDX 8 LF X CP LG PR 00:07:56

Figure 3-3. *Main menu of The Azusa Pacific College BBS*

access, while others will dim those options out or eliminate them from the display. (The last is preferable, because it doesn't waste your online time putting useless information onto the screen.)

Edit Tip Quote

If getting remote access is your main concern, see the description of DOORWAY that follows.

Setting up a BBS is an art form in its own right, whose practitioners are known to use a form of technobabble utterly baffling to a non-acolyte. The best we can tell you is if you want to start a BBS, either start with something you know—for example, if you use Qmodem, you might try Mustang Software's Wildcat! BBS—or get advice from the online community about the best shareware BBS products and give several of them a test before registering the one that works best for you.

Hack Facts

Doorway
Version 2.22
Marshall Dudley
TriMark Engineering
406 Monitor Lane
Knoxville, TN 37922
Orders: 1-800-676-3799
BBS: 615-966-3574
229,948 bytes
Shareware: $30
DRWY222.ZIP

Doorway is an elegant and economical hack that lets you log onto a remote computer by modem and control it from the remote keyboard. Originally designed for bulletin boards, it has become a sort of de facto standard in the BBS community, letting almost any program be run as a "door" in which everything behaves as if the remote caller was using the system's own keyboard—except for functions reserved by the BBS operator, such as breaking out of a program and dropping down to DOS. In other words, it is a safe way to assign system control to a remote user for specific purposes. If it's your system, on the other hand, you can set up a password to give you complete remote control, so you can do your hacking from the Pizza Hut™. To keep things fast by modem, DOORWAY won't handle bit-mapped graphics—in other words, it ain't for Windows (but neither is this book).

DOORWAY comes with a tiny comm program, DWCOMM, and a mated host mode program, DWHOST, that together operate seamlessly to let you log on, invoke DOORWAY to run your computer from afar, and log off again. To transfer files without relinquishing local operation of the remote computer, you can use DWXFER, also supplied. For reliable remote control using a good hack's clean lines and coding, DOORWAY is just the ticket.

Hack Facts

TinyHost
Version 3.31
Bruce A. Krobusek
5950 King Hill Drive
Farmington, NY 14425
BBS: 716-924-4193
CIS: 74106,1335
91,575 (TinyHost)
104,836 (TinyHost Plus)
Shareware: $25 (TinyHost), $35 (TinyHost Plus)
TH331.ZIP and THP111.ZIP

If Doorway's host mode doesn't have quite enough BBS flavor, take a look at TinyHost and TinyHost Plus. Both are quite capable BBS's—but they can run on a 1-floppy XT with only 256KB of total memory (150KB free). A superior hack! They won't do the job for you if you need to run 160 nodes with multiple high speed GIF file transfers. But they'll be terrific as a private small office or home BBS. Both support shell file transfers—meaning that you can send and receive files using DSZ or H/S Link—and both can be configured to provide limited or full access to your system when you or someone else phones in.

TinyHost Plus adds the ability to automate up to five file transfers between it and another TinyHost machine (20 files in the registered version), making it great for automated use between, for example, home and office. You can keep your work files synchronized that way. THP also supports personal directory access and recent activity stats.

Edit
Tip
Quote

ACK and you shall receive data.
—BBS Quote-of-the-Day Program

Both BBS systems are ready for ISDN fast phone lines, support multiple security access levels, can run on COM1 through COM4, and support various forms of messaging and passworded DOS access. These little programs are amazingly capable for their size.

Getting the Goodies from Here to There

If you're a BBSer, the kind of user who rides the wires from one small node to another instead of lurking around the mass consumption info services, you're probably one of three types: You might spend hours at the interactive games,

Edit
Tip
Quote

Baud barf: /bawd barf/ n. The garbage one gets on the monitor when using a modem connection with some protocol setting (esp. line speed) incorrect, or when someone picks up a voice extension...
—from "The Jargon File"

you might buzz around the message boards listening to the two cents' worth put in by others and adding your own dollar's worth, or you might collect shareware or information files. You've probably done all three at one time or another, but most BBSers settle down into one of these three areas to get their main fix.

If you're a file collector, you probably trade files for access time on BBSes, or just pass along files and programs because you like to share the wealth. It's surprising to us how many hardcore propeller-head computer techies settle for old fashion Xmodem or Ymodem to exchange files. It's like riding a bus when there's a free airline ticket collecting dust on your desk. We're including two of the best shareware file transfer protocols around, just in case you haven't gotten around to trying them. The bus is nice and slow and easygoing, but what a waste of time! Here, have a couple plane tickets for your file transfers:

Hack Facts

DSZ
Version Jan-23-94
Chuck Forsberg
Omen Technology
POB 4681
Portland OR 97208-4681
Modem: 503-621-3746
CIS: 70007,2304
GEnie: CAF
86874 bytes
Shareware: $20 (5.25" disk), $25 (3.5" disk)
DSZ.ZIP

The Zmodem file transfer protocol was first commissioned by Telenet (now SprintNet) and has become a near-universal standard. With Zmodem you can take advantage of fast file transfers on 99 percent of all BBSes and on Delphi and GEnie as well. Various Zmodem implementations are available, but the one we use is DSZ, by Chuck Forsberg. It's on the CD-ROM in both an EXE and a COM version. (The COM version is smaller, the EXE a bit faster on slow iron; see the docs for other differences.) Install DSZ, and forget the bumpy send-a-chunk, wait-for-a-reply rhythm of Xmodem and Ymodem. The data will stream through the wires instead. Look for DSZ*.ZIP.

DSZ also supports "true" Ymodem, which preserves true file size and sends/accepts the filename block. You can use it for automated batch downloads, just as you can Zmodem. Sometimes called "Ymodem batch" in other comm programs. See the various docs for more detail on the different transfer protocols supported by DSZ.

Also included in the DSZ collection:

- DSZEXE.ZIP: The .EXE (not .COM) version of DSZ, for slower iron. See READ.ME file.
- DSZBG.ZIP: Background on DSZ, an addendum to the DSZ manual in DSZ.ZIP.
- DSZNEW.ZIP: An addendum with technical information specific to this edition of DSZ.

Tip

What makes Forsberg's implementation superior is a series of features he's labeled Zmodem-90™. It improves considerably on the PD version, adding such features as data compression for speed transfers, frames that support 7-bit transfers when you're talking to a mainframe, auto-download, and more. Do read the docs to get best use of this protocol!

Brief Mention: H/S Link for Fast Two-Way Transfers

H/S Link is still less common on the boards than Zmodem, but it has been taking the BBS world by storm. It's great for general business use, because it gives the best bang for the long distance buck by sending files boths ways at once. HS/Link isn't the only protocol that can do this, but it's probably the fastest, faster even than modem-to-modem hardware correction when tested on some hardware and used only for one-way transfers. It's very easy to install, and if you often upload and download during the same session, it's a great way to go. Look for HS121.ZIP.

Edit
Tip
Quote

The {COMMO} telecomm program described earlier supports auto-downloading with H/S Link, making it a good choice if the host nodes you call have H/S Link installed.

The Major Online Services

The line between a BBS and an online service is blurry, now that hybrids like Channel 1, Exec PC and The Well have grown huge and offer diverse services. Nowadays they all access the Internet, where the true wireheads dwell. Want action on The Wires? Keep your beady eyes on Internet. It's amazing what you can do, just roaming around that worldwide service. For more structured access, use one of the major information services. CompuServe, AOL, GEnie, and even ad-littered Prodigy have beefed up their "I-Net" gateways, while the smaller Delphi service has provided complete I-Net access for years. Delphi is a good place to start exploring the I-Net, because it provides such powerful traveler's tools as gophers, archie, wais and other arcane resources. Delphi's menu system is very easy to use, so poking around the net is easy. If you can't find what you want on I-Net using Delphi's well conceived access portals, just post a question in Delphi's Internet SIG. Some real gurus of the I-Net hang out there. You might also check out *The Internet Yellow Pages* by fervent Net-a-zoids Harley Hahn and Rick Stout (Osborne/McGraw-Hill, 1994).

Edit
Tip
Quote

Go exploring! It's the only way to travel the wires, with a lot of fun added into the bargain.

For a somewhat more traditional style of information service, you may prefer the highly organized and well run CompuServe, where you can find an expert on any aspect of computing. Or the fast-growing, yeasty feel of America Online, where access isn't always easy, but you get an "it's happening here!" feel that resembles old-timers' descriptions of the golden days of The Source (R.I.P.). The sense of enthusiasm that AOLers convey is infectious, and as AOL continues to expand its I-Net gateway services it will become a good place to start exploring. Or you may prefer the more technical flavor of GEnie, which started out as a way for General Electric to make a buck on excess late-night computer capacity, but has grown into a full-time service in its own right. Some serious hackers have hung out there for years.

Quote

Computer networks encourage the active participation of individuals rather than the passive non-participation induced by television narcosis.

—Mitchell Kapor, Electronic Frontier Foundation

Don't Mutter—**Emote!**

Misunderstandings happen in cyberspace. Your correspondent in Geneva can't hear you chuckle or see you smile as you type some witticism involving bankers and large dogs. He might not realize you're joking. He might even be a banker with a large dog. Because of the lack of eye contact, even the most innocent remark can sometimes make someone "flame," to use a common term. Misunderstandings happen, and people who travel the wires learn to keep their voices down until they're sure they want to take offense.

There are ways around the problem. The best cyberspace solution is "emoticons," which can convey emotion and facial expressions to some extent. The most common emoticon is a smiley, which stands for—are you ready?—a smile. Use it to say "that was a joke" or "hey, lighten up, stop flaming at me." The simple smiley looks like this:

:-)

It's a smiley face if you tilt your head to the left. Other common emoticons include ;-) for a wink, :-(for sadness, :-< or >:-< for anger, :-0 for yelling, and a dunce-capped smiley <:-) . The simple smiley :) also is often used.

Some of these services, especially CompuServe, are beehives of support for users of commercial programs; dozens of firms keep their own support areas there, so you can find expert help on just about any question.

Accessing the Info Masters

Use these numbers (listed alphabetically, not by preference) to set up accounts on the major information services, if you decide you want to go that route:

- America Online: 800-827-6364
- CompuServe: 800-848-8990
- Delphi: 800-695-4005
- GEnie: 800-638-9636
- Prodigy: 800-776-3449

All are voice numbers, but some, like Delphi, also have modem numbers with which you can sign up. Ask about that when you call one of these numbers.

Next Up

In the next chapter, we open Part II, where we start to get a bit more technical. Hackers don't always like to use others' programs when they can roll their own, but everyone needs good tools. In Chapter 4, "Programmer Friendly," we offer a collection of editors and other tools guaranteed to make the hacker path a bit easier to follow.

011010 11000110 0011010 11001001 100010001

11010 11000110 0011010 11001001 100010001

0011010 11001001 100010001

part 2

Tools for the Hackmeister

4

Programmer Friendly

This chapter introduces some tools that will help your work sessions go more smoothly. Anyone seriously engaged in a job needs decent tools—tools that are fit for the task. For a programmer, writing code (and the docs that often go with it) begins with text editors, and we'll offer some superior examples here. We'll also show you some editing add-ons to make life easier, and we'll even include a terrific task-switching "shell" to let you jump around from this program to that without unloading the current task or putting up with the performance toll exacted by Windows and its gooey, er, GUI kin.

DOS Tools for DOS Programmers

Man is a tool-using animal. Without tools he is nothing, with tools he is all.
—Thomas Carlyle

Face it. It's hard to stay sane when you have to spend huge amounts of time getting around the limitations designed into your tools by others. Try writing some code—or even an ASCII "readme" file—using the Windows Notepad, for example. It's all double-clicks and multiple menu item selections. You can get used to it; humans can adjust to anything.

You have to be a real stud hombre cybermuffin to handle "Windows." I have spent countless hours trying to get my computer to perform even the most basic data-processing functions, such as letting me play "F-117A Stealth Fighter" on it.
—Dave Barry

But the Notepad becomes annoying, especially if you're used to the speed and convenience of single-key control toggles and other common features of the better text editors.

The same goes for your working environment. Simple is better, and it's always a good idea to do your work where you expect others to use the results. If you spend time writing, debugging, and testing code for DOS, why put ten layers of bad ideas between you and the computer by throwing in a hoggish GUI? That sort of folly can only waste resources and confuse both you and the computer, and when someone runs your programs under plain old DOS their machine might explode. (You wouldn't want that, unless it belonged to your boss or some politician.)

Granted, for years we've heard people complain about how "unfriendly" DOS is. That reputation has helped some people pile up some money, creating a trade for those who simplify the obvious. But hey, guys, DOS isn't unfriendly. It's just stark, economical, and minimal. Naturally it has a few drawbacks, as anyone who ever typed a long pathname will eagerly go into print to point out. You can only assume that such users have never heard of tricky tools like batch files and command macros. Maybe they just don't read much.

Sticking with DOS: EDIT and DOSSHELL

As with a lot of other computing areas, by the time Microsoft caught on that big bucks could be made giving people good tools to work with, others had made a major, money-making industry from that same idea. It wasn't until the DOS focus switched from pleasing the Intel hardware to pleasing PC users that anything like "user friendly" crept into the DOS list of goals. By the time DOS 5.0 rolled around, the MS minions were already engineering a Windows takeover; any bow they made to the DOS user at that point was bound to be perfunctory.

The DOS reputation never scared a hacker, but it played hell with users' attitudes. In a world where a book titled *Hey Dummy! Here's a DOS Book for You!* is a guaranteed best seller, you might suspect that someone burned their midnights to make DOS read like Greek to a Laplander.

Still, a few hardy souls in the dusty back rooms at Redmond, Washington finally ground out some fair to middling tools for working with files and programs. EDIT.COM (actually just a loader) does a halfway decent job on text files, if you don't mind the bloated QBASIC overhead it takes to tweak, say, a 60-byte batch file. And DOSSHELL, Microsoft's answer to DOS task switchers like Back and Forth and Software Carousel, is slow but it does save having to shell out or unload an application just to make a quick jump to some other program. A lot of people get along just fine with only those programs, thank you very much.

So, if you're a Microsoft loyalist, you might want to ignore this chapter. The tools we offer here are far superior to the native DOS versions, but hey, to each his/her/their own.

Fortunately for hackers, the minor inconveniences of DOS have a multitude of solutions, shortcuts, and work-arounds. Getting around DOS's limits is a fertile field that hackers love to cultivate. No doubt the satisfaction comes from the gardener in us all. To carry the gardening metaphor to truly ridiculous lengths, in this chapter we'll give you some choices, so if you don't like cauliflower, you can pick broccoli (just don't tell former President George Bush).

There's an almost limitless supply of general utility programs out there if you go looking for them. Why? Well, mostly because computer years, like dog years, go by at a mad pace (maybe not with the "blinding speed" that cliché-bound software reviewers gabble about, but still awfully fast). By now, we've had whole computer *generations* of hackers who've figured out better or easier ways to do this task or that, and some of their solutions to the hassles of working with Microsoft tools have been elegant indeed.

For ways to hook more of the good stuff in the DOS shareware stream, check out Chapter 3, "Walking the Wires."

Here, we'll concentrate on a few of the best DOS tools for general use. The programs in this section will help you start or switch between programs, edit files and program code, or enhance your work sessions in other useful ways. We'll start with a tool no hacker (whether of programs or words) can afford to be without—a superior text editor.

Quote

You can't always get what you want, but if you try sometimes, you might find you get what you need.

—The Rolling Stones

Getting What You Need

Maybe you've been told all your life that you can't have everything you want, and maybe it's even true, but in the world of shareware you can come awfully close. If you see something here that seems to be almost, but not quite, exactly what you've been looking for, you have a couple of ways to find something closer to your needs. You can spend the time writing a program that does exactly what you want (check out the CD-ROM for sample code that can make the job easier). Or you can spend time "on the wires" hunting for alternatives (see Chapter 3, "Walking the Wires"). Either way, you can have a lot of fun.

Caution

You may not want to have all that fun openly in front of your employer during the working day, unless you have a garden-variety boss whom you can easily fool or safely ignore.

Editors: Fast and Flexible

Back in the dark ages, some programmers actually did all their work using EDLIN, the old DOS line editor whose main virtue was that it worked like an extension of DEBUG. People wrote long, priestly essays on how to use EDLIN, usually with stock "There—wasn't that easy, dummy?" perorations. Still, normal people went to extreme lengths to avoid EDLIN, the ill-mannered child of haste and minimalism.

EDLIN was truly a bad hand to deal to programmers, but hey—they were programmers. If the Founding MS-DOS Cheese insisted on handing them a joker for an editor, programmers knew how to reshuffle the deck. And did they ever reshuffle the deck.

Within a couple of years, EDLIN was ignored by all but High Adepts of the DOS Mysteries and some lay-but-skilled devotees of on-the-fly DEBUG routines. A few years of independent programming had produced text editors with such handy features as whole-screen editing of pure ASCII files, global find and replace, cut and paste, and a host of other superior tools. What these features had in common was that they all made it much easier to write program code and simple, copy-to-your-printer documents such as memos and mash notes. Many of the best of the new editors were, and remain, shareware. They're better than their Windows counterparts even when used in a DOS box, and in DOS proper they really rocket around. Some of their more clever features, like automatic indenting and key word colorizing, can quickly become addicting. We guarantee that the highly configurable editors on this book's CD-ROM won't make you tear your hair out or bounce off the walls any more than is necessary or customary to your craft.

We'll start with one of the first and best of the shareware editors: the classic Qedit offered by SemWare. Then we'll throw in Boxer, an up-and-comer that some think of as a Qedit clone but which actually stands on its own and includes some nifty extra features. And if the ultimate speed of an editor in a .COM file format tickles your fancy, try VDE, an interesting, powerful little editor designed to work well on laptops and other limited iron.

Of course this section wouldn't be complete without a mention of the (hiss!) commercial editor, Brief™. If you're using Brief at the office and don't want to waste time shifting command sets to do your own work at home, you can emulate Brief in any of these editors. Macros and other features may not work exactly like your office system, but the keyboard commands can be quite effectively cloned.

We gave the earlier hiss not for the editor itself but for the fact that Brief is a commercial, retail product. It's a good program, just about the only commercial product we'll deal with directly in this book. Why this exception? Well, a lot of programmers swear by that particular editor. If you have Brief, if you love Brief, if you wouldn't try to write code without Brief, did you know there's stuff you can do with Brief macros that'll stand that program on its ear? The folks at The Software Annex have provided a free site license for this book's readers to use their Brief macro language database, CBRIEF (in the file BH_NGS.ZIP). It's done up in Norton Guides format, but if you don't have that program you can use NG_CLONE (also on the CD-ROM and described in Chapter 10, "A Bag of Other Goodies").

SO let's take a look at one of the most basic tools in a programmer's tool chest—the editors used for writing program code. Try our selections and pick the one you like best. Trust us, you can't go wrong with any of these programs.

Hack Facts

Qedit Advanced
Version 3.0
Sammy E. Mitchell
SemWare Corporation
4343 Shallowford Road
Suite C3A
Marietta, GA 30062-5022
800-467-3692
CIS: 75300,2710
206,317 bytes
Shareware: $59
QEDIT3C.ZIP

Qedit has by now become an "old standard" in the programming world. Many consider it the *de facto* standard for text editors, in much the way WordStar was at one time the *de facto* standard for word processors. And many loyalists wouldn't consider trying to work without it and the huge systems of macros that users have developed for it over the years.

If small, fast, and flexible are the hallmarks of a good editor, then Qedit fills the bill. It comes with a variety of configuration files, or you can configure it however you want. Almost every key on a 101-key "en-yucked" AT keyboard can take on any meaning you choose, from switching the colon and the semicolon or ESC and the tilde to assigning long, interactive macros that would qualify as small programs if written in C or Pascal. On the other hand, to run this little editor right out of the box, uh, ZIP file, all you need is the file Q.EXE. All of which makes Qedit a full-featured editor that fits on a travelin' 360K floppy, with room to spare for other files.

Qedit is fast because it operates all in memory, up to 640K—more than enough room for just about any program code and the docs that ride with them. You can edit as many files as will fit in memory, and you can put as many horizontal windows onscreen as will fit. You can use the pull-down menus if you want. You can cut and paste between files and save your clips for later use in umpteen different named clipboards that you can recall from a pick list.

We won't try to cover all of this classic's highlights here. Check out the docs in the distribution file—a bulleted list of notable features takes up more than two full pages. Qedit has set the standard for a long time now, with good reason. It's a great little editor.

Hack Facts

Boxer
Version 6.0A
David R. Hamel
Boxer Software
P.O. Box 3230
Peterborough, NH 03458-3230
Voice: 603-924-6602
Sales: 800-982-6937
CompuServe: 70242,2126
334,573 bytes
Shareware: $35-$50
BOXER60A.ZIP

Boxer may be a newcomer compared to Qedit, but it has gained a very large following very quickly. If you try it, you'll see why. At 126,460 bytes, the main executable program is slower to load than Qedit—you'll notice the difference—but the extra heft packs some very nice features. You can spot the care that author David Hamel takes with this program in the fine detail work.

Take the way Boxer handles keyboard info. All good editors have an ASCII chart, but Boxer's stands out from the rest. It's in a 128-character window. You toggle between 7- and 8-bit characters with PAGE UP, pick a character, and insert it directly into your text. Simple. But there's more. The SPACEBAR toggles between decimal, octal, hexadecimal, control equivalent symbols, and control mnemonics displays. (Figure 4-1 shows the control mnemonics chart.) Need keyboard values? The ASCII Value menu command shows values for the character under the cursor in four bases (hex, decimal, octal, and binary) plus the main, auxiliary, and shift status bytes for subsequent keypresses. All that information in one place when you need it—that's slick...and typical of this fine editor.

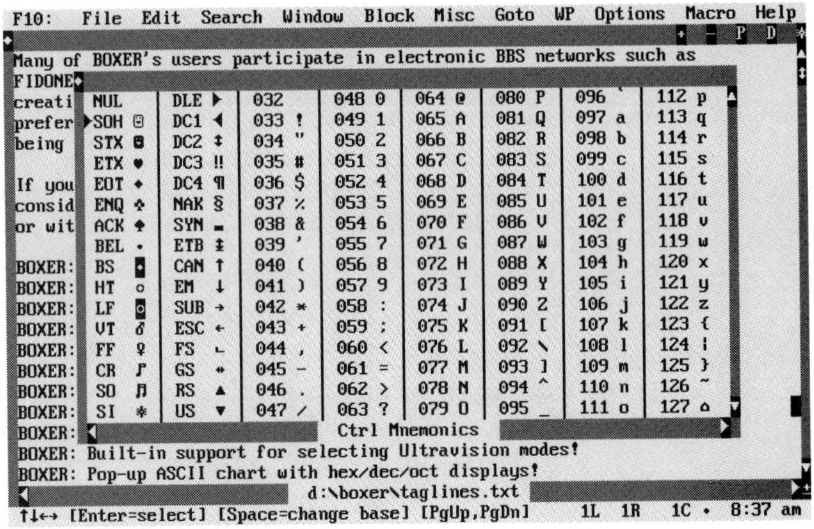
F10: File Edit Search Window Block Misc Goto WP Options Macro Help
Many of BOXER's users participate in electronic BBS networks such as
FIDONE
creati
prefer
being
If you
consid
or wit
NUL DLE 032 048 0 064 @ 080 P 096 ` 112 p
SOH DC1 033 ! 049 1 065 A 081 Q 097 a 113 q
STX DC2 034 " 050 2 066 B 082 R 098 b 114 r
ETX DC3 035 # 051 3 067 C 083 S 099 c 115 s
EOT DC4 036 $ 052 4 068 D 084 T 100 d 116 t
ENQ NAK 037 % 053 5 069 E 085 U 101 e 117 u
ACK SYN 038 & 054 6 070 F 086 V 102 f 118 v
BEL ETB 039 ' 055 7 071 G 087 W 103 g 119 w
BS CAN 040 (056 8 072 H 088 X 104 h 120 x
HT EM 041) 057 9 073 I 089 Y 105 i 121 y
LF SUB 042 * 058 : 074 J 090 Z 106 j 122 z
VT ESC 043 + 059 ; 075 K 091 [107 k 123 {
FF FS 044 , 060 < 076 L 092 \ 108 l 124 |
CR GS 045 - 061 = 077 M 093] 109 m 125 }
SO RS 046 . 062 > 078 N 094 ^ 110 n 126 ~
SI US 047 / 063 ? 079 O 095 _ 111 o 127
Ctrl Mnemonics
BOXER: Built-in support for selecting Ultravision modes!
BOXER: Pop-up ASCII chart with hex/dec/oct displays!
d:\boxer\taglines.txt
[Enter=select] [Space=change base] [PgUp,PgDn] 1L 1R 1C 8:37 am

Figure 4-1. *Boxer's ASCII chart (control mnemonics on left)*

Another reason Boxer spins our caps is its built-in colorizing of reserved words, comments, symbols, and constants in just about every major programming language. You can pick different colors if you don't like the defaults. Colorized text is very addictive—errors in closing statements, for example, leap right off the screen. Boxer recognizes the language you're using by a file's extension. If David forgot to include RIPIT, the Russian Interdependent Programmed International Transaction language, no big deal. Just add a section to the plain ASCII configuration file. Some high-end integrated design programs like Borland's IDE will color your code, but Boxer does it every bit as well, it only sets you back $35 or $50, and it lets you add any languages that David forgot.

boxer resembles high-end IDE programs in another notable respect—you can compile a program from within the editor and be placed automatically on any errors. Boxer has built-in support for the most popular compilers, and you can add others if you need to. When you correct mistakes, Boxer remembers the lines, so if fixing an error requires you to add or delete lines of code, subsequent error lines are not impacted by the change in line numbering. Try to get that kind of service from some other $35—or $235—text editor.

Here's the final touch that makes Boxer a must-try editor: you can split the screen vertically or horizontally and load before- and after-versions of a file, letting Boxer take you, in sequence, to each difference. Now that's *service!*

Have It Your Way

Everything about Boxer gives you choices. When you install the program, you choose from, not two or three, but 15 different editor and word processor emulations. Partial to PFS:Write? Fine! Want to use the Borland IDE command set on your laptop with the 20MB drive? No problem. Or pick Brief, Epsilon, Norton, WordStar, Multi-Edit, or MS Word emulations among the major DOS programs. If you just love EPM, the OS/2 editor, Boxer does that shtick too. It's even got ready-made emulations for Qedit and VDE, two other major shareware editors included on this book's CD-ROM.

The list may not include your personal favorite. Want something like your old Commodore 64 version of VolksWriter? Maybe you're partial to the way PC Write uses function keys, or you're a Dvorak keyboard speed demon. Hey, no problem; just roll your own keyboard configuration. And for icing on that particular cake, if you change the keyboard, then not only will the pull-down menus reflect the new settings, so will Boxer's context-sensitive F1 help system. Slick!

Boxer gives your life some color variation too, if you want it. You can change the entire color scheme without ever leaving your current editing session. Boxer comes with nine different prepared color schemes including Windows, but if bright green text on a magenta screen would make you happy, Boxer aims to please. We spent an hour designing the ugliest editing screen we could think of. Why not? When we got a headache, all we had to do was click on the Option menu and reset the screen to a sane and restful white on blue motif. Oh—did we forget to mention it? Boxer has built-in mouse support, too.

This is an editor that just begs you to have fun with it!

Hack Facts

VDE
Versions 1.72 and 1.65B (both on CD-ROM)
Eric Meyer
3541 Smuggler Way
Boulder, CO 80303
Order: 800-242-4775
CIS: 71355,470
152.212 bytes (VDE172)
140,809 (VDE165B)
Shareware: $35
VDE172.ZIP, VDE165B.ZIP

If you need a more general DOS file editor, one with close to the power of a full fledged word processor without the hassle of format-happy file bloating, VDE by Eric Meyer may be just the ticket. This is a small, clean program built on the familiar WordStar keyboard command set, though you can use its pull-down menus if you prefer.

VDE is very fast, and it's great for working with ASCII documents that need only mild word processing. It even handles proportional spacing fonts and auto-hyphenation—a remarkable accomplishment for a program so undemanding of your system's resources. As the manual points out, if you need more sophisticated page design, you can import your VDE-produced file into a real desktop publishing program. But you may not resort to file-bloating, disk-hogging mainstream word processors nearly as often after you get used to VDE.

VDE only handles a 64K data chunk of memory, which (with in-memory data compression) comes to about an 80K ASCII file. That's plenty for most purposes, but if you work with larger documents, you can break them into smaller parts that are faster to edit.

For Off-Trail Hardware

If your hardware puts special demands on your editor, VDE may be just the choice for you. It makes special provisions for systems that use 40-character-wide screens, for example. It also is friendly to special hardware like HP 95LX/100LX palmtops.

VDE version 1.65, also included on the CD-ROM, has a "generic" installation option that requires only ANSI screen sequence compatibility. If you have unusual or non-PC-compatible hardware that can, however, handle ANSI screen sequences, try VDE 1.65 instead of VDE 1.72.

Some Other Cushions for Working Hackers

Never deny yourself the comfort of a couple of soft cushions under your overburdened working hacker's posterior. Life is real, life is short, life is earnest. An added convenience or two can encourage a healthy, Bronx cheer attitude. Be good to yourself.

The next few programs, which we'll describe briefly, are designed to make your work go better and faster. The full manuals are included on the CD-ROM. These programs are luxuries for people who deserve binary pampering, like you.

Hack Facts

Back and Forth Professional

```
Version 2.14
Shane and Sandy Stump
CIS: 76702,1360
557,148 (BFP214A)
769,989 (BFP214B)
Shareware (fully enabled,
  trial version—no fee)
BFP214A.ZIP and
BFP214B.ZIP
```

Back and Forth Professional is probably still the finest task-switcher around—fully the equal of any commercial competitor, and far superior to DOSSHELL, the DOS equivalent. It's like Windows without concurrent processing, but also without the huge disk and performance overhead. B&F (or BNF as some call it) will run only one program at a time...but it makes up for that limitation with gonzo fast switching between tasks. It also lets you cut and paste between programs, run an alarm system, and even macro all your applications to run together. The version we include here is the fully enabled trial version that will load up to 20 tasks at once—more than enough for most users. You can run this program in a DOS box under Windows, or run Windows under B&F. It's also completely compatible with OS/2, and can provide some nifty extra services while inside the old DOS "penalty box." B&F is a truly great hack. Figure 4-2 shows what the B&F installation screen looks like as B&F installs Word Perfect Phone Notes with a hot key.

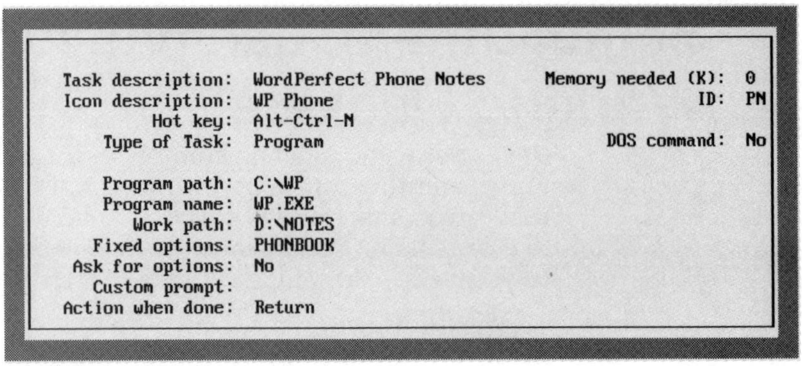
Task description: WordPerfect Phone Notes
Memory needed (K): 0
Icon description: WP Phone
ID: PN
Hot key: Alt-Ctrl-N
Type of Task: Program
DOS command: No
Program path: C:\WP
Program name: WP.EXE
Work path: D:\NOTES
Fixed options: PHONBOOK
Ask for options: No
Custom prompt:
Action when done: Return

Figure 4-2. *Back and Forth installing a program*

Note

This completely functional software is no longer directly supported by the authors, since the basic B&F engine was sold to a retail software house. You can, however, message the authors on CompuServe to get friendly answers to reasonable questions. B&F Pro is a fully developed, stable system that runs rings around DOSSHELL, its DOS equivalent. To remove memory limitations on this trial copy, use registration name *DOS Programmer's Cookbook* and serial number P-1994-0124-01 (as contained in file B&FPRO.SN, i nside file BNFKEY.ZIP).

Hack Facts

NewKey
Version 5.4
Frank A. Bell
FAB Software
P.O. Box 336
Wayland, MA 01778
508-358-6357
CIS: 75206,1366
202,557 bytes
Shareware: $43
NEWKEY54.ZIP

A few years ago, when SuperKey and ProKey pretty much ruled the keyboard macro roost, people flamed passionately at each other over the virtues of their favorite. Then applications began doing their own macros, command editors took over the DOS prompt, and the keyboard macro battles pretty much stopped. All the while, Frank Bell quietly continued to develop what has become the finest keyboard macro program available, bar none, and you can register it for only $43. At that price, it's a steal.

If you haven't used one of these beasts in a while, give NewKey a try. The convenience can become addictive. Among its many services, NewKey lets you customize any software package by attaching program-specific key sequences. It's great for entering boiler plate passages, and it provides you with custom help menus, redefines your keyboard, speeds up your cursor, acts as a screen saver, and extends the keyboard buffer. NewKey's pop-up menu, shown here, provides services like cutting and pasting between programs.

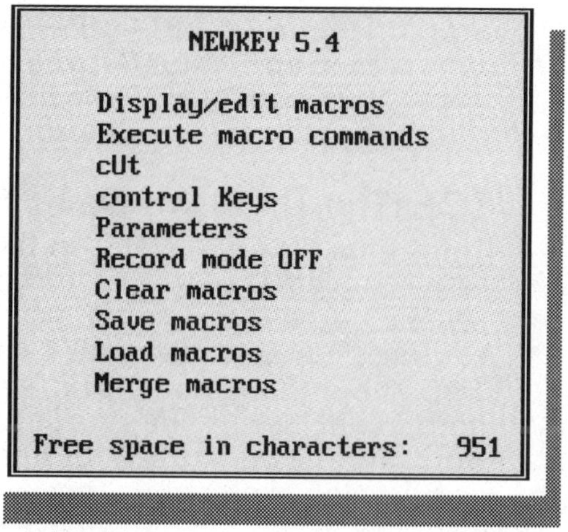
NEWKEY 5.4
Display/edit macros
Execute macro commands
cUt
control Keys
Parameters
Record mode OFF
Clear macros
Save macros
Load macros
Merge macros
Free space in characters: 951

NewKey's shorthand facility can provide both command aliases at the DOS prompt and word or phrase completion inside an editor. You can use the program to automate statement closure and other nettlesome requirements of the programming trade.

Tip

If the full program's 62K or so of memory overhead is a bit too steep for you, use one of the smaller versions of NewKey supplied in the distribution file; these go down to about 30K of memory and can load in upper memory on most machines.

Brief Mentions

Check out the following files, all of them included on this book's CD-ROM. These are add-ons, enhancements, and other attractions for anyone who hasn't yet found exactly the tools needed to turn code-writing from a chore to a breeze...or for the ambitious or adventuresome who want to take matters a step further.

Rainbow: The Color-It-Anywhere Utility

This little jewel (in RB14.ZIP) selectively colorizes your keywords in any editor. All you have to do is tell it which words and what color. If you love Qedit but covet the colorizing of Boxer, here's a sort of bridge between them.

TDE (The Thomson-Davis Editor)

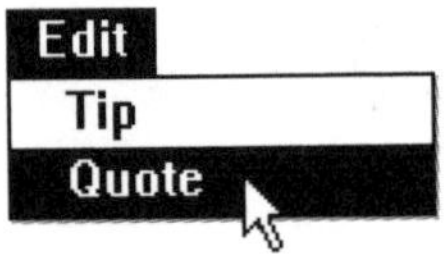
Edit
Tip
Quote

Give us the tools, and we will finish the job.
—Winston Churchill (Radio speech, 1941)

This editor (TDE32A.ZIP) is in the public domain and comes with complete C source code. Aside from being a very good general purpose text editor, you can use the source code as a starting point to create your own editor or just to modify TDE. The author, Frank Davis, says he put TDE in the public domain not because he's a saint but because he had to. He works for the Department of Agriculture, so the program was developed on public time and belongs to the public. He also says he has "an impressive collection of inflatable bed bunnies," and he calls his Atlanta, GA, company "Yank Software—Software you just can't beat."

ASavit: The Auto-Saver

This well executed little TSR (in ASAVITV3.ZIP) will stuff your keyboard buffer with the file-save keystrokes you specify (for example, CTRL-K, CTRL-S) at any interval you specify from 5 seconds up to about 18 hours. ASavit is for any application that lacks a periodic autosave, and it can be used to perform other timed functions (such as a network mail check) as well.

WCED: Command Editing and Aliasing

This DOS improver (WCED18C.ZIP) adopts a UNIX-like method of filename completion that saves hassles and typos when you need to type weird filenames: just type the first letter or two, then press the TAB key, and WCED provides the rest of the filename. If more than one filename fits the pattern, it lets you choose among them. The program also provides limited command aliasing, so it's a good choice if you don't want the more extensive operating changes and enhancements provided by NewKey (described above) or 4DOS (see Chapter 10, "A Bag of Other Goodies"). The distribution file includes WCEDLite, which is WCED without the command aliasing.

Next Up

In the next chapter, we'll delve into the arcane realm of data compression and file encryption. The two are not identical, but we're grouping them because they both allow you to change the form of a file to something unrecognizable without losing any of its contents. Of these two processes, compression is far and away the most important to programmers and developers, because it is central to program distribution—a legitimate practical (and commercial) concern.

5

Data Compression and Encryption

Quote

The problem with encrypting files is, people lose their keys. If they don't encrypt, they can lose their private data. Anyone who solves both problems will probably make a couple of bucks.
—Stephen B. Hicks, security consultant

At first glance, data compression and data encryption seem like a strange couple of subjects to treat as a married pair. But aside from the fact that both fields tend to attract mathematicians (who are known to make weirdness a way of life), there's nothing unnatural about pairing the two. They both involve transforming data into something radically different from the original without losing the original content. Lewis Carroll would have been right at home in either field. Of course, he was a practicing mathematician named Charles Dodgson when he wasn't sending Alice down rabbit holes for prototypical acidhead experiences. Mathematicians are like that.

Both data compression and encryption require finding repeated patterns and mutating them into something unrecognizable or something that takes less space to store, or both. Squeezing it down is the easy part. The hard part is getting your data back in its original form—no bugs, no glitches, nothing lost. It's tricky, and if the program fails, it can make a user very unhappy.

> *Don't worry. I'm fluent in weirdo.*
> *—Online message from a hacker*

The now standard data compression schemes serve most people fine. As for encryption—well, that's a specialty in its own right, although many of the file compressors will optionally encrypt as they compress, to keep your data safe from Mom, your spouse, or other prying eyes. Among the compressors, you can choose from the transparent whole-disk compressors like Stacker™ and (at least if you already have it) DoubleSpace, as well as a few others. Or you can work with the nontransparent, file-by-file variety that you control directly. These two types of compressors are different enough that most people who have the transparent kind can also use the file-by-file type.

So put away your attitudes and come with us, children, to an area where even hackers often fear to tread—or at least consider the company there to be spaced out a tad beyond the Outer Limits. Both compression and encryption have practical applications for the practicing hacker. We promise not to bore you with theoretical algorithms and transforms and like that. Ask your wild-eyed mathematical friends for those kinds of details, if you want them. What we will do here is take a short guided tour of compression, describe the best of what's out there in shareware, throw in a word or two on encryption just because it's a related field, and offer some of the reasons why a Complete Programmer should stay on top of what's going on in the field.

Compression Essentials

> *We're gonna teach you to put ten pounds of [expletive deleted] into a five-pound sack.*
> *—USMC Drill Instructor, ca. 1967*

Here's the essence of file compression: you take 50K of complex code, executable programs, or any other type of files and stuff them into a 25K or smaller space *without losing any of the original contents.* It's that last requirement that intrigues mathematicians, information theorists, and other sometimes lofty intellects; it's a realm for people who love puzzles and abstract analysis. It also attracts more than a few hackers, who love a real challenge.

The essence of transparent disk compression is that the user doesn't see it happen (your temp typist can't screw it up) and it operates across an entire logical drive. It's not selective, but it sure is easy. File compressors, on the other hand, work on one file (or wild-carded file) at a time. You tell the compression program what files to compress, what percentage to compress them by, where to store them, and whether to delete the uncompressed originals.

The field of compression is pretty stable now. We've included the main file compression programs plus some alternative choices on the CD-ROM, because they're shareware. Try them and pick the one you like best. For disk compression, you have to go retail.

For anyone who hasn't played around with compression, the next couple of sections will give a mercifully brief overview of what it's about.

Disk Compression

In disk compression, a program typically sets up a huge, hidden file and fools the system into believing the hidden file's contents actually reside on a separate, significantly larger logical drive. In other words, it plants a fake new drive on your hard disk and then stores what you put there in compressed form. As far as DOS is concerned, you've added new storage space to your system. This has the happy effect of letting you put double the data (well, typically a bit less, actually) onto your drive than you could normally store there.

This seemed like a good idea to people, so the main supplier of this type of compression, Stac Electronics, sold a *large* number of their Stacker software and add-in boards. So did several other thriving retailers. You might say they were in high cotton. This success naturally drew a little attention, and some honcho at Microsoft decreed that DOS should be able to do that type of compression as well. DoubleSpace, the native DOS disk compressor, was born with DOS 6.0. The people at Stac Electronics were very upset and sued Microsoft for infringing on their patents, and they were awarded a fairly hefty sum of money, but they also were told to pay Microsoft a lesser but still hefty sum of money to settle some other reckoning. You might say Stac won the fray, but the final score card wasn't very clear about who done what to whom.

DoubleSpace was knocked down but not out when users reported severe problems, such as badly munched data after using the DOS 6.0 version. In DOS 6.2 such problems were solved. DOS 6.2 also included some diagnostics that worked better than CHKDSK with compressed disks. Meanwhile, Stac came out with a new version of Stacker that gave better compression than DoubleSpace. Stac's victory in the court knocked Double Space out of the box in version 6.21, but if you got DoubleSpace with version 6.2, you can still use it...for now, at least.

The bottom line? Either product is cheaper than a new hard drive when you run out of storage room. As is usual with third-party products, Stacker is ahead of DOS in terms of compression ratio and nifty features. Stay tuned to your neighborhood computer magazine for future episodes in the continuing drama of Disk Compression Man, starring a huge cast of interesting, sometimes slightly weird characters.

File Compression

File compressors work on individual files. You name what files to compress and, depending upon the compressor, whether to go for maximum compression or for maximum speed (if you've used backup programs like Central Point Backup or Norton Backup, you've seen this option). In a nutshell, more compression takes more time, faster compression produces larger files. If you're working on or saving to floppy diskettes, you probably want the most compression you can get. The fewer 5-pound bags you need to handle, the better. If you're saving to a less limited medium like a hard disk or a tape drive, you can give up compression to gain what can be significantly faster operation. It'll take a 7-pound sack instead of a 5-pound one to hold your 10 pounds of *[expletive deleted],* but you'll wrap up the operation much sooner.

File Compression Benefits

The most obvious effect of compression (the one old Mrs. Grundy down at the high school would most likely understand) is that compression makes more files fit into less space. To a BBSer, it's just as obvious that a smaller file is faster to transmit over the phone—you have fewer total bytes to send. That's a *very* good effect, especially if one of Ma Bell's idiot children has been bugging you to pay for all those long-distance modem calls to some big BBS in the midwest. But we can tell you about other, less obvious benefits of file compression.

Minor Virus Protection

Some viruses are programmed to look for a certain sequence of bits in a specific host executable program. If the file is compressed, such a virus won't find the pattern it seeks and won't be able to make your program sick. Chances are you'd never even find out the virus was there looking for a home. (Compression won't, however, help against the general run of boot sector or other nonspecific viruses.)

Hack Shielding

Compressing your executables can help protect your software from data vandals or copycats, because it makes an executable harder to peek into or tweak in destructive ways. There are utilities out there to re-expand a compressed executable, but for distribution you can also use options in the registered version of some programs that will prevent re-expansion. It makes reverse engineering a bit harder even for determined pirates.

Trust in Allah, but tie your camel anyway.

—*Trad.*

Integrity Checking

Many compression utilities provide a way to self-check for changes since an archive was first created. You can use this to guard against hacks of your distribution files. If some pirate, or piece of hostile code for that matter, changes anything in the library of files, even the smallest detail in a README file, the program notifies the user that someone has diddled the data. Integrity verification can be done in a variety of ways, including "locking" an archive and comparing a current checksum against a stored value. A checksum system uses an algorithm to generate a number based on a file's contents and stores it in the archive itself for later comparison. When you expand the archive, a new checksum is generated and, if it differs from the original, the program warns the user.

Embedded Comments

Embedded comments are used to pass information to the person de-archiving (expanding) the file. The embedded comments are displayed, often followed by a prompt asking whether the user wants to continue with de-archiving. You can use this message to tell people about the contents of the archive, to remind them that they need to register shareware, or to provide installation information.

Password Encryption: Useful but Limited

Most of the good compression utilities (with the notable exception of LHA) provide password protection and member file encryption (or "garbling"); both features that a developer can find very useful. Member file encryption is not as secure as full encryption because the file titles remain unencrypted. A snooper can see what's in there. But to see a file's contents, unless you're a professional code-breaking spook, you'll need the correct password. A password keeps casual snoopers out and makes it a bit safer to exchange sensitive files on the public info systems or on a BBS. You aren't as likely to lose your work to pirates.

Password encryption can let you supply fully registered versions of your software on a CD-ROM or on the same floppy as the shareware or test version. If a user wants to register, he or she can call, use a credit card, and get a password that unzips the full, registered version of your program. If you distribute several versions—say, a basic and a deluxe version—you can use different passwords to control which level of registered program a user gains access to. In essence, you trade your key for their gold—a fair exchange.

A Penny Saved Is a Penny Saved

Compression will save some bucks when you distribute your brainchild to the public, by cutting down the number of disks it takes to hold the software. Fewer disks means fewer chances for copy errors, so to some extent compression may also cut back on returned disks and even on technical support calls from end users who received bad disks.

SFX: Making It Easy on Everyone

Most file compressors can make self-extracting or SFX archives that extract their contents automatically. Technically speaking, they have a small segment of code tacked onto the beginning that lets them run as executables whose purpose is to extract the archived contents. Some SFX files also accept user (or installation batch file) options of various types. An SFX file does not need the parent archiving program to extract its own contents, making life easier on users and distribution of a program easier as well. Anything that makes *anything* easier for end users, preferably by taking them out of the loop, makes life easier for the programmer. Hey, the more you can do *for* users, the less they can do *to* your software!

Compression and the Pirate

If you've created an excellent program, something with unique software technology you developed yourself, some bozo somewhere will probably try either to steal it or to copy it to market themselves. Integrity checking can't stop these bozos, but it can at least warn honest users (and you) that someone's been stealing the silverware. Just knowing about it can help.

Here's why. One of the simplest hacks—and most discouraging to honest programmers—doesn't take the brightest bulb in the lamp store, just a 20-watter who's bent wrong. What they do is hack the registration form to replace your name and address with their own. Then they lay around the shack 'til the mail train gets back with your registration checks—made out to them.

We are not making this up to alarm you. It happens more than people like to think about. Shortly after Marshall Magee released AutoMenu he found someone else marketing a program that looked just like AutoMenu. In fact it *was* AutoMenu—it just had a different registration payment address. It took Magee several years of legal action to stop the software thief. Diana Gruber, of Ted Gruber software, writes and publishes gambling and educational games. She's found many of her games hacked the same way. The idiots who perpetrate this hack can be prosecuted, since they must include their own names and addresses to receive the misdirected checks. But prosecution takes time and doesn't pay the rent. It's better to throw a stumbling block or two in the way of such sleazy simpletons.

Baffling the Bozos

One easy hurdle to throw in their path is to compress your files with an antitampering lock. It's not hard to change the text in an editable file. But if your compression program checks for changes, it can tell your honest users the program has been hacked. People are gradually learning to contact the ASP or some other software association when they see such notices.

Of course, any honest person's lock can be defeated by a determined crook. But the laws protecting authors have been improving, and in time—probably about the time software itself gets obsolete—everyone will be completely safe. Honk if you believe that.

Types of File Compression

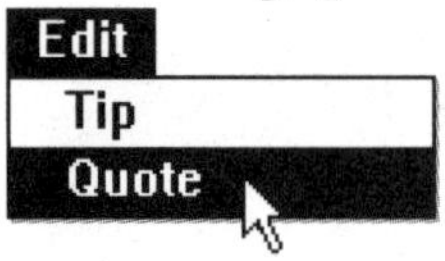
Edit
Tip
Quote

Oh oh, your ZIP file is open!
—from TAGLINE, a BBS program

File compression can be divided into two common categories. One type compresses groups of files into a single archive file. The other takes a single executable and converts it into a compressed executable that works as if it had never been compressed, that is, with no significant effects on how well or how fast the program runs. The resulting executable file uses less disk space but restores the relevant code to full size in memory, when run. Compression programs don't do both types of compression, though there's no logical reason why they couldn't. The two types have just always been programmed separately.

This section presents some of the better and more popular file compression programs available. All of these handy hacks are on the CD-ROM, and are either shareware or free.

Customers Are Always Right (But Users Can Be Idiots)

When you wear your programmer's hat as opposed to your marketer's hat, remember that many users are, shall we say, intellectually challenged. If you let them stand out in the rain with their mouths open, they'll drown. It's not your fault. They got that way long before they ever bought or downloaded your software.

Gotta Love 'em

These are wonderful, valued customers when they pull out their checkbooks, of course, and so they deserve all the help you can give them. But at times it will be a trial. They will try to do things to your software that a reject from a Three Stooges casting call would not try. They'll lose parts of the program, try to install it incorrectly, copy files to almost any place except where they belong, and in other ways prove they might have the IQ of a fence post if you spot them 15 points. Best of all, after having ignored the clear instructions on your distribution diskette, they won't be too shy to call you at 2:00 a.m. for help. Steve Hudgik, owner of HomeCraft Software, comments:

> Users of our software continually try to install it onto the master floppy disk. Our software has a very simple installation procedure that is plainly described in the manual. You just type **INSTALL**. Yet we continually get technical support calls from users who have directly copied the files to another disk, or tried to de-archive the files onto the master floppy disk itself—usually because they are afraid that installing a program on their hard disk will "use up all of the space."

Drool-Proof Installation

A good way to make your products idiot-friendly is to supply a compressed archive with the "read only" archive bit set. It keeps your valued customers out of trouble. So do this even if the files would fit on a single floppy disk without compression. It keeps all the files together and prevents a user from accidentally erasing files your software needs. And, combined with a good installation program, it lets you control the installation process and ensure that the proper files are installed as required. You'll get more uninterrupted sleep that way.

Hack Facts

PKZIP (with PKUNZIP, ZIP2EXE, PKZIPFIX)

Version 2.04g
Phil Katz
PKWare, Inc.
9025 North Deerwood Drive
Brown Deer, WI 53223
Voice: 414-354-8699
BBS: 414-354-8670
202,574 bytes
Shareware: $47
PK204G.EXE

If you are publishing software, get PKZIP even if you have to skip a few pizzas. If you're just out there exploring cyberspace on the BBSes and information services, you still can't get by without it. Not only is PKZIP good, it has become the archiving standard used throughout the industry. On many BBSs, you can't even upload program files unless they're in "zipped" form. If you only learn to use one file compressor, this is the one to learn.

PKZIP works by compressing files and then storing them in a single archive file. A "zipped" file has a filename extension of .ZIP and follows a standard compression format. As a result, you can peek into it using a variety of utilities. Just don't try to change a distributed ZIP file arbitrarily. If antitampering is turned on, the file will report to the next person who unzips it that something has been changed.

Edit
Tip
Quote

Everyone connected with shareware is actively using PKZIP.
—Article in ASPects, newsletter of the ASP

PKZIP is an excellent program. It's fast. It provides multiple levels of compression, letting you go for speed, a "normal" compromise between speed and compression, or maximum compression. It also includes extra features such as directory recursion and multiple-volume support, which means you can ZIP a huge directory branch, including all subdirectories, onto a series of floppy diskettes. That's a handy way to store "as-installed" program backups, much easier than restoring from tape if all you need is to put a deleted directory branch back onto a hard drive. PKZIP—or rather, its companion program, PKUNZIP, which comes with PKZIP—recreates your subdirectory branch, files and all, on demand. Slick.

The PKZIP package provides two additional utilities. PKZIPFIX can sometimes repair a damaged archive, although in our experience once you need a fix-it utility you probably won't get much useful out of a ZIP archive. And ZIP2EXE turns a ZIP file into a self-extracting executable, which can be a real boon to installation routines.

Tip

To make SFX files with options such as the ability to re-create original directory structures or extract only specified files, use ZIP2EXE. To make smaller SFX files without the extra options, use the ZIP2EXE -J option; it adds only 3K instead of about 13K to the size of the original ZIP file.

Hack Facts

LHA

```
Version 2.13
Haruyasu Yoshizaki ("Yoshi")
Send inquiries to
  K. Okubo at
CIS: 74100,2565
Internet:
c00236@sinet.ad.jp
44,381 bytes
Free
LHA213.EXE
```

LHA, by "Yoshi," is a terrific file compression program for which the author requests *no* registration fee at all. It's what most people think "freeware" means. LHA has a complete set of file archiving features, though it lacks some of PKZIP's advanced features such as password protection and other archiving security capabilities. Since LHA is free and may be included with software without paying a licensing fee, you might consider distributing it simply as a convenience to your users. You could even build in a backup feature using LHA that would remove or ameliorate some of the intellectually difficult aspects of making regular backups, such as remembering to do it. (Remember, users need help.)

Although it is free, the speed and compression provided by LHA compares favorably with other archiving utilities. In some cases, such as with some graphics files, LHA even provides the best compression of all the standard compression utilities. LHA also can make self-extracting archives, and you can include text to be displayed with a "shall I continue?" prompt when the SFX file is invoked. Archives created with LHA have filenames that end with .LZH.

Hack Facts

ARJ
Version 2.41
Robert and Susan Jung
2606 Village Road West
Norwood, MA 02062
CIS: 72077,445
robjung@world.std.com
223,856 bytes
Shareware:$40
ARJ241.EXE

If you want extreme reliability, or you just get tired of typing PK-this-and-that all the time, then ARJ is a good archiver to choose. In features and capabilities, ARJ is at least equal to the Phil Katz programs, although its compressed files are not always as small as PKZIP's. ARJ creates archive files with an .ARJ extension.

ARJ includes all of the standard features you should expect in a file archiving utility. And it includes advanced features such as the ability to make multiple-volume archives; provide file encryption and password protection; and create self-extracting archive files. But where ARJ really shines is in its reliability. ARJ can often recover useful files from a damaged archive where other archivers typically choke. PKZIP recommends using PKZIPFIX when it finds damage, but in our experience it doesn't usually help much. With ARJ, an archive can be "broken"—missing data or having a damaged part—and still selectively extract the remaining good files.

ARJ also provides security protection to prevent (as opposed to simply reporting) any changes to the files in the archive. Not even the comments can be changed. All files, and the archive file itself, must be left in their original condition. This feature can be very useful when distributing software as shareware, since it prevents other people, such as BBSs and disk vendors, from adding advertising and other messages to your archive files. It also may work against the simple-minded pirate hackers who simply want to change the address on the registration form.

Hack Facts

ZOO
Version 2.10
Rahul Dhesi
Ronald Gas Software
350 West 55th Street
New York, NY 10019
CIS: 71230,2500
56360 bytes
ZOO210.EXE

ZOO is similar to PKZIP and ARJ in its ability to create compressed files. It has many of the same features as these programs, such as multiple-volume archiving, but its standout feature is that it works across platforms. With ZOO you can create an archive on your Gateway DOS machine and extract its files on an Amiga or UNIX system, for example. That makes ZOO a natural choice if you expect your software to be used on a variety of platforms (a common characteristic of graphics files, for example). ZOO is not particularly fast, but its compression is comparable to that of other programs.

ZOO is also unique in that it can store multiple generations of a file in a single archive. This feature is very useful for software developers. ZOO automatically numbers and keeps track of each version of the file. You can then go back and extract any version you might need. Archive files created with ZOO have a filename extension of .ZOO.

Hack Facts

PKLite

Version 1.15
Phil Katz
PKWare, Inc.
9025 North Deerwood Drive
Brown Deer, WI 53223
Voice: 414-354-8699
BBS: 414-354-8670
Fax: 414-354-8559
54,066 bytes
Shareware: $46
PKL115.EXE

PKLite compresses files that have .EXE and .COM extensions, so they use less disk space. When the file is run, it decompresses itself into memory and expands to its full size. There's a trade-off involved. Uncompressing the file into memory so it can run takes computing cycles (read: more time). But a compressed file is smaller, so it's off the disk and into memory to be expanded sooner (read: less time). On balance, a compressed file will usually be up and running sooner, because accessing data on a hard drive typically acts as a data bottleneck. However, if you have a slow machine with a very fast hard drive, you may want to experiment to see whether a particular file loads faster or slower after you've processed it through PKLite. In terms of hack protection, the registered version provides an option that lets you encrypt an executable permanently, making the file impossible to re-expand. This will stop some pirates.

Tip

If you're using a disk compression utility like Stacker or DoubleSpace, don't use PKLite to save space. A file on a compressed disk is already compressed, so PKLite will only add a second layer of compression. More layers of decompression will reduce net speed.

Brief Mentions

The CD-ROM contains a variety of other compression and encryption utilities that have unique applications or are standouts in their area.

SHEZ: Compression Power Shell

SHEZ, for SHell EZ, is widely considered the premier shell for file compression utilities. This power shell (in SHEZ97.ZIP) gracefully handles any option in every major compression program, making it a painless task to, say, convert a ZIP file to an SFX or to select individual files to add or move to a compressed file. If you work a lot with compressed files, SHEZ is the shell to have.

TINYPROG: For Custom Apps

TINYPROG (in TINY39.ZIP), like PKLite, compresses EXE and COM files so they can be expanded and run directly from the disk. Its compression ratio is not as high as some of the others, but it is a very good choice if you're writing applications, because you can encrypt and apply password access to install and menu programs created with batch file compilers like TurboBat (also on the CD-ROM; see Chapter 10, "A Bag of Other Goodies"). Programs compressed with TINYPROG will check themselves for changes and generally quit gracefully if something has gone haywire. Author Alex Robinson really designed this compressor for independent programmers with corporate customers, but its features can be useful with nearly any type of program. Also, you can attach user data to the front of a compressed file, including copyright information, customer ID, and other customized data.

LZEXE: Good, Solid, No-Fee Compression

This no-fee program (in LZEXE91.ZIP) from France creates compressed EXE files but does not offer advanced features of the sort available in other programs. Still, it works well and is free. It typically compresses a file to about half its original size. We also include LZESHELL.EXE (in a ZIP file of the same name), a shell program that makes it easier to traverse LZEXE's prompts, which are in French. Finally, you'll find UNLZEXE (in UNLZEXE5.ZIP), which lets you reverse the effects of LZEXE if that's what you need to do.

CHK4COMP: Managing Compressed Executables

On an uncompressed disk, if you start running out of space, it can be easier to compress your executables to gain space than to start deleting stuff right and left. We hate getting into deletion binges, because Murphy always steps in: Start deleting stuff, and you'll need it within the week. But it helps to have a roadmap. What files have been compressed already? How many files haven't been compressed yet? That's the sort of information CHK4COMP (in CHK4COMP.ZIP) will tell you. It tests every EXE and COM file in a directory (or just the files you specify) for compression by all the major executable program compressors. You can use it to uncompress specific files, too, if compression causes a program to choke. A handy utility. (For a full-screen compressed executable manager, check out DIRX, described in Chapter 10.)

MAKEREAD: Automatic ASCII File Display

Although MAKEREAD (in MAKEREAD.COM) does not really fit into the category of file compression and archiving software, it can help protect you from pirate hacks. MAKEREAD converts ASCII text files into COM files that you can then compress using PKLite to make them harder to modify. This can be useful for README files and the like. It'll also help users who don't understand how to read a README file but are smart enough to run a COM file if you tell them they need to. MAKEREAD adds about 750 bytes to a file's length and permits scrolling in either direction.

ZipComment: Automated PKZIP Comments

This little utility (in ZC210.ZIP) can automatically use any specified ASCII file as a ZIP file comment. Intended for BBS operators, ZipComment is handy when you want to "brand" a ZIP file as your own, or just remove long comment files from something you've downloaded. It's also potentially helpful against "ANSI bombs"—comment files that contain keyboard reassignments. Such bombs can reassign a command like "ECHO Ha ha! Fooled you!" or worse to any key. (Create a comment file consisting only of a carriage return, and have ZC use it to eliminate existing comment lines without reading them into your system, to foil such bombs.) We used

ZCP (the "Plus" version) to insert the following comment in this book's CD-ROM ZIP files:

> This file was distributed on the CD-ROM accompanying *BYTE's DOS Programmer's Cookbook,* Osborne/McGraw-Hill, 1994

If you use ZCP with the -L switch, it won't change a ZIP file's existing date—a definite plus. Note that author Jeff Garzik requests only a $5 donation if you like this program.

Edit Tip Quote

What man can lock, man can unlock. Don't put too much faith in codes.
—Stephen B. Hicks, security consultant

ENCRYPT: Long Key Encryption

This little program (in ENCRYPT.ZIP) uses your password to generate a 256-character randomized encryption key. It would not be secure against your average code-busting spook, but it is fine for casual use. We include it because registration only costs $5 and it comes with full "C" source code. Use it as a model to roll your own, if you like, but do pay the measly $5 fee if you do.

Next Up

In the next chapter, we will introduce you to some of the best general file and disk management programs available as shareware. Some of them, such as 3_DRIVES, let you do things that have always been considered impossible on a PC, *and* can save you tons of money. With an intro like that, how can you pass it up?

6

Disk-O Magic

Calling your hard disk the most important component in your system is like calling your heart more important than your liver. You need it all; that's why they call it a system. But it's also true that hackers probably spend as much time tweaking, twanging, and twiddling their hard disk storage as they do their memory setup. Both are vital—the more you have of either, the more you can do, and either will cause headaches, heartaches, and bouncing off walls when it goes awry.

The disk is where the data live. Without it, you couldn't turn the box off at night, so you'd have to eat too much pizza and stay up all night and make the neighbors think you're strange. Disk storage lets you give the machine a rest so you can work on making the neighbors think you're strange for other reasons.

As a VIP (Very Important Part) of the system, the disk deserves to be treated well. That's why disk and file maintenance utilities have turned into a major industry wherever computers have taken over from typewriters and hand ledgers. That also explains why this is one of our book's longer chapters—there's a lot of interesting territory to cover.

Disk Utilities and the Big Cheese

It took Microsoft Corporation nearly forever to get wise to the heavy demand for third-party disk utilities. For almost ten years, users had to depend on local hackers and bulletin board junkies to augment the deficient Disk Operating System provided by the World's Main PC Cybermuffin in Seattle. But with MS DOS 5, the home hive of 10,000 buzzing system designers in Redmond, Washington shrewdly lifted data recovery and undelete functions from Central Point's PC Tools package, and marketers then promoted the improved DOS into a major bestseller.

O! it is excellent
To have a giant's strength, but it is tyrannous
To use it like a giant.
—*Shakespeare,* Measure for Measure

It worked so well that version 6 featured a cut-down version of Symantec's Norton Backup and antivirus programs plus a DoubleSpace disk compression module borrowed from Vertisoft and Stac Electronics, two successful smaller companies. (DoubleSpace was later removed from DOS 6.21 after a lawsuit.) Some malcontents have remarked on the similarity of the DOS disk utilities market to the end stages of a Monopoly game: The Big Cheese player has paid lesser players to release their rights to a few key properties, and it now has a solid wall of hotels that stretches from Kentucky to Pennsylvania Avenues. You wander into Big Cheese territory, you're gonna pay some hefty rent.

In the meantime, players out in the low-rent avenues, the shareware vendors and utility artists, continue to produce specialized disk utilities. These are packages with useful features for programmers, power-users, and other independent-minded consumers. It has gotten harder to avoid being eaten by the Giant, but a few dark corners remain where Jack can eke out a living without having his bones ground for meal.

For users, the payoff is more than just retaining a little independence from the Big Cheese. The reward can be a better, faster, tighter system. These independent programs still embody the essence of hacking, and all it takes to use them is a do-for-yourself frame of mind.

The utilities discussed in this section will let you do a host of things that you couldn't do as well, or at all, in a plain vanilla DOS system. They'll let you write-protect your C drive so your files don't get trashed when you try out that strange new C library you picked up on the "WaReZ WaRurZ" pirate board across town; or you'll be able to run debug against the BIOS in the unidentified IDE drive that you got at the swap meet down at the drive-in theater. Specialized backup utilities you won't find in commercial programs can clear your hard disk of unwanted files, copying them to floppies and creating indexed catalogs of the stuff you transfer. Other ingenious hacks let you load device drivers from the command line, change the way DOS assigns drive letters, and monitor or report on free and used disk space.

You'll also find utilities for data recovery and physical hard disk maintenance. If testing some new code made your hard drive plunge over the brink, our FAT and partition-editing tools may help bring both disk and files back from the dead.

The Disk-O Magic Goodie Box

The file and disk utilities in this chapter include quite a useful variety:

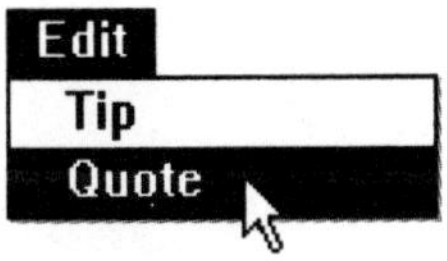
Edit
Tip
Quote

Any sufficiently advanced technology is indistinguishable from magic.
—Arthur C. Clarke

- *Speed-up Utilities,* including disk caches, plus hacks that enhance the flexibility of your controller subsystem.
- *Programming Aids,* such as TSRs that can save you from scurrying through printed tables and appendices when your time would be better spent compiling and testingcode.
- *Backup Utilities,* including specialized disk and data tools that Microsoft left out of DOS 6.
- *Disaster Control Utilities,* to help you recover lost files and data or directly edit your partitions.

Disk Enhancers: Faster is Better

In this section we'll show you some utilities to make your hard drives do things you may never have considered possible. Let's start with one of the niftiest tricks of all—making different types of drives coexist peacefully in the same system while improving the whole system's data handling performance. Sorcery, you say? Read on.

Device Drivers and Other Sorcery

Talk about arcane arts—most users don't even really know what a device driver is, much less how to write or modify one. For a long time, such tasks were reserved for the DOS high priests and acolytes. Device drivers were loaded at boot time and were a completely different class of code from TSRs or other resident software.

The art of programming disk-access device drivers under DOS still holds vast mysteries. Originally, Microsoft mostly provided slow, formal, but very stable algorithms to third-party software vendors but reserved a series of undocumented techniques and secret interrupts for in-house use. Year by year, programmers working for third-party vendors have delved fearlessly into the mysteries and found new and better ways to improve the speed and depth of hard disk transfers. They've used that knowledge to improve on DOS. The resulting code usually runs faster than it could under the "approved" interrupts, but every new version of DOS inspires a mad, hacking scramble to deal with new incompatibilities. It takes many post-midnight pizzas and six-packs to keep the hacks flowing during periods of DOS transition.

Microsoft finally broke its own formal rules for disk access in Windows 3.1 by inventing a technique to bypass the DOS software entirely. The mysteries of reading and writing directly through hardware and of using the ambiguous Interrupt 13 have forced disk cache and memory management vendors to mutate their products in strange new ways.

Nowadays, many companies issue free or low-cost compatibility fixes to keep the Microsoft upgrades from causing catastrophes. So you have to keep your eyes out for minor releases, which can be a hassle. The upside is that the software eventually becomes so efficient that it can even compensate for inferior hardware. One of this chapter's hacks, 3_Drives, is a brilliant example of turning sows' ears into silk purses (well, nylon purses anyway). Check it out.

Hack Facts

3_Drives
Version 2.60
Dustbowl Designs, Inc.
12600 S.E. 38th Street
Choctaw, OK 73020-6107
Voice: 405-741-4705
BBS: 405-741-2721
CIS # 71062,2542
70,577 bytes
Shareware: $40
3DRVS260.ZIP

The 3_Drives hard drive enhancement system is absolutely terrific. It can make up to three drives (or up to four drives, if you register for the 4_Drives upgrade) coexist on your system in a sort of electronic peaceable kingdom. You can combine any two MFM, RLL, ESDI, or IDE AT format controllers. (See "Putting the Hag Back in Harness," just pages ahead.)

But that's just the beginning. The authors wanted to include the speed advantages of their DiskQwik product (described below) in the registered version of the program. That idea worked, so when the publisher, Dustbowl Designs, Inc. turned one year old, they celebrated by releasing version 2.6 (the one on this book's CD-ROM) with the "READ FAST" routine enabled, which had formerly been available only in registered versions. If you run your IDE drive on the secondary controller card, READ FAST will give it the same speed it would have if run on the primary controller—up to twice as fast as without READ FAST. (The registered version comes with a WRITE FAST feature as well.)

Figure 6-1 shows the improvement achieved on a sample hard drive with a registered version of 4_Drives using no fast options, with READ FAST enabled, and with 32-block read-ahead enabled. This is hacking at its best.

Tip

Some of the performance-enhancing features tapped by 3_Drives are available in most newer IDE drives, but are ignored by DOS unless your system has 32-bit direct access. In that case you're already enjoying maximum performance, and 3_Drives won't increase your data transfer rates. The multiple-drives feature may still be very useful, though!

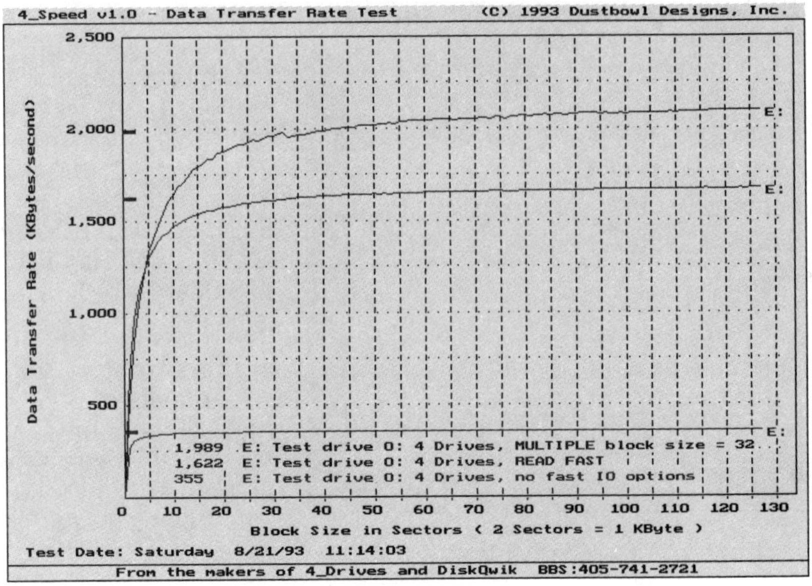
4_Speed v1.0 - Data Transfer Rate Test (C) 1993 Dustbowl Designs, Inc.
Data Transfer Rate (KBytes/second)
2,500
2,000
1,500
1,000
500
E:
E:
E:
1,989 E: Test drive 0: 4 Drives, MULTIPLE block size = 32
1,622 E: Test drive 0: 4 Drives, READ FAST
355 E: Test drive 0: 4 Drives, no fast IO options
0 10 20 30 40 50 60 70 80 90 100 110 120 130
Block Size in Sectors (2 Sectors = 1 KByte)
Test Date: Saturday 8/21/93 11:14:03
From the makers of 4_Drives and DiskQwik BBS:405-741-2721

Figure 6-1. *Performance improvements achieved with 4_Drives on a sample hard drive*

Mapping 3_Drives

Technically, 3_Drives v2.6 is a CONFIG.SYS block device driver that allows the utilization of a single hard disk drive (two, after you register) on the secondary port address using the standard DOS operating system. It also permits two incompatible controllers or host adapters to coexist. With the registered version, you can mix and match up to four drives, in up to two different formats, on a single machine. Figure 6-2, taken from the 3_Drives docs, shows various drive combinations you can use.

The advantages of 3_Drives are many. You can use an extra AT/IDE, MFM, RLL, or ESDI drive to perform image backups of your data. If you have two AT/IDE drives that refuse to cooperate in a master/slave relationship on one controller card (a common problem), you can install each as the master on its own controller card and they'll stop squabbling.

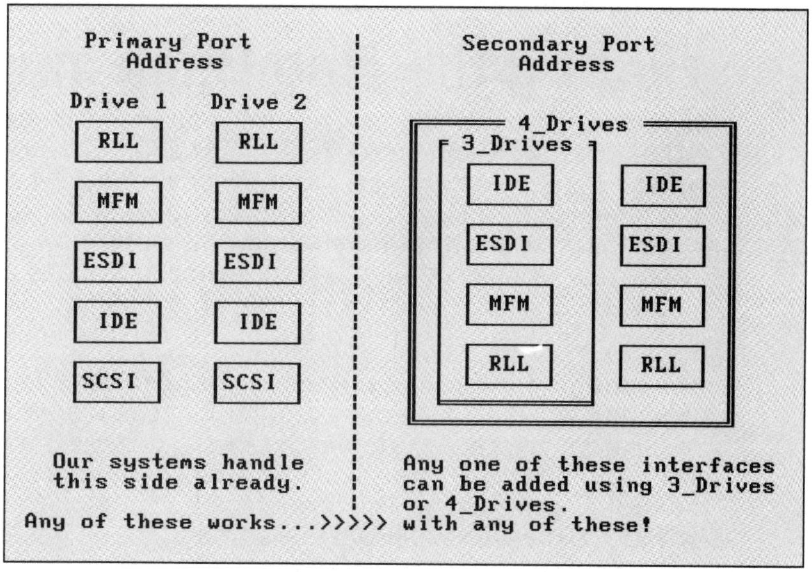
Primary Port
Address
Drive 1
Drive 2
RLL
RLL
MFM
MFM
ESDI
ESDI
IDE
IDE
SCSI
SCSI
Secondary Port
Address
4_Drives
3_Drives
IDE
IDE
ESDI
ESDI
MFM
MFM
RLL
RLL
Our systems handle
this side already.
Any of these works...>>>>>
Any one of these interfaces
can be added using 3_Drives
or 4_Drives.
with any of these!

Figure 6-2. *Combine drive types using universal driver in 3_Drives or 4_Drives.*

6

Edit
Tip
Quote

Dustbowl Designs has thoughtfully included diagrams of various generic types of IDE and MFM/RLL controller models. Find the one that fits best and proceed from there.

Other Goodies

The Dustbowl Designs programmers who wrote 3_Drives are also deeply enmeshed in other mysteries of hard disk access. The package on our CD-ROM includes a slick utility that queries the diagnostic cylinder of each hard drive. The information it discovers there may improve disk read/write speed and data transfer rates markedly. Many AT/IDE drives manufactured within the last two years have hidden capabilities built into them that DOS ignores completely. Some BIOS and controller card designers are getting hip to multiple sector reads and block mode transfer. That's fine, but 3_Drives goes a step further and implements these features on the secondary controller too (if it is IDE). The whole package can double your data transfer rate while it's doubling your storage. Now *that's* worth going to a little trouble to set it up properly.

Putting the Hag Back in Harness

If you were around PCs before 1990, you probably have a few old disk drive controllers and an MFM/RLL hard drive or two gathering dust and spiders in your garage. We know one hacker who took apart what he called his "Sea Hag 225," tied string to its shiny silver plates, and hung them on his front porch as a wind chime. He said his fast ESDI drive made the "Sea Hag" useless (he doesn't smoke and has no need of an ashtray), and he'd rather listen to a wind chime any day than to a head-grinding 225 with the power on.

His sour-grapes attitude is understandable. We've long been told by columnists, clone dealers, and other mavens that you can use only two hard drives in a system unless you go SCSI. You can't mix ESDI with IDE or MFM, we've learned. You can't use more than one standard controller per system. The formula is 1 ESDI + 1 MFM = 1 ESDI + 1 ASHTRAY. Everybody knows these things.

Everybody's Wrong

3_Drives throws out the wasteful formula and lets multiple disk controllers coexist, side-by-side, even if they're of different types. So if you've been thinking about chucking your old 100MB RLL off the nearest building, think again. Now you can dust it off, pop it into your system, and run it alongside your newer fast-access IDE drives.

The extra space will be great for storing ZIP files you've downloaded but haven't had time to check out. Or you can make it the office e-mail drive. Or keep on-the-fly backups of a day's work. An antique MFM or RLL may be slow, but it'll run at warp 9, Mr. Sulu, compared to shuffling floppies in and out of drive A at the end of a day.

Wind chimes are nice, but wouldn't you rather have the extra storage?

Secrets of 3_Drives' Success

We found a few technical facets of 3_Drives that weren't obvious the first time through. Pay attention to these tips and you'll have an easier time of it than we did.

Edit
Tip
Quote

Intelligence plans. Competence improvises.
—Graffito

Stop Interrupting

You'll probably need to disable Interrupt 14 on the secondary card. This maneuver can be a bit tricky. You can do it using a jumper on IDE cards or by placing a piece of Scotch Tape™ over one of the gold contacts where an ESDI or MFM card plugs into the motherboard. The one you want is the seventh contact on the 16-bit card connector—but a gain, don't worry; the diagram in the instructions makes it easy to locate.

Disconnect Slaves

After you plug both controller cards back into the motherboard, you can restore the CMOS primary drive types. If the primary controller is IDE, the BIOS may beep at you and refuse to boot the first drive. Most likely cause? IDE controllers are touchy about the master/slave relationship; the CMOS must register the master drive first. Disconnect the cables to any attached slave drive and your system should boot without a hitch. Then reset the CMOS, power off, and reconnect the slave drive. The system should now work fine.

Mo-o-ore Power

Figure that you'll need a 220 to 250 watt power supply to support four drives in one system. With that much power, you might want to install an auxiliary fan as well.

C D & E F

DOS will recognize the third and fourth drives once you load the 3_Drives/4_Drives device driver in the CONFIG.SYS. The secondary controller's logical drives will be assigned letters that follow the ones assigned to the system's primary drives.

Block Device Driver Functions

The 3_Drives/4_Drives block device driver talks directly to the second controller through the secondary port address. READ, WRITE, RECAL, and RESET functions are supported, but the FORMAT command option isn't recognized. Consequently, you must carefully follow the detailed procedures included with the docs.

Unformatted Disks

Format and partition any drives that will be hooked up to the *secondary* controller, using the *primary* port address. Once that's done, you can bump them over to the second address. You may have to remove the primary controller card, prepare the extra drives, and then reinstall the original controller card to make it work. DOS will then handle the secondary drives through the device driver, in much the same way as CD-ROM drives are recognized.

Int 13 and the Secondary Controller

Because DOS considers the secondary drives as additional block devices, cache programs that use direct-access Interrupt 13 routines won't recognize them. Fortunately, DOS's SMARTDrive is a slightly slower, less efficient program that caches disk writes through Interrupts 24 and 25. This means that SMARTDrive will cache the secondary controller with no problem. If you prefer a different cache program, make sure you can disable direct access by Int 13, or the cache won't work.

3_Drives in Windows

If you decide to place a permanent Windows swap file on a secondary controller drive, you'll need to disable (uncheck) the 32-bit disk access box in the Virtual Memory dialog box of the Control Panel. Even with 32-bit access disabled, you'll still see a speed improvement when using 3_Drives.

Hack Facts

DiskQwik
Version 1.10
Dustbowl Designs, Inc.
12600 S.E. 38th Street
Choctaw, OK 73020-6107
Voice: 405-741-4705
BBS: 405-741-2721
CIS: 71062,2542
129,003 bytes
Shareware: $25
DQWIK110.ZIP

DiskQwik, a companion to the 3_Drives package discussed above, takes advantage of secret capabilities implanted by elves at the disk drive manufacturing plants to activate the multiple sector block transfer mode built into most current IDE drives. Many or even most newer IDE drives include special data buffers, similar to the "look-ahead" buffers that DOS can set up in your system RAM. Here's how it works.

Normally, DOS processes read and write requests to the controller card one sector at a time. The typical Interrupt 13, Function 02 request is invoked once for each new sector of the disk. To avoid this time waster, DiskQwik sets up a scheme that gulps down more than a single sector of the disk each time a program generates a read or write interrupt request. DOS, and most BIOS chips for that matter, know nothing about this. But if you run Coretest or this package's included benchmark utility, you'll find dramatic increases in data transfer rates.

...carrying information from place to place, passing it around at the speed of light.
—Lewis Thomas, The Lives of a Cell

The shareware version of DiskQwik included with this book is hard-coded to turn on multiple block accesses and cache two sectors per block transfer (write request). This typically improves transfer rates by 15 to 25 percent on many IDE drives. The registered version of DiskQwik gives you broader control over the number of sectors cached per read/write request by enabling command-line switches. That can up the improvement by 40 to 50 percent. If that's not enough inducement to register the program, the authors have thoughtfully provided some tedious begware messages to encourage you.

If the thought of manually tweaking the CONFIG.SYS file seems daunting, don't worry. The 4_Drives (registered version) diagnostic utility included with the package on this book's CD-ROM reads the diagnostic cylinders on your drives and suggests an optimal configuration. You can just copy the suggestions into your CONFIG.SYS file and ponder the details later.

Hack Facts

Speedkit with Hyperdisk
Version 4.65
Roger Cross
Hyperware, Inc.
185 Berry Street
San Francisco, CA 94107
BBS: 415-882-1735
292,059 bytes
Shareware: $49.95
SPKT451S.ZIP

Hyperdisk, the main component of Roger Cross's Speedkit, bills itself as "The fastest disk cache west of the Pecos," and it is probably faster than anything east of the Pecos as well. Hyperdisk is the most successful cache we know of at bypassing DOS's Interrupt 24/25 read/write routines and talking straight to the BIOS for high-speed performance. If you're using good ol', slow ol' SMARTDrive, give Hyperdisk a try. It blows the socks off its other commercial competition, too.

Hyperdisk comes with separate modules to establish the cache in raw (unmanaged) extended memory, expanded memory, or Microsoft XMS memory. Once installed, you can resize the cache on the fly. You can also turn it on and off, or disable/enable the write-ahead feature (called staged writes) by using hot-key toggles. If you're working

I took a course in speed reading...and was able to read War and Peace in 20 minutes. It's about Russia.

—Woody Allen

on a master's degree in DOS disk access technology, you'll love the vast number of technical options that Hyperdisk can modify through command-line parameters: timer-delay, media check rate, sectors per buffer, and advanced A20 gate access, to name just a few. (If you're a disk access beginner, lazy, or just have better things to do, the install program will analyze your system and set up quite a good default configuration.)

Hyperdisk isn't just fast, it's flexible too. It will dance to just about any tune you specify. And its features aren't just bells and whistles—they're practical. For example, you can remove and reinstall the cache as many times as you like without rebooting the system. This is great for timing some piece of code's raw disk access efficiency. Hyperdisk gets along fine with all the standard DOS drive compression schemes, and the next versions will support CD-ROM caching. (You'll just have to register to get it!) You can install Hyperdisk modules as CONFIG.SYS device drivers or invoke them at the command line as executables.

Compatibility Notes

The Hyperdisk staged write feature is so efficient that older versions of some memory managers like 386MAX have installation difficulties unless staged writes are turned off. Quarterdeck's QEMM also had to go through a number of minor revisions to keep pace with Hyperdisk author Roger Cross's sophisticated Interrupt 13 algorithms. All versions of QEMM from version 6.02 up are completely compatible with Hyperdisk, as are the newest versions of 386MAX.

Hyperdisk won't work with secondary drives hooked up through the 3_Drives utility that we discussed earlier, though the authors say the next version will be able to. Using the version (4.65) on this book's CD-ROM, however, you'll need to run your secondaries with no disk cache—not a big deal if you don't often need access—or you'll need to install a second cache (such as SMARTDrive) for the secondary drives.

Other Goodies

Hyperdisk comes as part of the Speedkit package, which also features Hyperkey and Hyperscreen, utilities to speed up the keyboard and screen display. They are written to the same high standard as Hyperdisk and are worth checking out if your screen and keyboard aren't already running in the Mach double-digit region.

Edit
Tip
Quote

The superfluous, a very necessary thing.

—*Voltaire*

Programming Aids

The next few programs are aids for working programmers. They range from simple command line device drive loaders to direct-disk subdirectory editors, and more. They're utilities to get you around the nagging little hassles that can break up the smooth flow of a work session.

Hack Facts

Devload
Version 1.8
Raintree Computer Systems
P.O. Box 2339
Mill Valley, CA 94942
3074 bytes
Shareware: $7.00
DEVLOD18.ZIP

Some DOS device drivers are not much more than dead weight in a CONFIG.SYS file most of the time. We went for years keeping stuff like ANSI drivers and the like in memory just for that 10 percent of the time when we needed them. But now watch out—here come sound boards, CD-ROM drives, special graphics devices, and other memory-gobbling drivers. With DOS and UMBs limited to 1MB, you may need a reboot just to switch from your soundboard to your scanner. Not to mention standard DOS utilities such as SETVER, COUNTRY.SYS, and the like that you might use once in a blue moon (if that often).

If you're like us, you dearly hate to reboot just to look up a phone number or a compiler README file on CD-ROM (or to take a game-playing break when the boss goes out to meet with a client). Enter Devload. This little gem is a file loader that lets you load device drivers from the command line instead of from inside your CONFIG.SYS file. With this

A happy and gracious flexibility....
—Pericles

program, anytime you encounter, say, that pain-in-the-neck message "Wrong Version of DOS," you don't have to reboot. Instead, just type

```
Devload C:\DOS\SETVER.EXE
```

to patch the driver into memory from the command line. Same with your ANSI or mouse drivers: Load 'em when you need 'em, and forget about 'em the rest of the time.

The Devload hack is not quite as sophisticated as device driver loading-equivalent utilities that come bundled with some commercial memory managers, nor can it compete with the DMC package discussed in Chapter 7, "Don't Forget Your Memory!". It will not load borderline block devices like EMM386.EXE, for example. But it can load HIMEM.SYS after bootup, and it's useful also for loading any less picky driver on the fly.

Hack Facts

Meathook
Version 2.01
Keith P. Graham
BBS: 914-623-0039
2670 bytes
Free
MEATHOOK.ZIP

Meathook is an old-timer that's making a comeback. Author Keith Graham originally wrote it to combat the undesirable side effects of loading the SHARE.EXE network utility under DOS 4.0, and we thought DOS 5.0 had made it obsolete. But Microsoft now insists that you load SHARE.EXE before you can use applications like Word for Windows 6.0 that use OLE 2.0.

This won't affect you if you work in DOS 100 percent of the time, but who can do that anymore? And while OLE 2.0 may require SHARE, once it's installed, SHARE is nothing but a lurking headache for most other applications, not to mention power users.

SHARE was originally intended to manage file handling on large disks and in network environments, but anyone who ever used it came to curse all the "sharing violation errors" and system crashes that occurred when two competing processes tried to access the same file. One of DOS 5's improvements was to do away with mandatory loading of SHARE, and words can't express the relief felt at that time by people who were using DESQview or other multitasking environments.

It's Ba-a-a-ck

Due to a bug in the OLE 2.0 handling procedures—at least it seems like a bug to us and everyone else we know—Word 6.0 and other OLE 2.0-using programs have again forced Microsoft's faithful customers to load SHARE; without it, these programs will refuse to load. And the install routines for these programs put a SHARE loading line right into your AUTOEXEC.BAT.

Okay, so it's an easy hack to delete the AUTOEXEC.BAT line and put it into a separate WIN.COM-loading batch file instead. But if you use DOS boxes in Windows, or you go back and forth a lot, you'll once again curse the dreaded "sharing violation" message whenever you try to do something simple like read a file into a TSR browser during an editing session. You also won't be able to upload a file with a telecommunications program while it is also open in a word processor or file viewer.

Word for Windows may be able to merrily open duplicate instances of itself for animated tutorials, but so what? How often do you *really* work with OLE 2.0?

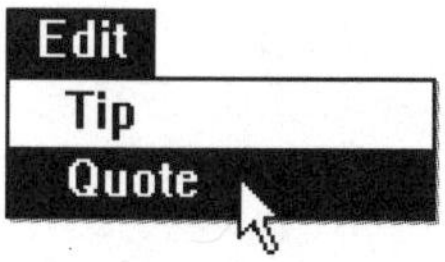
Edit
Tip
Quote

It is quiet here and restful and the air is delicious. There are gardens everywhere, nightingales sing in the gardens and police spies lie in the bushes.
—Maxim Gorky

It's Meathook to the rescue...again. Meathook is a small TSR that alleviates SHAREd suffering by intercepting read/write requests before SHARE ever sees them. You can open as many browsers as you like, and edit away.

Bribing the Chief of the DOS Police

Using Meathook is kind of like bribing—or maybe tranquilizing—the Chief of the DOS Police, in order to zoom past his cop shop at 90 m.p.h. When the effects wear off, the Chief may be annoyed and start issuing random arrest warrants. SHARE operates at very low levels, and you need to be both selective and judicious about using it, or the DOS police will inevitably come after you.

The Meathook file included on our CD-ROM gives you a couple of choices. MHR.COM installs as a permanent interceptor of read/write requests, effectively disabling SHARE for the rest of the session unless you use TSR management utilities to remove it (see Chapter 7). However, there are times when denying access to a file really does protect you from nasty consequences. You may not want to hack around SHARE completely. MHP.COM is a safer, non-TSR version that you load separately for each program you wish to immunize against SHARE.

MHP.COM works much like the command shell syntax:

```
COMMAND.COM /C [Command]
```

To Outwit SHARE When Even Meathook Fails

A cute and time-saving trick that telecommunications junkies love is to read a string of messages off a bulletin board and compose replies even before the capture file has finished coming in through the wires. Loading SHARE ruins this trick beyond even Meathook's capacity to fix things, because the open message file is constantly being written to by the telecommunications program. SHARE won't let you copy the partial message file to a RAMdisk or even permit another file viewer to read it until the telecomm program is finished capturing. It's frustrating.

Never Say Die

Defeat, you say? Not even close! Here's a way to get around the tyrant SHARE and read messages while you're still downloading. Say you're capturing messages to a file called SF.MSG on drive C. This command defeats SHARE:

```
TYPE C:\DOWNLOAD\SF.MSG > [d:\path\]SFMSGS
```

The TYPE command loftily ignores SHARE, because the pipe and redirection symbols (<, > and |) take a higher priority than COPY. Now you can open SFMSGS1 in a file viewer or word processor and work on a beginning set of messages, while the telecomm package continues to write to the original capture file.

Edit
Tip
Quote

I'm not against the police; I'm just afraid of them.
—Alfred Hitchcock

MHP bypasses SHARE just long enough to run a specified command, then deinstalls itself when done. For instance, if SHARE won't let you copy a file to a RAMdisk because it's currently open in LIST, you can type the following:

```
C:\>MHP /2 COPY [Filename.Ext]  [d:].
```

Meathook will let the COPY command access the file, and will then return control to SHARE. This process is much safer than completely disabling SHARE, and the DOS police should leave you alone.

If you want to allow only one application (say, the telecommunications program QMODEM) to defeat SHARE, you can use Meathook to load it:

```
MHP/1 QMODEM.EXE
```

SHARE will still police all read/write activities except those done by QMODEM.

Hack Facts

Eddy
Version 7.1C
John Scofield
117 West Harrison Bldg.
Sixth Floor, Dept. S-678
Chicago, IL 60605
CIS: 70162.2357
Orders: 1-800-2424-PsL
232,287 bytes
Shareware: $25.00
EDDY7C.ZIP

Have you ever wished you could just call up a directory and edit file names, extensions, dates, or attributes the way you do an ASCII file? It can be a real hassle to go through an endless series of REN commands just to change, say, version numbers buried randomly in the middle of filenames. Somebody oughtta write a program to make it easier!

Somebody did. Eddy, a terrific hack that only recently has started to gain the broad BBS distribution it deserves, is, as the docs put it, "ready when you are." With this slick directory management tool, you can call up a directory onscreen and cursor around, changing just about anything you want. When you're done, press RETURN, and all your changes are made at once, automatically.

"Eddy" stands for EDit DirectorY, but in its more recent versions it lets you do much more than its original name implies. You can alter directories, the files themselves, and even the disks they rode in on. Here's a partial list of this remarkable utility's abilities:

- Full-screen directory editor
- Disk and directory manager
- DOS shell
- Sector editor
- RAM editor
- File finder (by name, attributes and/or timestamp)
- File viewer/patcher/comparer
- File backup utility
- String finder/replacer (hex and/or ASCII)
- Data recovery utility

Eddy offers an easy, intuitive interface for most common file-management operations. But it doesn't stop there. Some of its capabilities may surprise you when you first encounter them in the program's extensive help system. The Help index screen in Figure 6-3 will give a sense of how much this modestly named utility can do.

Eddy does take a bit of getting used to, but it's worth the effort. We don't know of any other program that does what Eddy does, and Eddy does it so gracefully.

Hack Facts

Palert
Version 2.4
Patri-Soft
(Norman Patriquin)
P.O. Box 8263
San Bernardino, CA 92412
CIS: 76347,2477
BBS: 909-352-2825
30,211 bytes
Shareware: $20
PALERT24.ZIP

Palert monitors the status of your conventional memory and the amount of free space left on your hard drive. You can call it from the command line or invoke it in batch files. Because it returns errorlevels (depending upon whatever minimum space you set) for "disk full" or "memory full" or "plenty of room left," Palert is useful for determining whether a program will have enough memory to start up, or enough disk space to save a data file or swap file. You can use that info to branch to the appropriate command line options. Palert can search for free disk space using either a specified

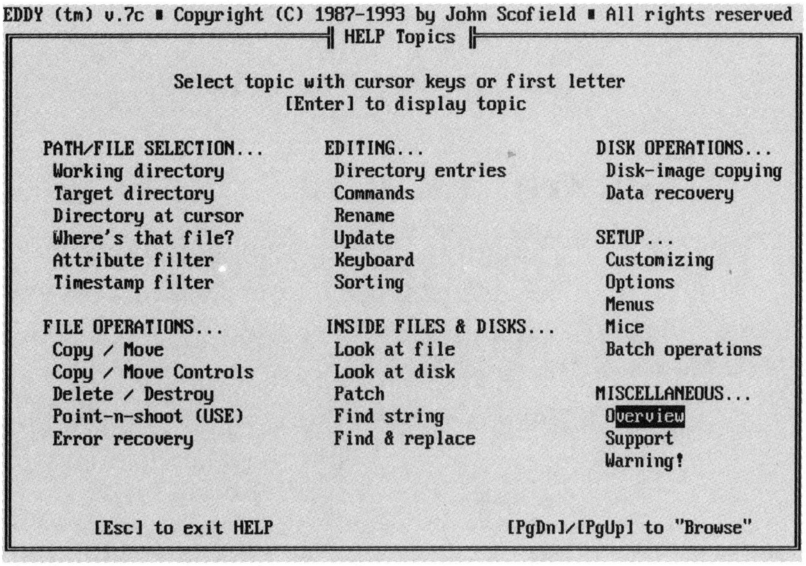

EDDY (tm) v.7c ▪ Copyright (C) 1987-1993 by John Scofield ▪ All rights reserved
HELP Topics
Select topic with cursor keys or first letter
[Enter] to display topic
PATH/FILE SELECTION...
Working directory
Target directory
Directory at cursor
Where's that file?
Attribute filter
Timestamp filter
FILE OPERATIONS...
Copy / Move
Copy / Move Controls
Delete / Destroy
Point-n-shoot (USE)
Error recovery
EDITING...
Directory entries
Commands
Rename
Update
Keyboard
Sorting
INSIDE FILES & DISKS...
Look at file
Look at disk
Patch
Find string
Find & replace
DISK OPERATIONS...
Disk-image copying
Data recovery
SETUP...
Customizing
Options
Menus
Mice
Batch operations
MISCELLANEOUS...
Overview
Support
Warning!
[Esc] to exit HELP
[PgDn]/[PgUp] to "Browse"

Figure 6-3. *Eddy's Help screen*

number of kilobytes or a specified percentage of the total storage space. It can also let your programs know the system date or trigger alternative commands, depending upon the test outcomes.

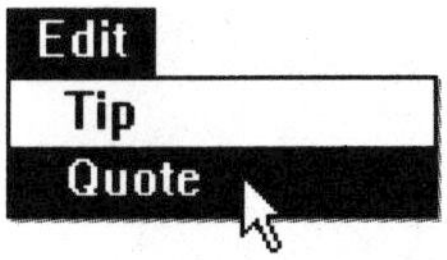

Edit
Tip
Quote

All a poet can do is warn.
—Wilfred Owen

Here's a simple example. The following batch file warns you if Lotus 1-2-3 will not have sufficient work space to create a large spreadsheet:

```
echo off
cls
Palert /b2000/m
if errorlevel 1 goto error
123
goto end
:error
ECHO Aborted due to insufficient disk space
:end
```

Palert can search multiple drives and show a nice little graph showing free disk space, sound a beep, or confine itself to error levels. If you are developing a DOS or Windows masterwork that swaps part of itself out to disk in order to conserve memory, Palert can help you debug the code. Or you can use the day-of-the-week feature to automate periodic tasks like disk backups.

Backup Utilities

Although MS-DOS 6 now contains a useful backup program borrowed from Symantec's Norton Utilities, the following specialized programs can perform tasks that DOS isn't up to yet.

Hack Facts

Stowaway
Version 2.20
Patri-Soft
(Norman Patriquin)
P.O. Box 8263
San Bernardino, CA 92412
CIS: 76347,2477
BBS: 909-352-2825
252,032 bytes
Shareware: $39
(with Auto-Restore:$69)
STOW220.ZIP

Stowaway is another great little utility from Norm Patriquin, who gave us Palert. It's for people who need to clear some valuable junk off their hard disk in a hurry without losing track of it all. You can set up Stowaway so that it automatically generates file backup lists, or you can do it manually. The program lets you type one-line descriptions of your files if you want, and then compresses all the specified files, moves the archive to floppy diskettes, and clears the files off your hard drive, keeping a database of what goes where.

One difference between Stowaway and an ordinary backup program is that Stowaway lets you add one-line on-the-fly file descriptions in the middle of backing up. If you want to remember the difference between IGNATZ.ZIP, IGGY.LZH, and IGNATZ2.ARJ, just type your comments into the catalog. It'll still be there in six months to remind you exactly what you swept off your disk, and how to get it back.

Edit
Tip
Quote

A man should keep his little brain attic stocked with all the furniture that he is likely to use, and the rest he can put away in the lumber room of his library, where he can get it if he wants it.
—Sir Arthur Conan Doyle

Stowaway is easy to use. Nested menus let you select drives or directories to clear, enable or disable the one-line description option, specify the degree of file compression in the archives, and select a target destination (floppy diskette, another hard drive, or a Bernoulli drive). The catalog is kept in the original file location so you can see what was originally stored in a given subdirectory. You can also use the catalog to manually point and click to restore individual files. Or you can use Norm's customary broad set of selection criteria from the command line or batch files to fine-tune the sweep according to a range of dates, the state of the archive bit, and so on. You can even use the catalog to delete obsolete or unwanted data from the set after archiving. A file viewer lets you inspect text files or review WordPerfect 5.1 files if you're not sure whether you want to save them.

Edit
Tip
Quote

Time is the fire that burns you.
—Tennessee Williams

The Auto-Restore Companion

Auto-Restore (in AUTOR11.ZIP) is a companion Patriquin TSR utility that cooperates with Stowaway to make it easier to retrieve archived files. Configure Stowaway to keep 0-byte versions of archived files—that is, just the filenames—on your hard disk in their original locations. If you then try to read data or launch a program that's been archived, Auto Restore prompts you to insert the correct Stowaway floppy, restores the file to your hard disk, then launches the program. Slick!

Hack Facts

Preback
Version 1.3
Patri-Soft
(Norman Patriquin)
P.O. Box 8263
San Bernardino, CA 92412
CIS: 76347,2477
BBS: 909-352-2825
37,418 bytes
Shareware: $15
PREBACK.ZIP

Preback is yet another utility by Norm Patriquin. If you get the impression that we like Norm's utilities, you're right. To some extent Norm's utilities are an acquired taste, because they're not designed for users who want gorilla-friendly programs that wouldn't challenge anyone with an IQ over 30. They *are* designed for people who aren't afraid to write a batch file or two and who know a bit about what they're doing.

This particular utility was originally intended for Norm's private use, to help keep track of when the last backup was made and to nag for another one from time to time. You install it in AUTOEXEC.BAT and, at intervals you specify, it'll tell you it's time for a backup or, if you prefer, even force a backup (for systems under the care and feeding of heedless employees, temp typists, 13-year-old game junkies, or the like). It'll work with any backup program you invoke directly from the command line.

Like all Patriquin utilities, Preback has a raft of option switches to let you tweak it into doing just about anything you want, including summarizing files that have the archive bit set, excluding some files from a backup, and other nifty tricks. A fine utility.

Disaster Control

Everyone knows that the Norton Utilities include a number of features designed to bring hard disk data back from the dead. The following shareware packages emulate many of the Norton features, like partition editing and display of the FAT table, plus some added wrinkles.

Hack Facts

```
FixMBR
Version 2.1
Padgett Peterson
P.O. Box 1203
Windermere, FL 34786
Internet:
padgett@tccslr.dnet@mmc.com
13,414 bytes
Shareware: $5.00
  ($20.00 with tech support)
FIXMBR21.ZIP
```

Once upon a time, a lot of pompous corporate types thought computer viruses were in a class with bogeymen—you wouldn't want to meet one, so it's a good thing they don't exist. Then the spokesmen for one company after another started getting all tight-jawed and sweaty whenever the topic came up in public. "Viruses are not a problem to us," they would declare, running their fingers around their collars like Rodney Dangerfield talking about his wife. After a while, the denials stopped and antivirus hackers gained some deserved respectability. As usual, it just took corporate America some time to catch up with reality.

A virus is a nasty little miniature of malicious programming. Viruses wreak havoc with any kind of system. A lot of antivirus programs are now around, including some classic shareware programs, but they tend to be awkward to use and often take a long time to run. They also tend to become obsolete rather quickly, so we haven't even included any of the catch-'em-all omnibus programs on the CD-ROM.

Edit
Tip
Quote

No rampart will hold out against malice.
—Molière

However, we have included FixMBR, a nice little antivirus and anticrash hack that is simple but effective against the most common class of virus infections—those that infect a disk's boot section.

Here's what FixMBR (for Fix Master Boot Record) does. The more common viruses like STONED, JOSHI, and others often work by moving the partition table to a higher disk sector, then rewriting or writing over the master boot record (MBR) in sector 0. You may apparently lose all pointers to your FAT and directory tables, even though both they and the individual files are still intact.

FixMBR makes a backup of your original (uninfected) boot sectors from both physical hard drives in a system. The data files it saves with your boot record information can actually be renamed with the .COM extension and run as self-executing mini-programs to restore the original boot record to each disk, including the pointers to partitions, FAT, and directory information. FixMBR is very slick, and it's a good answer to this type of virus.

The authors of this program have also written a second utility, SAFEMBR, that writes a "safe" master boot record to any disk, including floppies. The "safe" MBR resists infection by known viruses. SAFEMBR is available to registered users of FixMBR.

Hack Facts

PartEd
Version 2.3f
Paul Glanville
9245 E. 14th Street
Oakland, CA 94603
Voice: 510-632-0999
51,438 bytes
PARTED2F.ZIP

If a virus does attack your system, a poorly programmed antivirus scanning program may "disinfect" you by erasing the partition table entirely. It's like using nitro to kill the little spider living in the corner of your living room. It works, but jeez, Fred, did you have to blow up the house?

When one of these ham-handed programs has had its way with your disk, you'll find that one or more of your logical drives has simply disappeared. When this happened to the author of PartEd, he wrote this combined partition editor/disk sector editor to bring back his hard disk without resorting to DEBUG. Then he wrote one of the best manuals we've seen on the various magicks you can perform on this critical area of a hard drive. We're happy to pass his neat little hack, and the terrific technical info that comes with it, along to you. It's like a FixMBR for the "More Power!" set.

Figure 6-4 shows the PartEd editing screen.

Edit
Tip
Quote

The greatest danger of bombs is in the explosion of stupidity that they provoke.
—Octave Mirabeau

Searching Out the Missing Info

PartEd can perform a sector-by-sector search of your hard drive to locate missing partition information. It can specify drive type, starting and ending addresses, and partition size to manually reconstruct damaged partition information, or it can serve as a Super-FDISK to let you edit existing information. Like FixMBR, it can make copies of the Master Boot Record, load them, and restore a damaged drive.

PartEd includes a sector editor (not as sophisticated as the one in ZipZap, described later in this chapter) that toggles between write-over and push-ahead HEX and ASCII editing modes. It lets you make tentative changes in the master boot record and then view the MBR that's actually present on the disk, toggling back and forth until you're sure you want to save your work.

```
        PARTED v2.3f - Disk partition editor by Paul Glanville

 Up, Down arrows select partition      Right, Left arrows select field
 Plus key increments an item           Minus key decrements an item
 Enter key selects an item             Escape key to exit program
 F1  Set/Clear Boot Indicator          F2  Sector editor/Load RMBR
 F3  Next/Prev auto-correction mode    F4        /Scan for partitions
 F5  Link field toggle                 F6  Swap/Sort Entries
 F7  Drive parameter toggle            F8  Zoom into Extended Partition
 F9  Load/Save Master Boot Record     F10  Load/Save MBR from/to file


Partition information :        Start          End
Num     System              Cyl  Hd Sec   Cyl  Hd Sec       Offset      Length
 0*  DOS 16-bit, >=32Mb       0   1   1  1008  11 55            55      665885
 1
 2
 3

  End Address relative auto-correction selected
  Linked fields       Drive parameters are partition maximums
```

Figure 6-4. *The PartEd partition editor*

Also like FixMBR, PartEd can create a virus-resistant Master Boot Record and substitute it for the weaker one normally created by DOS FDISK. PartEd's replacement master boot record (RMBR) alerts you if a virus tries to make changes in the MBR's vector table pointer file, letting you choose between accepting the changes, aborting the operation, or actively restoring the system to the state it was in before the warning was issued.

Changing Vectors

There are only two normal occasions to change a vector. Vectors will change the first time the system boots up with a new RMBR vector table, because all of the pointers will initially be set to zero. The system then displays an error message and resets the vector table correctly. Second, vectors can change when you add or remove a bus card in your system. Any video or disk interface card with a BIOS extension ROM on it will seek to connect to the appropriate vector. So changes do happen. Before using the RMBR feature, make PartEd backups of your original MBRs so you can restore them later if you need to.

Hack Facts

BackInfo/RestInfo

Version 1.26
Nemrod Kedem
Ksoft Development
Chief Data Recovery, Ltd.
P.O. Box 499
Nes-Ziona 70400, ISRAEL
Voice: +972-8-400070
BBS: +972-3-9667562
47,378 bytes
Shareware: $25
BRINF126.ZIP

BackInfo and RestInfo (both components of the BackInfo utility suite) work in much the same way as the Norton Utilities Emergency Rescue Disk. BackInfo automatically copies the system boot record, partition table, and CMOS information to files on drive A, then essential DOS utilities like FDISK, SYS.COM, and FORMAT.COM to the floppy along with your AUTOEXEC.BAT and CONFIG.SYS files. It also copies all device drivers specified in the CONFIG.SYS to give you a full-featured emergency boot-up. It knows about DoubleSpace and will copy Stacker files, memory managers, or other utilities.

After you perform a floppy boot, RESTINFO restores the boot record and partition table to drive C and refreshes the CMOS information. The package also includes a rather simple virus-checker TSR named VIRBOOT.

Hack Facts

ShowFAT
Version 2.51
D.J. Murdoch
337 Willingdon Avenue
Kingston, Ontario, CANADA
CompuServe: 71631,122
Internet:
dmurdoch@mast.queensu.ca
31,310 bytes
Shareware: $20.00
SHOWF251.ZIP

ShowFAT provides an ASCII-graphics display of a hard disk's File Allocation Table, showing information that may help you to reconstruct a lost FAT or directory table using a sector editor like Eddy (discussed earlier) or ZipZap (discussed next). If CHKDSK reports cross-linked files or invalid cluster allocations, ShowFat lets you cruise the FAT (see Figure 6-5) looking for a file entry, so you can determine the true cluster allocation. ShowFAT is smart enough to detect end-of-file markers, and the information can be displayed in both ASCII and HEX windows in addition to the ASCII graphics in the main window.

Edit
Tip
Quote

Journey over all the universe in a map, without the expense and fatigue of traveling...

—Miguel de Cervantes

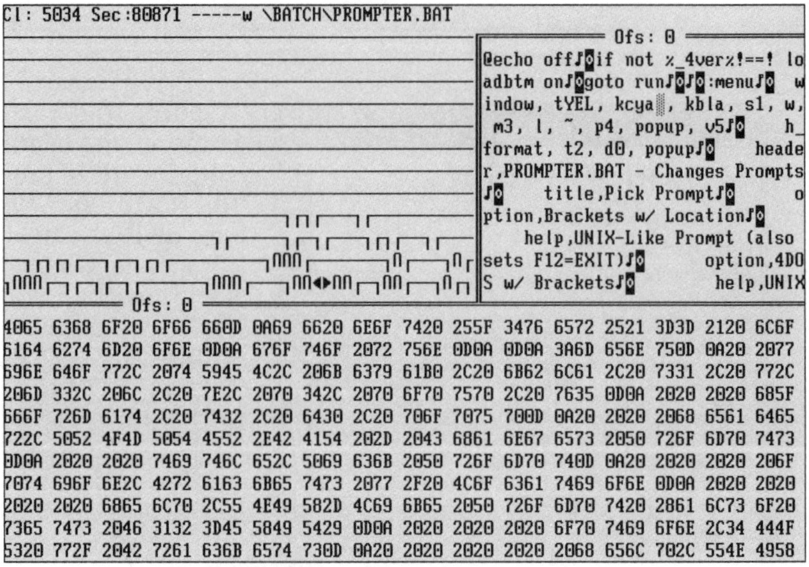
Cl: 5034 Sec:80871 -----w \BATCH\PROMPTER.BAT
Ofs: 0
@echo off if not %_4ver%!==! lo
adbtm on goto run :menu w
indow, tYEL, kcya , kbla, s1, w,
m3, l, ~, p4, popup, v5 h_
format, t2, d0, popup heade
r,PROMPTER.BAT - Changes Prompts
title,Pick Prompt o
ption,Brackets w/ Location
help,UNIX-Like Prompt (also
sets F12=EXIT) option,4DO
S w/ Brackets help,UNIX
Ofs: 0
4065 6368 6F20 6F66 660D 0A69 6620 6E6F 7420 255F 3476 6572 2521 3D3D 2120 6C6F
6164 6274 6D20 6F6E 0D0A 676F 746F 2072 756E 0D0A 0D0A 3A6D 656E 750D 0A20 2077
696E 646F 772C 2074 5945 4C2C 206B 6379 61B0 2C20 6B62 6C61 2C20 7331 2C20 772C
206D 332C 206C 2C20 7E2C 2070 342C 2070 6F70 7570 2C20 7635 0D0A 2020 2020 685F
666F 726D 6174 2C20 7432 2C20 6430 2C20 706F 7075 700D 0A20 2020 2068 6561 6465
722C 5052 4F4D 5054 4552 2E42 4154 202D 2043 6861 6E67 6573 2050 726F 6D70 7473
0D0A 2020 2020 7469 746C 652C 5069 636B 2050 726F 6D70 740D 0A20 2020 2020 206F
7074 696F 6E2C 4272 6163 6B65 7473 2077 2F20 4C6F 6361 7469 6F6E 0D0A 2020 2020
2020 2020 6865 6C70 2C55 4E49 582D 4C69 6B65 2050 726F 6D70 7420 2861 6C73 6F20
7365 7473 2046 3132 3D45 5849 5429 0D0A 2020 2020 2020 6F70 7469 6F6E 2C34 444F
5320 772F 2042 7261 636B 6574 730D 0A20 2020 2020 2020 2068 656C 702C 554E 4958

Figure 6-5. *The ShowFAT display, with hex and ASCII windows toggled on*

Hack Facts

ZipZap
Version 7.15
Keith G. Chuvala
Keystrokes Computer Works
812 East 15th
Winfield, Kansas 67156
Voice: 316-221-0814
CompuServe: 71600,2033
54,100 bytes
Shareware: $15.00
ZIPZP715.ZIP

Priced at just $15, ZipZap makes an invaluable addition to your arsenal of disk recovery tools. It is a sector editor that lets you search for either hexadecimal or text strings in any hard drive sector. ZipZap isn't designed to actually repair a damaged drive, although it does permit you to enter hexadecimal strings directly to the boot sector. Rather, ZipZap is a "search and write" utility to use when FAT or directory information is damaged or missing. It'll save your sanity when the 500 PKZIP files in your storage directory, not to mention your thousands of spreadsheets and word processing files, show up in your directories as nightmare lists of random high-bit characters.

ZipZap searches for document keywords in ASCII and dumps a designated series of raw sectors to a disk file on a floppy. So when you know that drive C contains a 10,000-word dissertation on the breeding habits of Australian wombats, but DOS shows zilch on the drive, you can use ZipZap to search for "wombats," "Australia," or "hot nights at Alice Rock." When ZipZap spots the text, it lets you selectively scrape the road-kill sectors off the disk and shovel them onto the floppy for medical treatment or burial.

Even better, you can use the hex search capability to look for file header signatures left in data files by applications. If you know the disk contains some WordPerfect files, you can tell ZipZap to search for the string FF 57 50 (WPC). Lotus 1-2-3 spreadsheets start with the heading 00 00 1A 00. PKZIP files begin with the string 50 4B 03 and usually have the name of the first compressed file in ASCII immediately after the header signature. Use ZipZap to identify the header signatures in your own applications' files.

If you were conscientious about defragmenting your drive before it crashed, chances are that the sectors following a file header belong to the same file as the header. (This logic is not infallible, but the more frequently you optimize your drive, the more likely all of the files will be intact, with their sectors in sequential order.)

Using ZipZap to Recover Binary Data

To recover a data file with binary header information, tell ZipZap to save the sector with the header in a cumulative file. Then go on to the next sector and dump it in the same file. Inspect the successive sectors in both the HEX and ASCII windows for tell-tale signs that they belong to the same document. WordPerfect files have some printer information, eventually followed by the text . PKZIP files have the name of the archived file, followed by machine-language characters until you get to the next archived filename. At the end of a PKZIP file is an ASCII listing of all the files contained in the archive. Other programs leave their own signatures.

Just use ZipZap to keep dumping successive sectors until you get to a bunch of zeros or other information that suggests you've reached the end. If it's a data file, chances are good that you'll be able to load it into the original application and recover part or all of its information. If a ZIP file contains clusters in consecutive order, PKZIP will decompress it even if you shoot past the end-of-file marker and include some extraneous information.

Brief Mentions

DrivePad

DrivePad is a tiny null block device (in DRVPAD.ZIP) that reserves a specified block of logical drive designators to a specified removable device, so that when the device is not installed, DOS won't assign its letter to something else and make your batch files, application paths, etc., error out. Especially handy for use with SCSI subsystems.

IDE Interrogator

This little program—DUG_IDE, in DUGIDE10.ZIP—will interrogate a system's IDE drives and report what it finds in what author Doug Merrett describes as "quick and dirty fashion." A small, handy program for when your CMOS forgets what drives you've got or for interrogating that strange, used IDE drive you got at the pawn shop.

HDTest: Hard Disk Test and Repair Utility

This shareware classic by P.R. Fletcher (in HDTST535.ZIP) contains one of the best hard drive diagnostic and restoration programs available for any price. The distribution file also includes HDChek, a small utility that checks compatibility with your system. Useful when your drive is getting unreliable and you want to find out why (and maybe even restore it to normal duty).

The Patriquin Utility Set

Because they stand out as useful hacks, we've included some components of this suite separately (in PTQNUTIL.ZIP). However, we also include this large file because it contains the entire set of Patriquin disk utilities, fresh from the Patriquin home BBS (909-352-2825). You can register all of them for $45, compared to $20 apiece if registered individually. Try three or four of them and, if you come to depend on them, get the whole set. It'll save you money. Here are the programs in the complete set:

- PCOPY93: File copy/move utility
- PALERT24: Disk/memory space reporting
- PATTR15: File attribute program
- PS52B: Search program
- PPRINT55: Printer utility
- PREBAK13: Backup reminder utility
- PDEL44: File delete utility
- PTOUCH: File dating utility

Next Up

If your hard disk is important as a data storage area, so is your memory—or, at least, your computer's memory. We can't do anything about whatever memory problems you may have personally, but the memory in most PCs is simply not used at maximum warp speed or efficiency. In the next chapter, we'll take a look at some super utilities to help you make faster, more efficient use of your computer.

7

Don't Forget Your Memory!

How much memory have you got? One brain, one memory.
—from TAGLINES, a BBS utility

Most PC users view DOS memory management as a job for failed rocket scientists. It's too intricate for normal people, but no one really smart would want to have anything to do with it. Give an average DOS memory guru a few more IQ points and he could revolutionize quantum physics or redesign the mouse trap instead of trying to make Windows 3.1 and AutoCAD coexist.

The pressure exerted on simple DOS by memory-hungry users and software vendors has altered its relationship to the PC far beyond what the original IBM and Microsoft system architects intended. Don't get us wrong—the space where DOS operates hasn't gotten any larger. It's still stuck below the 1MB limit. But the relationship between DOS, the hardware, and your programs has mutated into something vaguely resembling a bonsai logical monster.

One reason is the increasingly creative use of upper memory. Loading programs up there is kind of like solving those arrange-the-squares plastic puzzles sold at truck stops and pharmacies. You move the pieces sideways, or up and down, until they're arranged like the picture on the back of the box. Some people cheat. They pry out the plastic pieces and cram them back in sideways, often breaking the puzzle in the process. We, ahem, don't know anybody like that. But the practice does resemble the way programmers and power users cram square programs into the round spaces of upper memory. It ain't natural, but it works...more or less.

The utilities in this chapter increase the power and flexibility of the basic DOS operating environment. They make it easier to manage the monster in the UMB attic, and so they can help you reserve much more of the lower 640K for programs to use. The slick TSRs in the next section let you load and unload device drivers from batch files without rebooting the system, configure a RAMdisk or resize it on the fly, examine the current memory state while a program is running, and switch between tasks without a task-switching environment. (But see the section on Back and Forth in Chapter 4, "Programmer Friendly," for a good whole-environment approach to task switching.) This chapter's utilities make it easier to solve the memory puzzle, enhance what you can do, and reduce time wasted rebooting. These are productivity tools, folks, and if you're not already using something equivalent, you're missing out on some of the good stuff. Give them a try.

Reading the Alphabet Memory Soup

What with EMS, XMS, UMB, and HMA, it's no wonder people go bonkers trying to figure out where all the memory went. The name of the game, now, in memory management, is to arrange all those DOS alphabet pieces in the correct order without breaking the puzzle box.

A programmer at Quarterdeck Office Systems showed how to load programs high when he found what amounted to an IBM hardware bug that let DOS recognize the first 64K of extended memory on 80286/386 computing platforms. This was contrary to all the programming manuals. Microsoft quickly appropriated the new technology with the XMS/High Memory Area Specification. Many programmers groused that the Goliath of Redmond was taking an attitude of "this is how it is because this is how it is, so live in it." Such attitudes had long been considered IBM's private reserve. *Plus ça change, plus la même chose...*

Independents Still in the Game

Quarterdeck and Qualitas, the pioneer third-party vendors who actually developed high memory technology, continue to work independently. New versions of DOS do limit an independent's options. The area between 640K and 1MB is now called "Upper Memory Blocks," per Microsoft directives, because that's how it is, and it doesn't make sense not to be compatible.

Let's not forget the contributions of the Digital Research, Inc. staffers, who figured out how to stuff the DOS command kernel itself above 1MB into the Quarterdeck/Microsoft HMA. Digital's DR-DOS 5.0 stood Microsoft DOS 4 on its head by combining UMB and HMA tricks to net more conventional memory than users had ever seen.

Microsoft Recognizes Another Good Thing

Microsoft saw the handwriting on the wall and incorporated every new memory trick in sight into their DOS 5 and DOS 6 upgrades. Whether you love Microsoft for finally paying attention to users or hate the Chief Cybermuffin for aggressively pursuing what some see as monopolistic practices, there's no denying that the face of computing under DOS has changed.

Memory Management Utilities

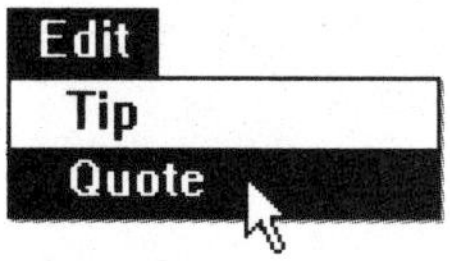
Edit
Tip
Quote

I think I can.
I think I can.
—Little Engine That Could, on managing memory under DOS

In MS DOS 5/6, the now famous DOS=HIGH,UMB statement means that the 35K to 45K command kernel, DOS files, and buffers are all placed "high" in extended memory, above 1MB. The "UMB" instructs the Microsoft EMM386 driver to reserve space *between* 640K and 1MB for drivers and TSRs loaded with the DEVICEHIGH and LOADHIGH statements. If all is not magically clear now, check out the terrific online memory tutorial in the Qualitas ASQ free package discussed next.

Hack Facts

ASQ
Version 1.30
Qualitas, Inc.
7101 Wisconsin Ave.
Bethesda, MD 20814
301-907-6700
Sales: 800-733-1377
178,081 bytes
Free
ASQ130.ZIP

ASQ is a combination online tutorial and system diagnostic utility distributed freely by Qualitas, Inc., authors of the 386MAX memory manager. It is a super snooper and classroom for the whole PC system, not just memory matters. Qualitas is one of the premier memory management vendors, and it shows. ASQ will tell you everything you want to know about expanded memory vs. extended memory, resident drivers and TSRs, or installed hardware peripherals. You can use it to test an expanded memory driver for information about mapping registers, pageframe, EMS version, and active EMS handles. It generates a complete address map for conventional and upper memory and scans the system for ROM addresses reserved by peripheral cards. Figure 7-1 shows the System Analysis Menu, which includes a quick reference window. The program also offers a series of performance benchmarks and hints for tweaking CONFIG.SYS to get binary hot rod performance levels.

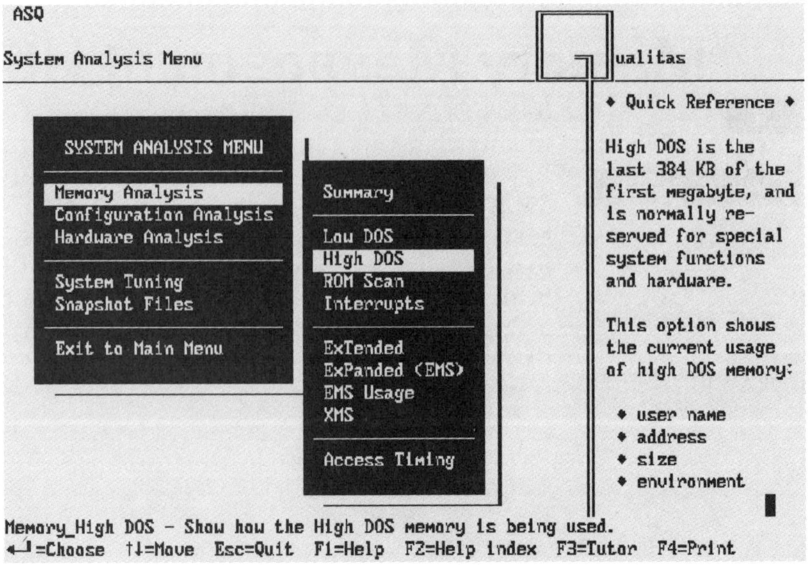
ASQ
System Analysis Menu
ualitas
SYSTEM ANALYSIS MENU
Memory Analysis
Configuration Analysis
Hardware Analysis
System Tuning
Snapshot Files
Exit to Main Menu
Summary
Low DOS
High DOS
ROM Scan
Interrupts
ExTended
ExPanded (EMS)
EMS Usage
XMS
Access Timing
♦ Quick Reference ♦
High DOS is the last 384 KB of the first megabyte, and is normally reserved for special system functions and hardware.
This option shows the current usage of high DOS memory:
♦ user name
♦ address
♦ size
♦ environment
Memory_High DOS - Show how the High DOS memory is being used.
↵=Choose ↑↓=Move Esc=Quit F1=Help F2=Help index F3=Tutor F4=Print

Figure 7-1. *The ASQ system analysis menu*

If you're not quite up to rocket scientist mode on how all of these things affect program performance, the online memory tutorial offers an excellent brush-up/refresher course. The tutorial contains lessons on memory, configuration, and hardware, as well as a good glossary of terms. It makes a fine point-by-point refresher on the intricacies of DOS memory.

Hack Facts

Dynamic Memory Control(DMC)
Version 3.5
Adlersparre & Associates
#304-1803 Douglas Street
Victoria, BC,
Canada V8T 5C3
BBS: 604-384-3564
74,861 bytes
Shareware: $50 U.S.
DMC35.ZIP

Dozens of memory-watching utilities let you load a TSR program, mark its position in memory, and later remove the TSR so you can use the memory for something else. Of them all, Dynamic Memory Control, or DMC, has got to be the champ. It lets you load and release TSRs in either conventional or upper memory, and—catch this—you can load and unload device drivers from the command line, too. We're not just talking stray ANSI or mouse drivers, but CD-ROM drivers, RAMdisks, even full-blown third-party memory managers. The DMC utility suite is a memory management tour de force.

Here's an example. Microsoft's CD-ROM device driver MSCDEX is a memory hog that everyone loves to hate. DMC lets you two-platoon this offense against clean coding. Just boot without the Microsoft driver and use Note and LDevice to load it from the command line only when you need it, without rebooting. Then use FreeNote to remove the driver when you're done. You can do the memory dance as many times as you like. Do you prefer the less hoggish CorelDraw CD-ROM driver to MSCDEX for everything but picky programs like Borland C++ 4.0? DMC can switch between them painlessly, no reboots required.

Edit
Tip
Quote

They say memory is the second thing to go. I can't remember the first thing.
—Vaudeville gag

DMC is perfect for testing program compatibility with memory managers, because you can do it on the fly, without rebooting. Start your system in plain vanilla DOS with no memory manager at all, then use DMC from the command line or from a batch file to switch between Microsoft's HIMEM/EMM386 combo and third-party retail products like 386MAX and QEMM, or the shareware product The Last Byte (described later in this chapter). You can load QEMM into upper memory, stealth and all, then remove it without even disturbing the vector interrupt table. It's a brilliant hack.

Edit Tip Quote

Using DMC, you can load device drivers inside DOS boxes in Windows. Closing the window gets rid of the driver. However, the DOS box environment is touchy, so be aware that it may take some experimentation to make certain drivers work right.

The version of DMC included with this book is a suite of command-line utilities. If you decide (like we did) that you can't imagine working without DMC, pay the $50 registration and get a conversion utility to transform any DOS program file *or device driver* into a self-executing *and self-removing* TSR. Pow! Take *that*, all you "reboot to remove" TSR programs and CONFIG.SYS drivers! The registered DMC's point-and-shoot interface also lets you mark, install, and remove TSRs en masse. It displays extensive information about your memory, showing the names and memory allocations for all resident programs and drivers. Figure 7-2 shows the registered shell reporting on a system.

Hack Facts

DOSMAX
Version 2.1
Philip B. Gardner
10461 Lever Street
Circle Pines, MN 55014
Voice: 612-785-9439
84,349 bytes
Shareware: $15
DOSM21.ZIP

DOSMAX gives fine control over upper memory blocks that you won't find even in retail packages like 386MAX and QEMM. You can use it to place the COMMAND.COM kernel, command environment space, and various DOS sub-segments (FILES, BUFFERS, FCBS, STACKS, LASTDRIV, INSTALL) into upper memory blocks. This greater flexibility can give you more conventional memory, both for single applications and for larger DOS sessions in multitasking environments. DOSMAX cooperates with Microsoft's EMM386 or any third-party EMS/XMS memory manager.

Under DOS versions 3.1 through 4.01, DOSMAX can simulate the DOS=HIGH feature built into more recent DOS versions. As long as the system provides expanded memory or mappable shadow RAM, DOSMAX will fit the command kernel snugly into upper memory instead of occupying conventional memory or

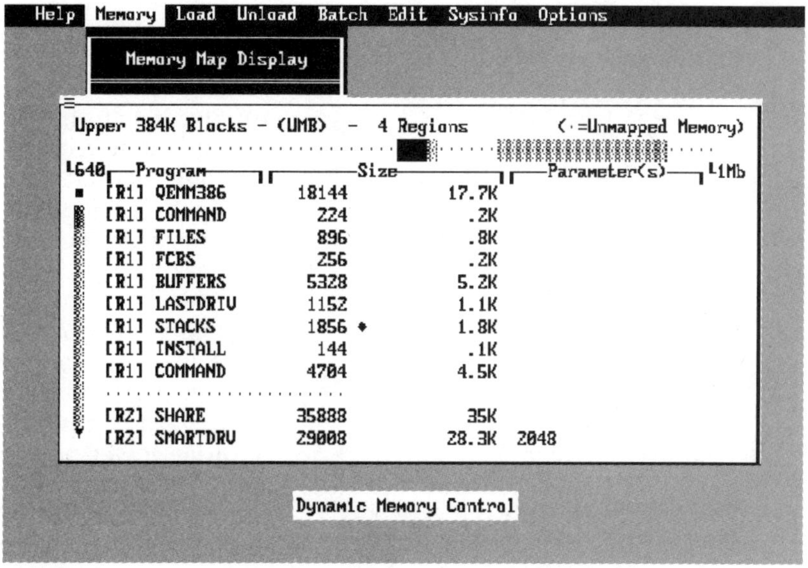
Help Memory Load Unload Batch Edit Sysinfo Options
Memory Map Display
Upper 384K Blocks - (UMB) - 4 Regions
(· =Unmapped Memory)
640 Program Size Parameter(s) 1Mb
[R1] QEMM386 18144 17.7K
[R1] COMMAND 224 .2K
[R1] FILES 896 .8K
[R1] FCBS 256 .2K
[R1] BUFFERS 5328 5.2K
[R1] LASTDRIV 1152 1.1K
[R1] STACKS 1856 1.8K
[R1] INSTALL 144 .1K
[R1] COMMAND 4704 4.5K
[R2] SHARE 35888 35K
[R2] SMARTDRV 29008 28.3K 2048
Dynamic Memory Control

Figure 7-2. *The DMC memory map (registered version)*

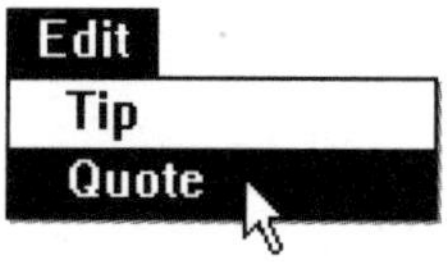
Edit
Tip
Quote

Back then, memory was memory—it didn't go away when the power went off. Today, memory either forgets things when you don't want it to, or remembers things long after they're better forgotten.
—Ed Post

the HMA. Under DOS 5 and 6, loading DOS between 640K and 1MB frees the HMA for applications like DESQview or Windows. Both multitasking environments can use more of the HMA than DOS, because they fill the entire 64K address segment with code. When you load DOS 5 or DOS 6 high, it occupies only 37K to 45K of the HMA, wasting the rest. Under DOS 5+, DOSMAX has an option to split the command kernel between conventional and upper memory. And QEMM users pressed for memory, or who just appreciate a superior hack, will like the bundled FREELOAD utility. FREELOAD scrapes up an additional 2K to 4K of conventional memory by removing the Quarterdeck LOADHI stub from programs loaded into UMBs.

The DOSMAX docs thoughtfully include configuration models for use with The Last Byte, QEMM, 386MAX, and the DOS 5/6 memory management drivers.

Hack Facts

The Last Byte
Version 2.30
Key Software Products
440 Ninth Avenue
Menlo Park, CA 94025
Internet:
Tech.support@ksp.com
BBS: 415-364-9847
Basic Package: 395,082
bytes, Advanced Utilities:
227,407 bytes
Shareware: $29.95
TLB-V230.ZIP and TLBA230.ZIP

The Last Byte shareware utility suite is like buying a blue-plate special and getting caviar and fine champagne. You get the sophisticated memory management options of a commercial package without having to pay much at all for it. The Last Byte is an upper memory manager, which means that it cooperates with DOS 5/6 or a third-party expanded memory manager to fit programs in your CONFIG.SYS and AUTOEXEC.BAT above 640K. The strongest feature of this package is its downward compatibility with a variety of older, lower-powered systems. Even an old 286 with 1MB of RAM can load programs above 640K if the motherboard contains a compatible shadow RAM chip set. The installation program can examine your machine for over 100 varieties of shadow RAM, along with standard EMS 4.0 memory management.

To make more contiguous address space available in upper memory, The Last Byte driver can remap video BIOS and system ROM to alternate address spaces. On systems that relocate the shadow RAM from UMB to the top of extended memory, The Last Byte can even override the default chip instructions to provide loadhigh capability. Like full-featured commercial packages, and unlike MS DOS 5/6, The Last Byte can shadow the system and video BIOS into expanded memory if your system doesn't provide hardwired shadow RAM. Also, you can tell the HIGHDRIVR and HIGHTSR modules to seek a UMB "best fit" for exploding device drivers, so they can load into smaller blocks. If a stubborn mouse driver refuses to load high with EMM386, for example, HIGHTSR can probably shoehorn it in.

Edit
Tip
Quote

Do what you can, with what you have, where you are.
—Theodore Roosevelt

The Last Byte Advanced Utilities is a supplemental package that provides sophisticated memory management tricks. It can append and reallocate monochrome video space to DOS, giving you up to 768K of conventional memory for text-based applications. A set of bookmark TSRs similar to those in DMC can load and remove programs in upper

Edit
Tip
Quote

When is a mouse a rat? When it eats memory!
—from TAGLINES, a BBS utility

memory on the fly. (These bookmarks are less sophisticated than the ones in DMC, since they can't handle block devices or other CONFIG.SYS based drivers.) The HIGHBFRS and HIGHFILES utilities place DOS buffers and file handles above 640K. The package also includes an expanded memory emulator for 286 systems, an upper memory RAMdisk, and a decent print spooler.

The main fly in the ointment with The Last Byte is that you must be willing to read the docs and experiment a bit to find the best utilities and command options for your system. There is no DOS MemMaker or QEMM Optimize program to do it for you. But the docs are clear, so even if you haven't graduated to Ninth Level Hackerdom and can't read a core dump directly, configuration is more a pleasant puzzle than an intimidating chore.

Hack Facts

SRDISK (Sizeable RAMDisk)
Version 2.05
Mark Kohtala
PL 115
FIN-01451 Vantaa
Finland
Marko.Kohtala@compart.fi
BBS: 708-776-1063
72,400 bytes
Shareware: $12
SRDSK205.ZIP

RAMdisks, RAMdisks, and more RAMdisks! There are hundreds of them out there, but this is one of the most interesting RAMdisk packages we've seen. SRDISK features XMS RAMdisks, EMS RAMdisks, dummy RAMdisks, and true DISKCOPY support. The kernel block driver in CONFIG.SYS occupies less than 1K, and once loaded, any of the SRDISK modules can be resized dynamically from the command line or removed from memory. SRDISK is compatible with MS DOS versions 3 to 6 and DR DOS 5 to 6. It supports 32-bit sector addressing, meaning that you can have RAMdisks of over 32MB, if you have the memory. The large module drivers are completely compatible with DOS DISKCOPY, which can be very handy if you have a spare megabyte or two but only one floppy drive on your system. Command-line switches automatically reformat or clear the disk contents or adjust the amount of memory it consumes. The driver can use combinations of conventional, extended, and XMS memory. Very slick little utility from Finland.

7

Setting Up a RAMdisk on the Fly

If you've unzipped Dynamic Memory Control (discussed earlier in this chapter), you don't even have to load a device driver in your CONFIG.SYS to create an on-the-fly, super-flexible RAMdisk. Just use DMC's LDEVICE module to load SRDXMS.SYS from the command line. Then run the SRDISK.EXE program to allocate memory precisely how you want it for the drive. On another tack, if you run Hyperware's Hyperdisk disk cache (see Chapter 6, "Disk-O Magic"), you can dynamically shift your extended memory between the disk cache and one or more SRDISK RAMdrives.

More Memory Tools

The next few programs help analyze and manipulate memory from inside running programs. You'll find them handy when testing code or tweaking your project to take maximum advantage of system resources.

Hack Facts

Memory Allocation Manager (MAM)
Version 1.09
Marc Mulders
c/o CCS
160 Summit Avenue
Montvale, NJ 07645
CIS: 76040,1420
64,758 bytes
Shareware: $20
MAM1_09.ZIP

MAM is a diagnostic utility which, coincidentally, you can use to save CMOS information and mark the location of upper memory device drivers. The true value of this little utility is that it can display virtually anything you want to know about the low-level configuration of your system's memory. In addition to presenting memory maps, it creates a table of the vector interrupts used by resident programs, memory control blocks, the chain of device drivers with default and remapped addresses, and hardware port usage. Command-line parameters allow you to look up information for all memory or for specific regions. Good little memory snooper.

Hack Facts

MemScan

Version 1
C. F. Martin
NoVaSoft
3239 Riverview Drive
Triangle, VA 22172-1421
703-221-1833 or
703-221-1471 (voice)
CIS: 72130,1400
2928 bytes
Free
MSCAN.ZIP

You can pop up this little memory-resident utility in the middle of another program, or at the DOS command-line for that matter, to display a hexadecimal map of the first megabyte of memory. The cursor keys let you page through addresses by incrementing either the segment or offset address. It also displays the current set of the principal PC hardware registers. MemScan is a fine little utility for ranging around your memory when something is stepping on something else, somewhere, for unexplained reasons...or just to see in detail how your programs are using memory resources.

Hack Facts

LegRoom

Version 2.0
Phil Grenetz
Ivden Technologies
87 Arbor Road
Churchville, PA 18966-1007
610-328-1145
CIS: 71221, 3602
144,534 bytes
Shareware: $35
LGROOM.ZIP

LegRoom lets you swap out your current application to XMS, EMS, or disk, then shell to a DOS command prompt with plenty of, well, leg room in which to run something else. A TSR, the program occupies less than 5K of memory and uses a hotkey that you specify. You can use it as a primitive task-switching utility while you edit files or compile code, with almost no performance or memory overhead.

LegRoom's hotkeys also work within graphic-based applications, and you can use it to automatically launch another program as a pop-up TSR if you like. Those abilities can come in handy if, say, you're in the middle of a session with your C compiler. Just hit a hot-key and the compiler, its data, video memory, mouse state, floating point coprocessor state, and the rest, are saved to RAM or a disk file. Run a second program, and when you're ready, LegRoom restores the compiler and all its data. Even if most of your applications have a built-in shell, you may prefer to use LegRoom. It can yield more memory—only 5K to 10K less than the conventional memory available to the primary command processor when you exit a progam entirely.

Brief Mentions

We've included the following programs, described only in brief, on the CD-ROM because we felt they would be of interest or useful in special circumstances.

(A)bort, (R)etry, (S)mack the @#$&~ thing!*
—from TAGLINES, a BBS utility

HiRam

HiRam (in HI-RAM.ZIP) is a full-blown memory manager in shareware form. It uses the memory control features of EMS 4.0 expanded memory or Chips & Technologies shadow RAM to fill unused memory addresses in high memory. In solving its "fit the most pieces into a limited space" puzzle, it can create up to 944K of DOS memory. This translates to up to 96K of additional low DOS memory.

TSR Management Utilities

The TSR management utilities by TurboPower Software (located in TSRCOM35.ZIP), were among the first such utilities around, and are still among the best. This suite includes Mark and Release, the basic two utilities that mark a place in memory so you can install your TSR, then remove the TSR by releasing its memory to other applications. You'll also find nine other TSR management utilities, including network and high memory management versions. Faster than DMC memory utilities, especially in lower memory areas.

For a similar program that works from the command line, not as a TSR, see SHROOM, described in Chapter 10, "A Bag of Other Goodies."

FastLoad

FastLoad (in FL150.ZIP) lets you read COMMAND.COM or any seven other frequently needed programs into XMS or EMS memory, and when your system invokes a stored program, it loads from memory instead of from a hard or floppy drive. Eliminates the magnetic medium data transfer bottleneck, resulting in tremendous boosts in speed for specified programs. You can specify overlay or batch files, too. Registering FastLoad removes the seven program limit. Try this hack sometime on a system with slow disk accesses.

You can't have everything. Where would you put it?
—Steven Wright (among others)

FakeHi

This little .COM program (located in FAKEHI.ZIP) fakes the HIMEM.SYS driver to let you run SMARTDrive version 4 on XT's and AT's with only 640K and a chunk of EMS memory, but no extended memory. Comes with complete source. Very useful if you're running DOS 5+ on an XT or other limited iron.

MemKit

This little utility suite (in MEMKT202.ZIP) lets you load device drivers and TSRs into upper memory on 8088 and 80286 machines, create up to 32MB of virtual expanded memory on your disk drive, load TSRs into expanded or extended memory, and more. Includes an earlier version of HRam (discussed earlier) as well.

Next Up

In the next chapter, we'll cover an area that can get every bit as snarled up as memory management—the care and feeding of a PC's ports, including the whole range of dedicated and user-definable hardware addresses.

8

Ports of Call

When you deal directly with I/O ports, you're at the electronic underbelly of the machine, working with low-level code and the most basic aspects of data handling. By "ports," we don't exclusively mean the multipin mechanical serial and parallel interface connectors familiar to most users. We also include the dedicated memory addresses through which software communicates with devices as well as the host of user-definable addresses.

When a lubber k'opens a port and doesn't k'has any spinach, I is always got to rescue him.
—Popeye the Sailorman

A more protective operating system than DOS would wrap any direct access to a computer's I/O ports in protective layers of device drivers, OS kernels, and authorizations. MS-DOS, though, is easy to program right down to the silicon. It's often said that "real hackers" don't use high-level languages and prefer a soldering iron to assembly language. We won't go that far, since we consider advanced DOS users to be a subspecies of hacker in their own right. Anyone happier at the command line than in some point-and-drool menu system or watching Windows run out of resources has been blessed with at least a few drops of hacker blood.

"Safer" systems include OS/2, NT, and UNIX, all of which set ring 0 privileges and rights and raise other barriers to careless access by "lusers," the computer innocents of the world. In DOS, a running program has complete access to *all* of a computer's resources. The C:\> prompt in DOS automatically gives you "super-user" rights. This is not necessarily good, if a luser can't tell a safe move from a dangerous one and doesn't realize there's no safety net. DOS does not cherish lusers.

There is, in real life, a need for user-obsequious, WIMP* interfaces. Lusers can be amazingly inept and don't always understand the need for caution. The following story comes from programmer Keith Graham:

> Once in 1985 I was working the PC help desk on the day after Thanksgiving. The company had kept its offices open by hiring temporary help to do word processing. I had five cases across the country of secretaries who had accidentally formatted their hard disks. It seems that Chapter 2 of the PC-DOS guide distributed to the offices described the process. The temps had made it through Chapter 1 and by noon had started on Chapter 2. "Format" must have seemed like a pretty nifty term. I spent the rest of the day trying to reinstall their software over the phone.

From such experiences came the take-'em-to-a-menu-and-lock-'em-there school of corporate computing. As a hacker, you have considerably more tools—and risk—at your disposal.

Basics of the Port

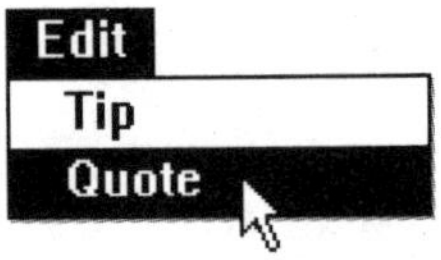
Edit
Tip
Quote

To reach the port of heaven, we must sail sometimes with the wind and sometimes against it—but we must sail.
—Oliver Wendell Holmes

The PC architecture inherited through the IBM/Intel generations allows 1024 I/O ports. In practice, a single device uses 4, 8, or 16 I/O ports at a clip. The motherboard reserves the first 512 of the available ports, though 256 of these are not usable (don't ask why). The remaining 512 ports are available to cards through contacts on a computer's expansion card slots.

The first 256 ports have some interesting properties. Playing with these ports will often crash a system—but then, crashing your system in unique and interesting ways is one of the joys of being a hacker, and one of the frustrations of programming in DOS.

A machine's parallel and serial ports are the computer's gateway to communications with the outside world. This data stream is subject to analysis, and we'll offer a variety of

*WIMP stands for Window, Icon, Menu, Pointing device—generic user-friendly (but hacker-hostile) interface tools.

Edit
Tip
Quote

A single bomb of this type, carried by boat and exploded in a port, might very well destroy the whole port, together with some of the surrounding territory.
—Albert Einstein (Letter to President Franklin D. Roosevelt about possible atomic bomb)

tools to monitor and diagnose what's going on at that level. You may want to check their status and configure a variety of defaults for telecommunications, printing, and remote control or file transfer. Since many programs access ports at a low level to circumvent the need to make stodgy, high-level DOS calls, you may also want to study their techniques while program code executes.

The utilities discussed in this chapter include diagnostic TSRs that allow you to examine the data flow through any port at your leisure. You'll also find modem diagnostic programs, information on high-speed modem configuration, file transfer and remote control programs, a shareware mini-LAN that works through serial port connections, and some TSRs that will let you control a high-speed 16550 UART from the DOS command line.

Serial/Diagnostic Programs

You'll need these diagnostic tools if your comm program bombs, your modem won't connect, or if you're having other serial port problems. They'll also help debug programs to improve speed and reliability. Use these utilities to optimize, debug, and generally improve your code. They'll let you defuse your bombing programs before they go atomic.

Hack Facts

comTAP
Version 2.1
Paladin Software
3945 Kenosha Software, Inc.
San Diego, CA 92117
Voice: 619-490-0368
Fax: 619-490-0177
132,383 bytes
Shareware: $169
COMTAP21.ZIP

comTAP is a serial communications analyzer, a spyglass on the dataflow. In a repair shop, they'd most likely use a special hardware monitor to do what this fine hack does in memory, and the MicroTAP "professional" release available as a registered upgrade version is an even more impressive tool. Here's how comTAP works.

When you connect two PCs by serial cable, comTAP turns one of them into a dedicated serial-line monitor. (This requires a null-modem or a serial cable with pin 2-to-pin 3 output). You can use comTAP to inspect character timing and other serial events, to test a modem, or to debug a communications program or subroutine. You can monitor output to several ports simultaneously and specify non-standard address and interrupt information.

The program includes color, monochrome, and LCD video drivers, so you can easily read screen windows on laptops and monochrome systems. The comTAP display windows deliver a byte-by-byte display of data flow through the serial ports. You can track information entered through the keyboard on the host computer, information sent over cable from a remote serial port, or data received through a modem. If you choose the "interactive" feature, source data is displayed in a separate window so you can compare it to what's received through the serial port. Various filters let you select a low-level record of the DCE/DTE transactions or a graphic log of the quantity of data received. You can toggle up to nine windows that display real-time or previously logged data flow through the ports. Live displays can be placed on hold to prevent scrolling or overwriting while you examine information. And if you get a bit lost in the wealth of information at your fingertips, just go into the hypertext help system and look up all the information you'll need on any of comTAP's various monitoring features. Figure 8-1 shows the display as the string "Now is the time" streams out the port.

Edit | Tip | Quote

The diagnosis . . . is often easy, often difficult, and often impossible.

—Peter Mere Latham

comTAP lets you monitor throughput for several ports simultaneously, compiling statistics and comparing the data to source output. MicroTAP, a registered version upgrade, adds a large number of additional capabilities.

Hack Facts

IO Monitor

Version 1.0
TurboPower Software distribution file
Portions of code copyright ASMicro Co.
35,758 bytes
Free
IOMON2.ZIP

IO Monitor, a fine hack from TurboPower Software based on code by ASMicro Co., tracks all accesses to a specified range of I/O ports on a 386 machine. The distribution includes full ASM, C and PAS source code, hackers. IOMON was designed chiefly to keep a log of I/O commands directed to a serial port by communications programs. You can use it to monitor a communications program as it runs, without interfering with or delaying any data transmitted or received

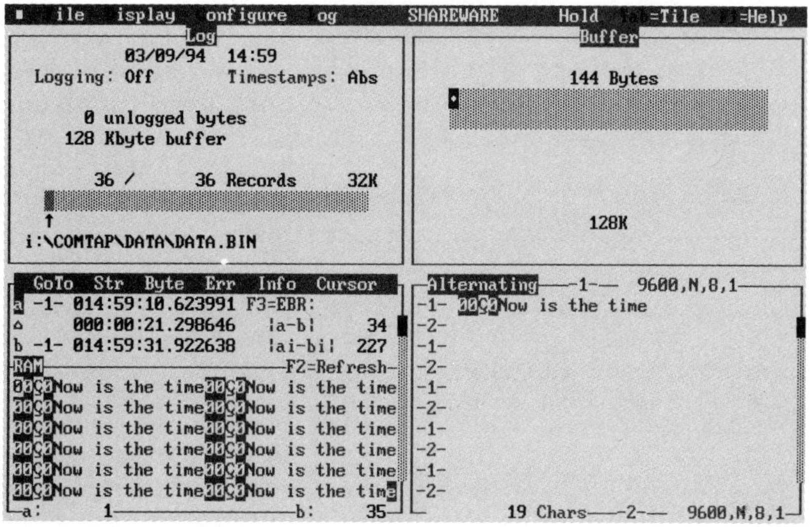

ile isplay onfigure og SHAREWARE Hold =Tile =Help
Log
03/09/94 14:59
Logging: Off Timestamps: Abs
0 unlogged bytes
128 Kbyte buffer
36 / 36 Records 32K
i:\COMTAP\DATA\DATA.BIN
Buffer
144 Bytes
128K
GoTo Str Byte Err Info Cursor
a -1- 014:59:10.623991 F3=EBR:
000:00:21.298646 |a-b| 34
b -1- 014:59:31.922638 |ai-bi| 227
RAM F2=Refresh
Now is the time Now is the time
Now is the time Now is the time
Now is the time Now is the time
Now is the time Now is the time
Now is the time Now is the time
Now is the time Now is the tim
a: 1 b: 35
Alternating -1- 9600,N,8,1
-1- Now is the time
19 Chars -2- 9600,N,8,1

Figure 8-1. *A moment of "Now is the time" frozen by comTAP*

through the port. The program maintains an internal 8K buffer of information about accesses to the port address you specify. IOMON.EXE, the executable as provided, produces both a log of Hayes commands and modem responses and a byte-by-byte log report of changes in the status of the specified port address. Since IOMON does its trick by running in a virtual 8086 machine, you will need to disable memory managers such as HIMEM, QEMM, or 386MAX in order to use it. But if you need precise information about what's coming and going through the port, that's a small price to pay.

this utility should be perfect for debugging communications scripts and tracing calls made to the UART on a byte-by-byte basis.

Hack Facts

CTS Serial Port Utilities
Version 1.3
Computer Telecommunication Systems, Inc.
3847 Foxwood Road, Suite 1000
Duluth, GA 30136-6100
404-263-8623
CompuServe: 76662,2315
104,216 bytes
Shareware: $20 (Personal), $35 (Personal Plus w/ manual)
CTSSPU13.ZIP

This suite of 10 utilities is a Swiss Army knife tool kit that can configure, reset, examine, and control serial port settings directly from the DOS command line. We'll describe some of them below, just to give you an idea of what this utility suite can do, but for the real experience, unzip the distribution file and try them out.

PortInfo is an interesting member of the set, and its centerpiece. Like some of the newer commercial system snooper packages, PortInfo detects multiple ports installed at the same address. It reports address and interrupt conflicts between serial ports and other installed devices. PortInfo generates a display of programmable port parameters including speed, format, parity, and current RTS/DTR settings. Its diagnostics also identify serial ports that share a common interrupt or that can't generate an interrupt. If disparities exist between your low-level hardware configuration and the way DOS sees the port setup, PortInfo will alert you. For instance, a programmable fax/modem might cause DOS to list COM1, 2, and 4 as available serial ports, while the hardware sees the third port as COM3. Knowing about this can help you resolve port addressing problems.

Edit
Tip
Quote

Nothing can have value without being an object of utility.
—*Karl Marx*

Hacking Around SMARTDrive's Brain Damage

Microsoft's SMARTDrive disk caching utility is famous for dropping characters from the serial line while doing disk reads and writes. It happens because SMARTDrive turns off interrupts for a fraction of a second while working, and the UART can drop a byte if it is not serviced quickly enough. Loss of data at speeds over 9600 bps can become a real problem, particularly in multitasking environments. With modems starting to connect at 115k baud and with throughput up to 28.8k bps, you really *need* a 16550 UART. Once you have one, the Buffers hack in the CTS Serial Port Utilities will find it and turn it on, so your I/O will be properly buffered.

PortInfo identifies the UARTs built into all serial ports. If it sees a 16550 UART, PortInfo displays the status of the FIFO buffer (off/on) and the buffer's current receive depth. The CTS Buffers utility then lets you modify the FIFO buffer setting on-the-fly. Figure 8-2 shows PortInfo's extensive diagnostic report on addresses, interrupts, and status of each serial port installed in a system with the mouse on COM1 and a modem on a COM2 16550 UART.

Other things you can do with the CTS Utilities include forcing DOS to recognize an added hardware port and swapping the addresses assigned by DOS to any two serial ports. The latter is particularly handy for working with a finicky software package or with a modem that demands access to a specific port.

The registered version of the utilities includes a program called SWAPIRQ, which remaps the basic hardware interrupt for a port to higher or lower IRQ values for DOS. If you own a serial card that operates on IRQ 10 or IRQ 14 but you have no software that recognizes this configuration, SWAPIRQ can remap the port for DOS to IRQ 3 through 5. Our CD-ROM includes ALADIRQ, a limited version of SWAPIRQ designed

PortInfo Summary Screen

	Serial1	Serial2	Serial3	Serial4
Port Address (Hex)	3F8	2F8	N/A	2E8
Interrupt (IRQ)	4	3		3
IRQ (Out2) Enabled	No	No		No
DOS uses port as	Mouse	Com2	N/A	Com4
Type of Port	16450	16550A		16450
Buffer - Trigger	None	Off		None
Speed (BPS)	1200	2400		2400
Bits / Character	7	8		8
Parity	None	None		None
Stop Bits	1	1		1
Clear to Send	On-RTS	On		On
Data Set Ready	Off	On		On
Ring Indicator	On-RTS	Off		Off
Data Carrier Detect	On-RTS	Off		Off
Data Terminal Ready	On	Off		Off
Request to Send	On	Off		Off

Press any key to continue....

Figure 8-2. *A PortInfo status report on serial ports*

for use with Aladdin, the proprietary front-end program for the GEnie Information Service. Aladdin recognizes only the standard system defaults of IRQ 4 and IRQ 3 for COM1 through COM4. ALADIRQ lets Aladdin recognize a hardware port on an alternate IRQ, for instance, COM3 at IRQ5 or COM4 at IRQ10.

About the 16550 UART

Most stock PC serial ports use UART chips like the 8250 or 16450, which have a hard time handling high-speed data transfer over about 4800 bps. Some high-speed cards use a buffered I/O UART replacement such as NEC's 16550AFN, but too many people get a high-speed card and see no improvement. The problem is that the 16550 defaults to the off setting. In that state it works just like an 8250. You need to switch the buffers on to get the benefits. (The CTS Buffers utility will handle that chore for you. Use it in a batch file when you start your comm software.)

Working with the FIFO Buffers

Once turned on, the 16550 UART buffers data sent and received through the serial line, using a FIFO (first in, first out) receive buffer. This action can add up to a 10 percent increase in data transfer speed and put an end to data overrun errors. If you've got an older serial card with socketed UARTs, you can often upgrade it simply by purchasing a three-chip 16550 UART kit from your local computer store, popping the 8250, 1488, and 1489 chips out and plugging the replacements in. If your serial ports are bundled on one of the newer IDE multi-I/O cards, they're probably soldered in. You can usually replace the whole card with a "high-speed" I/O card for under $50. It's worth doing, if you expect to communicate any faster than 4800 bps or use streaming protocols. (See Chapter 3, "Walking the Wires," for more on matters of data transfer and modeming.)

The FIFO buffer can cache both transmitted and received data. When setting your buffers, the range for received data is 1, 4, 8, or 14 bytes before the FIFO generates an interrupt request to the host system. Generally, 8 is a good, generic setting for the FIFO buffers. On very busy or multitasking systems, you'll want to generate an interrupt sooner (set the buffer to 4 bytes). On a fast or dedicated system, you can safely set the interrupt to 14 bytes and gain a marginal throughput increase.

Hack Facts

Cybercom
Version 1.1.00P
Cybersoft Corporation
P.O. Box 407 Vaucluse
New South Wales, 2030
Australia
CIS: 100033,1723
8775 bytes
Shareware
CYBDRV11.ZIP

Got a 16550AF UART on your serial port and *still* having trouble with file transfers inside of Windows? You're not alone. The Microsoft communication driver bundled with Windows 3.1 (and even with the 3.11 upgrade) is barely aware that a high-speed UART exists. As a result, if you do file transfers at 9600 bps or higher, whether using a Windows program or working inside a DOS box, your communications program is likely to enter the Twilight Zone. Your modem will report a happy 14.4 connection, and you'll suffer lost data, overruns, and other glitches typical of what some call *frogging* (that's when your program or hardware goes off its trolley).

Edit
Tip
Quote

I use windows—on my car, on my house, but not on my...
—from TAGLINES, a BBS program

SO if you defenestrate yourself a lot—jump in and out of Windows—use Cybercom. It will alleviate some of your file transfer problems by informing your Windows programs that a "virtual port" with a 16550 UART is available. See the docs on how to edit the Windows SYSTEM.INI file.

Working with Your Modem

If you've ever tried to install a new modem, whether internal or external, you'll know what we mean when we describe the process as a frustrating experience. If you're not changing brands it's usually easier, but when you go from one modem to another—or even from one comm program to another—it can turn into a major hassle. The following program can do a lot to help you through the transition, or to cure any other kind of modem blues.

Edit
Tip
Quote

PCDOS&MSDOS&CP/M&WINDOWS I'LLFIDDLEWITHOS/2 WOULDN'TYOU
—from TAGLINES, a BBS program

Hack Facts

Modem Doctor

Version 5.2
Hank Volpe
P.O. Box 43214
Baltimore, MD 21236
Voice: 410-256-5767
BBS: 410-256-3631
Shareware: $19.95
134,041 bytes
MODEMD52.ZIP

Modem Doctor is a super diagnostic program for curing the modem blues. It examines first the port, then the modem attached to the port. Besides providing address, IRQ, and UART status, Modem Doctor conducts a series of tests on any attached modem microprocessor, checking its ROM memory, identifying its maximum speed, and performing various register tests. The basic S-register values for the modem are displayed in one window while another window reports on line control, line status, modem control, plus the interrupt ID, enable and mask registers.

Once a modem passes initial diagnostics, you can select more specialized tests from Modem Doctor's pull-down menus. You can run UART register diagnostics, test the originate and answer frequencies on the modem, or perform a series of loopback tests including an RTS/CTS echo test, analog loopback on the port with a plug, or digital loopback to the modem's UARTs. A series of external modem drivers makes it possible to test special modems that might not use the standard Hayes AT command set. When problems are detected, the program issues detailed diagnostic messages. These are lucidly explained in a superior reference manual.

Edit
Tip
Quote

My doctor gave me six months to live but when I couldn't pay the bill be gave me six months more.
—*Walter Matthau*

The registered version of Modem Doctor can also check the modem's response to a hardware (RTS/CTS) or software (Xon/Xoff) handshake, perform diagnostics at up to 57,600 bps, or automatically program and set up a variety of high-speed modems from different vendors. Figure 8-3 shows that a modem attached to COM2 has passed the Modem Doctor's preliminary microprocessor diagnostic tests.

Incidentally, one of Modem Doctor's most useful screens for diagnosing comm problems gives detailed information on the modem's hardware S-registers for both settings and performance. Figure 8-4 shows this screen for one sample system.

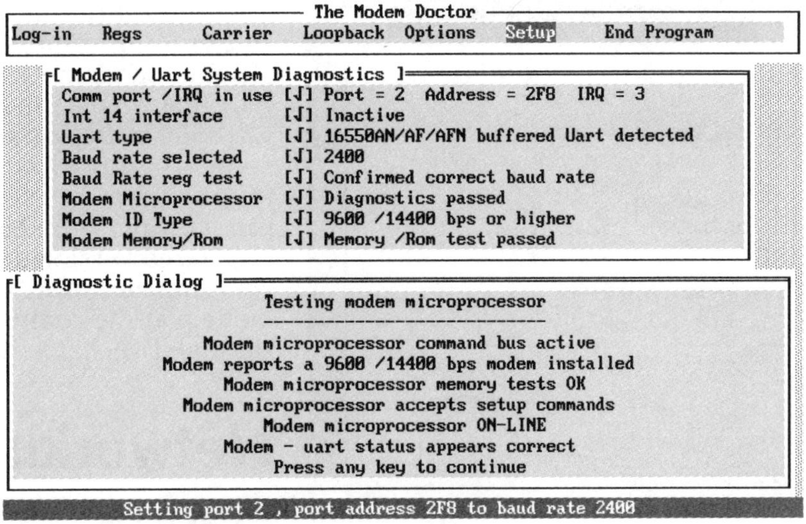
The Modem Doctor
Log-in Regs Carrier Loopback Options Setup End Program
[Modem / Uart System Diagnostics]
Comm port /IRQ in use [√] Port = 2 Address = 2F8 IRQ = 3
Int 14 interface [√] Inactive
Uart type [√] 16550AN/AF/AFN buffered Uart detected
Baud rate selected [√] 2400
Baud Rate reg test [√] Confirmed correct baud rate
Modem Microprocessor [√] Diagnostics passed
Modem ID Type [√] 9600 /14400 bps or higher
Modem Memory/Rom [√] Memory /Rom test passed
[Diagnostic Dialog]
Testing modem microprocessor
Modem microprocessor command bus active
Modem reports a 9600 /14400 bps modem installed
Modem microprocessor memory tests OK
Modem microprocessor accepts setup commands
Modem microprocessor ON-LINE
Modem - uart status appears correct
Press any key to continue
Setting port 2 , port address 2F8 to baud rate 2400

Figure 8-3. *Modem Doctor examines a port and tests a connected modem.*

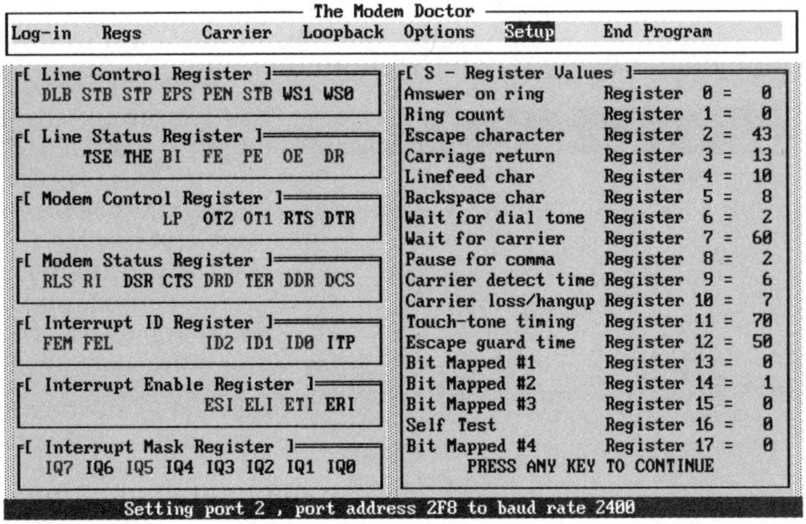
The Modem Doctor
Log-in Regs Carrier Loopback Options Setup End Program
[Line Control Register]
DLB STB STP EPS PEN STB WS1 WS0
[Line Status Register]
TSE THE BI FE PE OE DR
[Modem Control Register]
LP OT2 OT1 RTS DTR
[Modem Status Register]
RLS RI DSR CTS DRD TER DDR DCS
[Interrupt ID Register]
FEM FEL ID2 ID1 ID0 ITP
[Interrupt Enable Register]
ESI ELI ETI ERI
[Interrupt Mask Register]
IQ7 IQ6 IQ5 IQ4 IQ3 IQ2 IQ1 IQ0
[S - Register Values]
Answer on ring Register 0 = 0
Ring count Register 1 = 0
Escape character Register 2 = 43
Carriage return Register 3 = 13
Linefeed char Register 4 = 10
Backspace char Register 5 = 8
Wait for dial tone Register 6 = 2
Wait for carrier Register 7 = 60
Pause for comma Register 8 = 2
Carrier detect time Register 9 = 6
Carrier loss/hangup Register 10 = 7
Touch-tone timing Register 11 = 70
Escape guard time Register 12 = 50
Bit Mapped #1 Register 13 = 0
Bit Mapped #2 Register 14 = 1
Bit Mapped #3 Register 15 = 0
Self Test Register 16 = 0
Bit Mapped #4 Register 17 = 0
PRESS ANY KEY TO CONTINUE
Setting port 2 , port address 2F8 to baud rate 2400

Figure 8-4. *A Modem Doctor S-register screen report*

Hack Facts

Comset
Version 12
Hank Volpe
P.O. Box 43214
Baltimore, MD 21236
BBS: (410) 256-3631
Shareware: $10
25,718 bytes
COMST12.ZIP

Another utility from Modem Doctor author Hank Volpe, Comset wakes up sleeping modems. It can reset a serial port to any specified baud rate, turn an NS16550 buffer on and off, or send the modem an initialization string. It returns errorlevel codes to DOS, so you can use Comset in batch files. The registered version supports sending any sequence of AT commands to a modem at the command line or through DOS batch files.

Networking on a Budget

The next program gets its own major category because it's close to unique—a very smooth working local area network (LAN) system for two computers, linked by a null-modem serial cable. Since it's dated 1988 we double-checked the contact information in the file and were unable to contact the program authors. Still, this slick little program deserves to be included on the CD-ROM. Let us know if you find the EasyNet authors!

Hack Facts

EasyNet
Version 12
EasyNet Systems, Inc.
117,583 bytes
Shareware: $49.95
EASYNET.ZIP

Using a computer remotely by telephone, as DOORWAY permits (see Chapter 3), may often be all you need. But sometimes it's handier to network a couple of machines locally without resorting to the telephone. For that, you can go out and spend hundreds of dollars on a LAN. Or you can hook up a null modem cable and install EasyNet.

EasyNet is a two-computer local area peer-to-peer network that runs through an RS-232 serial port at up to 56,700 bps. It works well for a laptop-to-desktop connection, allowing two PCs to share programs, disk drives, RAMdisks, and printers. The connection requires a null modem cable (pins 2 and 3 reversed, pin 7 straight through). If you're not into changing cable pins yourself, you can pick one up cheap at the computer store. EasyNet is a budget LAN for small operations or on-the-fly installation.

Brief Mentions

CommChek

COMMCHK.EXE (in COMCHK18.ZIP) will analyze information on a serial line by intercepting the data flow. You can view the captured information in either a HEX or an ASCII format, or save it to a file.

Network management is like trying to herd cats.
—from TAGLINES, a BBS program

Set

This handy little non-TSR utility (in COMSET.ZIP) installs COM3 and 4 in the DOS BIOS area, making them available to programs that use DOS functions rather than the actual device addresses. It also makes the ports visible to DOS, which checks only for the first two ports at startup. Companion programs in the distribution file will swap your ports around to accommodate software that addresses only COM1 or 2.

Next Up

In the next chapter, we'll show you some nifty tricks to use with printers, including some utilities guaranteed to make life easier when it's time to print docs or put printer interfaces into your programs.

9

Taming the Wild Printer

What do you want your printer to do? Weed your garden? Groom your dog? The high-end printers may be able to accommodate you; some of the new products can do amazing things. Meanwhile, low-end products are just low-end products. But you can still do some pretty nifty things with them, if you have the right tools.

Thou hast most traitorously corrupted the youth of the realm in erecting a grammar-school... [and] thou hast caused printing to be used.
—Shakespeare, King Henry the Sixth, *Part II*

At one time, all you could really expect from a printer was plain text. If you wanted to lift your little finger and show some class, you'd use a daisy-wheel printer to make the output look like a secretary had typed it by hand. It might drive you (or your secretary) deaf, but it looked pretty good. You might even insert an intentional typo to keep recipients from thinking you had sent them something "done by computer."

Today, most printers can do much more than print the alphabet and the standard symbols. A low-end 24-pin printer (now almost obsolete technology) can print passable graphics, though it takes slow, grinding, multiple passes of the printer head. Laser and bubble-jet printers are capable of near-typeset quality output. The newest 600-dots-per-inch printers might as well be typeset—the human eye can't make out the difference.

The trouble is, many of us lack the knowledge or the resources to make our printers sing and dance as they should. In this chapter we'll help you get the best use out of your printer, whatever type it may be. What is "best use"? Well, for one thing it's getting the most performance for the money you've sunk into the hardware. For example, laser printers have long produced the best looking output available for less than it takes to buy a typesetting machine. The trouble is, laser printers are also among the most expensive printers. And, like copy machines, they run both hot and messy.

the tilt toward laser printers is changing. Many of the new "bubble jet" inkjet printers can produce output that looks virtually identical to that of laser printers, and bubble jets cost much less to buy. The best of the bubble jets are not as fast as a high-end laser, but their output is every bit as good. They also run quietly, and are much cooler than laser printers. The cost per page of inkjet printer output can run higher than that of a laser printer, because the ink cartridges cost a lot to replace. But that too is changing, and you can do some unauthorized things (*shhhh!*) to bring that cost down. Given an empty inkjet cartridge, for example, it doesn't take a dope fiend to find a non-medically approved use for hypodermic syringes.

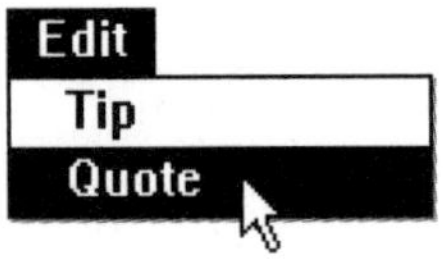
Edit
Tip
Quote

A Penny Saved is A Penny Earned.
—Trad.

How to save money on inkjet cartridges is exactly the subject of one of the utilities in this section. Beyond that we'll look at utilities that let you print Japanese characters or sheet music, bar codes and envelopes, and ones that will squeeze the text of four or five pages onto a single sheet of paper. Printers are document-oriented, so these utilities are all canted in the direction of making it easier to produce documents in a variety of useful ways. (For more on how docs affect shareware and the DOS hack, check out Chapter 2, "The Art of the Gem," and Chapter 14, "Hacker Graduation.")

Hack Facts
DownLoad
Version 1.10
Bill Goelkel
CIS: 71725,455
7584 bytes
Free
DL110.ZIP

The DownLoad printer utility downloads non-native fonts to a Hewlett Packard laser printer or compatible. It can handle automatic downloads of up to 32 fonts, as specified in a user-prepared text list. If the designated fonts in the list are not numbered in the text file, they will be automatically numbered from 1 up to 32 (if that many fonts are listed). The text file that the program uses can specify a different starting number or each font can have a totally different ID number as long as the number is between 0 and 32767.

The utility is quite easy to use and makes most sense when used in a batch file prior to loading a word processor or other application needing a special set of fonts.

Hack Facts
DeskJet Color Cartridge Refill
Doug Kron
P.O. Box 25591
Garfield Heights, OH 44125
Voice: 216-587-2024
7814 bytes
DJCLRFL.ZIP

Ever run out of a single color in one of those expensive DeskJet color cartridges? If one color goes, the whole cartridge is basically dead. Unlike black inkjet cartridges that have a refill hole (assuming you can find the "right tool" with which to puncture the plastic bag and inject some ink—see the text file, and ask at a nearby animal feed store, if you're not too scruffy looking), color cartridges are sealed.

This text file unlocks the mystery of the HP color cartridges, outlining exactly how to refill them. It includes a detailed drawing showing where to drill holes in the cartridges and how to maintain the cartridge for repeated use. The author also offers to sell cartridge-friendly inks, handy if you have no other supply. The whole file can be viewed and/or printed using a word processor such as MS Word. Figure 9-1, from the distribution file, shows where to drill a color cartridge and where to inject the ink.

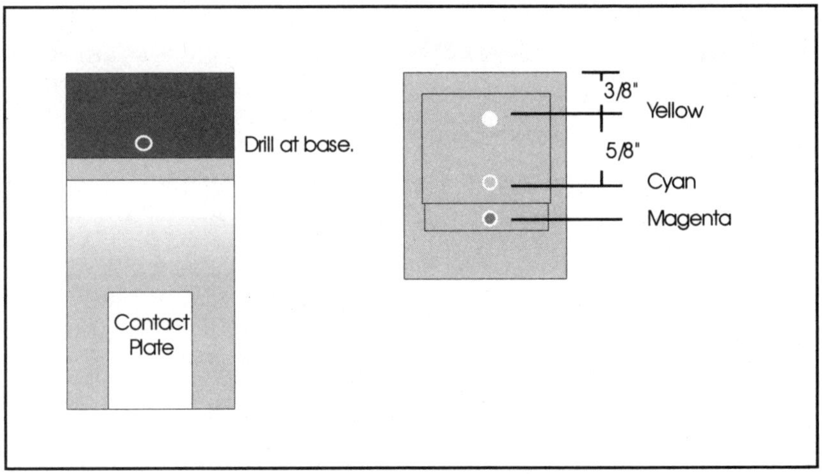
Drill at base.
Contact Plate
3/8"
5/8"
Yellow
Cyan
Magenta

Figure 9-1. *Drill 'n fill those cartridges yourself.*

Hack Facts

CodPr
Version 4.2
John W. Grothman
14,617 bytes
CP42.ZIP

This simple program is designed to format C-code and print it out in highly readable form. It produces a left-hand margin and line numbers to make programs easier to read and debug. C programmers will find the program useful and can use it as a good example of formatting and printing as well—and full source code is included. Some additional features in CodPr are optional page headers, selection of printer ports (LPT1-3 or PRN), or output to file. The program supports a number of different printers, including Epson-compatible printers and HP-compatible printers.

One of the best features in CodPr is its ability to identify long code lines. Since program code is usually indented, it often goes well beyond the right margin even if the total character count is less than 80 columns. CodPr correctly wraps lines that go beyond the right margin, without incrementing the line numbers.

Hack Facts

NewPrint
Version 1.0
Jeffrey R. Brenton
13,519 bytes
Free
NPRN10.ZIP

This formatting and printing utility can format text files into columns, adjust margins, and so on, for one or more files at a time. The program includes the C program source code, which makes it easy to modify for custom applications. It's a nice, simple program that takes care of one of a programmer's more persistent headaches—getting code and documentation onto paper in quick-and-dirty fashion, reliably, without needing to be a DTP expert. That's what NewPrint does. It is probably best used for formatting program files, to make them easier to read and modify at a later date (when even you have forgotten how your code worked). The program also provides an excellent example of pain-free printer and file control.

Hack Facts

DMP
Version 2.05
DMP Software
204 East 2nd Avenue, Suite 610
San Mateo, CA 94401
800-242-4775 (PsL voice order line)
Shareware: $29
56,284 bytes
DMP205.ZIP

DMP is a versatile and widely respected printer spooling program that can make long, repetitive print jobs quicker and much easier to set up. DMP's main claim to fame is its ability to direct output that would have gone directly to a printer to another target—for example, to a block of RAM dedicated to the purpose, or to a hard drive.

Printing is a notorious bottleneck. We hate it when some gremlin (certainly not us) hits CTRL-PRINT SCREEN when the printer's turned off; it hangs the machine. It's just as bad when the printer's turned on, since it can waste whole forests printing DOS prompts and error messages.

RAM caches and hard disks are much faster than any printer and give you an intervening layer that doesn't care if the printer is turned off. When you do intend to print, you can let DMP take care of the chore. Once the process of "printing to disk or RAM" is complete, the computer sends the data to the printer in the background while you go on to other things.

Edit Tip Quote

Without books God is silent.
—Thomas Bartholin

Done correctly, a print spooler can make the computer printing process quick and totally transparent to the user. DMP does this quite well. It manages the background tasks well without seeming to interrupt foreground tasks or making them slow down at all, if you have a fast computer. On slower systems like XTs or 286s, DMP's activity becomes more apparent, but none of the systems we tested showed any detectable slow-down using WordPerfect, MS Word, or WordStar. It's a very efficient spooler.

In addition to its spooling capabilities, DMP can make modifications in the data stream to set printer controls, make some automatic formatting changes, cue up batches of files for printing, and in other ways make it easier to keep your work flow smooth and printer distractions at a minimum. Give this one a try.

Hack Facts

DiskEnvelope
Version 1.00
Rod Barnes
9580 bytes
DSKVLP10.ZIP

This little disk envelope utility is one of dozens available; we include it here as an example of the genre. It produces 5 1/4-inch diskette envelopes that list all of the files contained on the diskette. Although 3 1/2-inch diskettes are dominant these days, most of us still use some 5 1/4-inch diskettes, and there's no law that says we can't drop the smaller diskettes into the 5 1/4-inch envelopes as a filing scheme. They can be a lot easier to keep track of that way.

Here's how the program works: you set your printer by default to a 12-pitch (i.e., characters per inch) type style, load the utility, and then insert the diskette you want to catalog. The program prints out everything on the diskette on a "cut-out-and-tape (or paste) together" diskette envelope. DiskEnvelope can include or not include subdirectories in its listings, can include a title-like comment above the file listing, and can send custom codes to switch your printer's output between pica and condensed type sizes (you specify the codes in a configuration file). This simple utility provides a fine way to catalog your diskette library while avoiding the hassles of writing everything down by hand or including separate pieces of paper in the jackets to indicate file contents.

Hack Facts

DocSmash
Version 3.26
David W. Rettger
5304 Johnson Avenue
Western Springs, IL 60558
CIS: 71131,3253
Orchard Hills
BBS: 708-361-4547
69,491 bytes
Shareware: $10.00
DOCSM326.ZIP

For computer users who do a LOT of printing, DocSmash can be a real forest saver. It takes standard ASCII text output and prints it in small type, four pages to an 8 1/2 by 11-inch piece of paper. The output, in default mode, prints text in two even columns of text, evenly divided into two pages of text per column.

Although DocSmash is fairly quick and versatile, it does have a few limitations. First of all, it only works with straight ASCII files. Anything produced on a typical word processor must be converted to ASCII before DocSmash can work with it. Also, be aware that DocSmash works (as delivered) with only a limited number of printers: either Epson-compatible or HP LaserJet-compatible. These make up a large enough proportion of the printer universe to justify including this clean little utility here. Your printer probably has a compatibility mode with one or the other of those two brands. If not, you can specify different printer codes in a simple configuration file. Finally, it insists on planting the configuration file in the drive's root directory, though you can get around this by using the DOS SUBST command.

Edit
Tip
Quote

From the moment I picked up your book until I laid it down I was convulsed with laughter. Some day I intend reading it.
—Groucho Marx

Despite its limitations, DocSmash provides a fair number of print options, including line-wrap control, line spacing (called *leading* by printers), and number (and size) of columns per page.

Hack Facts

KnowBars
Version 2.0
Simon M. Camtden-Main,
Client Services
Computer Resources Group
629 Silverdale Drive
Claremont, CA 91711
Voice: 909-624-8734
BBS: 909-626-1054
68,623 bytes
Free
KNOWBARS.ZIP

Like diskette label printers, the hapless bar code printing program can have a hard time making it into the market. We're not talking about programs to put postal bar codes onto envelopes here, though there are dozens of them too. These are programs that print bar codes for use by applications such as inventory control and employee time logging. We include KnowBars here because it illustrates the principal and it comes from the Computer Resources Group, which has about a ton of good, adaptable code and libraries in ASM, C, Pascal, BASIC, and dBase available for programmers to use in applications.

The KnowBars companion program, KnowWedge, replaces expensive barcode-reading mechanical devices normally "wedged" between a PC keyboard and system box. Using KnowBars, you can create the barcode; using KnowWedge, you can read it back into the machine using any dumb barcode reading device (such as a scanner) that can emulate a reader wand—about 80 percent of all such devices. The KnowBars version on the CD-ROM works with a 9- or 24-pin Epson-compatible printer, so you can use your old dot matrix printer to produce your machine-readable bar code listings. However, this suite of programs is constantly being updated so, if this technology will add value to your applications, call the authors' BBS.

There's a treasure of barcode programs and programming resources in the Computer Resources Group BBS, library 5. Look there for the most recently upgraded demos of both KnowBars and KnowWedge. You'll also find all sorts of linkable libraries in C, Pascal, BASIC, and dBase. Use these resources to enhance your point of sale, inventory, employee ID logging and other barcode-friendly applications. The source is free for personal use or during development, and licensing is negotiable for shareware authors—read: No money owed until your product starts to make bucks in the marketplace. The KnowBars authors are friendly and will negotiate.

The KnowBars/KnowWedge programs can handle code 39, with or without check data, and both Modulus 43 and Weighted Modulus 43 encoding. KnowBars will print labels in five sizes, with or without additional independent text. It will concatenate several bar code labels, allowing you to store important data in a series of labels. The docs include a clear description of the program plus a good tutorial on how bar coding works and how to use it. That's one good reason why we selected this little utility for the CD-ROM.

This program, by the way, is free as long as you don't use it as a part of another program that *is* sold. (If you plan to do this, pay the licensing fee.) KnowBars offers a terrific way to get started incorporating barcodes into your applications without having to invest an arm and a leg in offbeat hardware.

Hack Facts

AccuMusic
Version 1.2
Kevin Fischer
13234 Vinter Way
Poway, CA 92064-1216
34302 bytes
Shareware: $5.00-$20.00+
AC12MUSC.ZIP

Here's a nifty little specialty item that—if you need something like this—can save you many hours browsing through software outlets or ranging around the BBS wires, trying to find it. Do you need to print out "real" sheet music with your computer? Well, here's your problem solver. AccuMusic lets you write songs using a standard word processor and print them as music on a number of different printers. Printers that it directly supports are:

- Panasonic 1091i (and similar models)
- Epson RX-80 (and similar graphics models)
- Gemini 10
- HP LaserJet II-D

Many printers can emulate one or another of these printers. The program also includes drivers for quite a few additional printers, and in many cases one or another of these drivers will work pretty well. For example, a generic HP driver works well on a DeskJet (inkjet) printer.

Here's the crowning touch. The author recognizes that the program is a bit weak in the printer driver department, and has included an extensive description of how to adapt other drivers to this program. With this help, you should be able to use almost any printer if you're willing to invest a little time.

The only real drawback to AccuMusic is its input routine. Every note must be entered using a clumsy coding scheme that includes the note (A-G), its octave, and an assortment of other parameters such as its length, and so on. And while the program needs to know what note to print where, you may think there should be a more intuitive way to enter the music. Hackers, take note.

Brief Mentions

The following programs are mentioned briefly, because we thought them interesting enough to include on the CD-ROM, but very specialized, niche type programs.

JPRT: Codes In, Kanji Out

This utility (in JPRT11.ZIP) is one to use at your own risk. Well, actually there's very little risk, but it may take awhile to figure out how to use it effectively. But we live in a global village now, and this is an interesting hack.

> *In the Far East, calligraphy is done with a pointed brush held vertically. In America, it's done with a paint program viewed vertically, a typeface and a printer.*
>
> *—from a CompuServe message thread*

This program converts lists of special "JIS" codes into Japanese character output (kanji) as graphics output to an Epson-compatible printer. With the registered version, you can send the output into a .PCX file that you can e-mail or fax to someone. Or you can print the file directly on any Epson-compatible printer (most dot-matrix printers and quite a few others will work).

The biggest problem with this utility is that the docs are not clear on how to produce the data files that create Japanese text. With some work (and a good understanding of Japanese) you can probably figure out how to accomplish the translation, using the example data file included with the program. If you do have trouble with the data format, according to the docs, the registered version has additional features—and the author will help you out with any problems.

Nenscript: An ASCII to PostScript Converter

Edit
Tip
Quote

...and give the appearance of a certain greatness and stateliness.
—*Plutarch's* Lives

The Nenscript utility (in NENSC113.ZIP) converts ASCII text files directly into Adobe-PostScript compatible output. Nenscript, by Craig Southeren (whom you can reach care of geoffw@extro.ucc.oz.au), is a public domain clone of Adobe's Enscript program. The program is written in C and includes all of the source code, so you can make modifications as you need. The distribution file contains compiled versions by Darrel Hankerson (hank@ducvax.auburn.edu) for DOS and OS/2. Additionally, the program makes a good tutorial on how PostScript works and how to make direct changes to PostScript files produced by other applications such as PageMaker or FreeHand.

NJNLQ: Near Letter Quality from a 9-Pin Printer

Are you a low-budget computerist? Or would you just like to take the old 9-pin printer out of your closet and put it to good use? It's hard to tolerate the long, straight-element, 9-pin printing effect. Text Docs printed out that way makes you feel like you're reading a long document on 7-element LED displays, all angular and not quite like the alphabet you grew up with.

Edit
Tip
Quote

It is most true, stilus virum arguit—our style betrays us.
—*Robert Burton,* The Anatomy of Melancholy

This fine utility (in NJNLQ143.ZIP) for graphics-capable, Epson-compatible 9-pin printers was written by "Nifty James," or Mike Blaszczak (as some have reported his secret identity to be). "Nifty" first gained hacker prominence as a teen-ager on The Source information service (R.I.P.) and has since then produced a series of slick utilities, all beginning with the letters NJ. This one will give you more than simple dot-matrix output from a 9-pin printer. NJNLQ stands for "Nifty James Near Letter Quality," and its output comes surprisingly close to the NLQ output of a 24-pin printer. The only real drawback is that the output files (which are totally graphics files) grow by a factor of about 24 from the original text file size.

Like all the Nifty James utilities, NJNLQ is written in assembly code and includes a revised outline of all the source code for reference. When you range out on the wires, look for the NJ utilities; they are uniformly high in quality—good hacks for good hackers.

LPTMON: A Port Monitor

This assembly language TSR utility (in LPTMON10.ZIP) monitors activity on a parallel printer port. Full assembly source code is included, as well as a complete description of every signal on the parallel port. LPTMON is a nice little info treasure trove as well as a useful utility if you're having trouble with parallel port functions. The implementation as it stands is fairly simple, but if you start here, it wouldn't be too hard to springboard to some very useful utilities to control and monitor parallel ports.

Next Up

As noted elsewhere, we've found so many first-rate goodies that there was no way to fit them all in this book. There are just too many gems out there in the shareware universe. The next chapter gives brief descriptions of some of the best programs that didn't fit elsewhere in the book.

10

A Bag of Other Goodies

This chapter ends Part II of the book. You'll find a raft of useful, interesting files and programs here, plus some that either didn't quite fit elsewhere or that we came across too late to include in another chapter. In any case, we didn't want the CD-ROM to miss these programs. So expect a potpourri of files and programs, many described briefly but a few with longer descriptions. Some support files for the larger programs won't have their own headlines or hack fact boxes, but unless otherwise specified, all the distribution files mentioned in this chapter are included on the CD-ROM.

If you're a browser, you'll enjoy this chapter. If you're not, just skip to Chapter 11.

DOS and Batch File Tools

We start with some very good DOS and batch file utility tools. First up is probably the most comprehensive and powerful keyboard buffer program anyone has created to date—Stackey, the best of the keyboard automators.

Hack Facts

Stackey

Barry Simon
CTRLALT Associates
Suite 133
260 South Lake Ave.
Pasadena, CA. 91101
Orders: 800-872-4768
CIS: 76004,1664
Shareware: $49
361,775 bytes
SKEY40.ZIP

Stackey is, according to author Barry Simon, "a keyboard stuffer with English language syntax, record capability, pauses for text, and more." This is a remarkable program that adds a lot of power to a PC. It lets you automate just about any part of a routine session so you can concentrate on doing useful work. Stackey will put a keypress (or whole phrase, for that matter) into the keyboard buffer immediately, wait for an input request, wait a set amount of time, or wait for a specific prompt (such as "press a key when ready") to appear on the screen. The progam also fills in the blanks for a large assortment of variables, including many system values.

Use the associated utility Skres (also in SKEY40.ZIP) to install Stackey's memory-resident portion into just a few hundred bytes of memory, or load it high if you like. Another associated program, Filekey (in SKREST.ZIP) runs scripts that can automate entire sessions, for example, load a database for you to read remotely when you're on the road, then do an incremental tape backup after you hang up. Stackey also comes with several screen and palette control utilities. You can glitz up your system with tones of mauve and camel pink, if that's your style.

A second major program in SKEY40.ZIP is the do-everything batch file program BatUtil. This program is so-o-o comprehensive it even implements its own language, called BUSIC. BatUtil does some things especially well, such as date arithmetic. How many days has it been since Judge Newton sent cousin Orville to jail? Tell BatUtil the day the judge threw away the key and BatUtil will figure out how many days, months, or years Orville has spent on the road gang. The program's fun to play with, though we find it too bulky and slow loading for frequent casual use. BatUtil's online Help files are in BUHELP.EXE.

Hack Facts

Screen Wizard
Version 4.6
Warren Small
Shareware: $15
68,059 bytes
SW-46.ZIP

We like the companion batch file utilities Screen Wizard (in SW-46.ZIP) and BatMenu (in BATMNU23.ZIP) for the terrific screen control and menus they add to batch files. Screen Wizard is the easier utility to use; just tell it in quotes what to put on the screen and up it pops, in a very good looking box. Its Help screen and very complete docs will let you quickly produce screen displays that would take hours to produce using the ECHO command. You can also use it to access the DOS environment, to interact directly with users, and even to create small, ASCII-based animations.

Hack Facts

BatMenu
Version 2.3a
Warren Small
35 Benjamin Street
Manchester, NH 03109-4319
CIS: 71076,407
AOL: WKSmall
Shareware: $15
45.776 bytes
BATMNU23.ZIP

BatMenu is for menus, not screen displays, and is a bit more complex to use at first. The registered version comes with a very well-designed menu-building utility that makes it easy to create menus with moving light bars, mouse support, nesting, and other powerful options directly in your batch files. No littering the disk with cryptic little menu files—though you have that option too, if you prefer to maintain your menu designs separately from their batch files. The BatMnu command line options are very similar to those of Screen Wizard, making the two a natural set.

Edit
Tip
Quote

Check out SWSAMP.ZIP for some flashy examples of what Screen Wizard can do for a batch file.

These utilities by Warren Small are really the only batch enhancers you'll need for writing professional quality, user-interactive batch files. The Screen Wizard distribution file also contains DI.EXE, a drive-testing utility with many useful options.

Hack Facts

GET
Version 2.6
Bob Stephan
Monterey Bay Disk Data
1021 San Carlos Road
Pebble Beach, CA 93953
Voice: 408-646-1899
CIS: 72357,2276
bob.stephan@nitelog.com
Shareware: $15
GET25.ZIP: 80,309 bytes
GET26U.ZIP: 30,821 bytes

GET.EXE version 2.6, Bob Stephan's DOS batch file enhancer for environment and errorlevel batch services, concentrates amazing functionality into a tiny package (runtime version about 5K). Version 2.6 needs two files: GET25.ZIP for the manual, and GET26U.ZIP for the upgraded version. Take everything but the manual from GET26U.ZIP, then rename GET26.EXE to simple GET.EXE. The version 2.6 upgrade includes a variety of new user-requested features, which are detailed in the docs.

GET's features include string handling, environment variables, hardware testing, simple arithmetic, file dates, return codes from other programs, branching, simple keyboard buffer input, ANSI code translation in no-CRLF echoes, and much more. Stephan has made it his goal to keep this terrific hack as small as possible, so it can fit onto crowded installation diskettes. He's been known to recode whole sections, and even change his executable compression scheme, to keep the runtime version size below his target limit. Hackers, here's a challenge: try to get this much power into a smaller package than GET. Good luck.

Hack Facts

PocketD
Version 4.0
Jeff Rollason
PocketWare
PO Box 2369
Hendon
London NW4 1NR, England
Voice: +44 81 203 3731
CIS: 100031,3537
Shareware: $54
164,837 bytes
POCK40.ZIP

PocketD is a deceptively small file display and management tool that arrived with a splash in 1992, when it immediately started garnering awards and long, positive reviews. Author Jeff Rollason calls it "a small color directory listing program & exceptionally powerful DOS file manager." That's a fair description. This little do-anything file manager has more than 220 options for the power user, though at its simplest you can just enter the command D to produce a double-column directory listing that is color coded by file type.

for complex operations such as managing compressed files or making highly selective backups, you can use the front-end program MenuD. This well-designed, full-screen interface has more than 60 menus and can create fully commented batch files once you've finished telling the program what files to operate on.

Figure 10-1 shows the screen that resulted when we told MenuD to create a list of all files in the current directory that had been modified in the last two hours. Notice the rather complex actual command line displayed in the lower left window. PocketD is a great power hack.

Quote

If his office were half as organized as his disk drive, maybe he'd stop asking me where he left his glasses.

—*Sami Menefee*

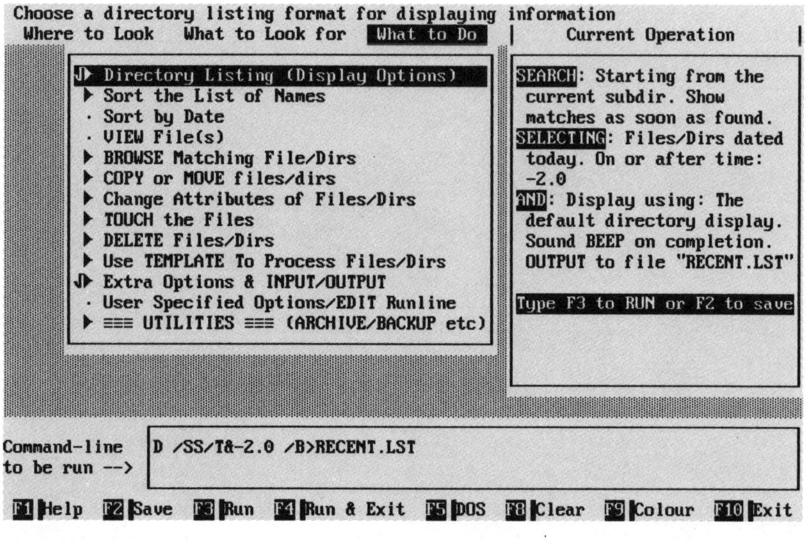
Choose a directory listing format for displaying information
Where to Look
What to Look for
What to Do
Current Operation
Directory Listing (Display Options)
Sort the List of Names
Sort by Date
VIEW File(s)
BROWSE Matching File/Dirs
COPY or MOVE files/dirs
Change Attributes of Files/Dirs
TOUCH the Files
DELETE Files/Dirs
Use TEMPLATE To Process Files/Dirs
Extra Options & INPUT/OUTPUT
User Specified Options/EDIT Runline
=== UTILITIES === (ARCHIVE/BACKUP etc)
SEARCH: Starting from the current subdir. Show matches as soon as found.
SELECTING: Files/Dirs dated today. On or after time: -2.0
AND: Display using: The default directory display. Sound BEEP on completion. OUTPUT to file "RECENT.LST"
Type F3 to RUN or F2 to save
Command-line to be run -->
D /SS/T&-2.0 /B>RECENT.LST
F1 Help F2 Save F3 Run F4 Run & Exit F5 DOS F8 Clear F9 Colour F10 Exit

Figure 10-1. *MenuD's complex file selection, with save to file*

Hack Facts

FFF and FF2
Version 4.5
James Derr
California Software Design
P.O. Box 15248
Santa Rosa, Ca. 95402
707-575-9868
Shareware: $25
192,194 bytes
FFF45.ZIP

This Fast File Finder utility by SHEZ author Jim Derr is the fastest file-finding program we know of and it has a raft of features. Whereas PocketD emphasizes file and directory management but also doubles as a file finder, FFF is for quick searches of multiple drives and directories but can also do file management if you want it to. It comes in a full-screen version (FFF.EXE) and a command line, scroll-up-the-screen version (FF2.EXE). Either is very fast and has a large set of options. We tend to use PocketD for quick 'n dirty local file management or highly selective file searches, and FF2 or FFF for simpler pan-galactic file searches and incidental management. The distribution file also contains FFD, a directory searching utility, and BRZ.COM, a small but capable file browser.

Tip

For another fast file and string-inside-file finder, see Norm Patriquin's PSearch, included with the Patriquin Utility Set described in Chapter 6.

Hack Facts

TurboBat
Version 3.23
Foley Hi-Tech Systems
185 Berry Street
San Francisco, CA 94107
Voice: 415-882-1730
BBS: 415-882-1735
110,190 bytes
Shareware: $19.95
ExtraDOS Toolkit: $59.95
TBT323.ZIP

TurboBat, one of about 50 useful utilities in the ExtraDOS Toolkit utility suite, turns standard DOS batch files into fast-executing COM files. This is no great deal for simple, line-at-a-time batch commands with no branching. But when you get to the outer limits of what native batch files can do with their slow excruciation techniques, then a good compiler can be hard to find. Compiling complex batch files so they run successfully is tricky, and TurboBat is the best compiler we've found for the job. It handles branching and looping with aplomb. It also fully supports the 4DOS/NDOS enhancements of the MS-DOS command set (4DOS is described in the "Other Superior General Tools" section following).

If your batch files tend to use little tricks like combining label lines with comments, TurboBat is very forgiving. It doesn't balk at the double-colon "Hey DOS, ignore this" commenting technique, either. And it provides a host of its own DOS-extending power commands, such as WHILE/WEND structures that can nest up to 15 levels of conditional commands using the Pascal-like form:

```
WHILE "%1" NE ""
     ECHO Deleting %1
     DEL %1
     SHIFT
WEND
```

The program's error checking is very good, and if something bombs, TurboBat can trace execution by source line number or write a full symbolic trace to a file you specify. This is a superior enhancement to the neglected DOS batch language.

Caution

Don't load TSRs from compiled batch files. When the compiled program exits, the system might become unstable.

Inside the TBT323.ZIP distribution file you'll also find TTX400.ZIP, which contains TurboText. Like MAKEREAD (described in Chapter 5, "Data Compression and Encryption"), TurboText turns text files into self-executing files—in this case, EXE instead of COM files. The increase in file size is larger than for MAKEREAD but TurboText has sophisticated extra capabilities, such as Find and Print. A self-executing TurboText file can be compressed using PKLite or a similar utility, but unlike a MAKEREAD file, the contents are not readable using a standard ASCII file lister.

Other Superior General Tools

The next set of programs includes some that rank among the very best in shareware—or retail, for that matter—and some that are minor but useful, interesting in how they handle problems, or are simply good hacks. They're all worth looking at to decide if they'd enhance your own time at the keyboard.

Hack Facts

4DOS
Version 5.0
Rex Conn and Tom Rawson
JP Software, Inc.
P.O. Box 1470
East Arlington, MA 02174
Voice: 617-646-3975
Orders: 800-368-8777
CIS: "GO JPSOFT"
Shareware: $69
4DOS*.ZIP

4DOS is...the best word we can come up with is *magical*. It's one of those rare offerings that does everything so right that once you try it, you won't dream of regressing to plain vanilla MS-DOS. Put over-simply, it replaces COMMAND.COM as the running command interpreter. But 4DOS is much more than that. It provides a complete computing environment for all 21 versions of MS-DOS and PC-DOS from 2.0 to 6.2; with DR-DOS 3.4, 5.0, 6.0, and above; and for OS/2 1.*x* and 2.0 DOS sessions. It is fully compatible with Microsoft Windows and with task-switching programs such as DESQview and Back and Forth (see Chapter 4, "Programmer Friendly"). And the things you can do with it are incredible. The complete set of 4DOS files is on the CD-ROM (look for files starting with "4DOS").

Don't get the impression that using 4DOS is like switching to UNIX or an equally un-DOS-like system. 4DOS is completely compatible with traditional DOS commands, and we've never run across an application that won't run under it. But it adds dozens of new features to DOS that we guarantee you'll quickly come to depend on. And to top it all off, it takes less memory than its competition, because it takes advantage of extended memory, expanded memory, and memory managers for 80286, 386, and 486 computers that let programs "load high." If you load both 4DOS and the environment "high," 4DOS uses only 256 bytes of base memory. Put that in your hat, COMMAND.COM.

Quote

The other major kind of computer is the "Apple," which I do not recommend, because it is a wuss-o-rama New-Age computer that you basically just plug in and use. This means that you don't get to participate in the most entertaining aspect of computer-owning, which is trying to get the computer to work. This is where "DOS" really shines.

—*Dave Barry*

Other Features

4DOS has an extremely powerful command editing and command macro capability built right in. The closest thing to it in vanilla DOS is DOSKEY or Cove Software's much better retail command editor, PCED (an extended version of the shareware classic CED). But you can't use PCED's synonyms (equivalent to 4DOS aliases) in batch files without invoking an auxiliary utility, and you can't use DOSKEY's command macros in batch files at all. 4DOS also adds powerful conditional command nesting to batch files, and other features including

- Context-sensitive help that pops up when you press F1 (see Figure 10-2)
- Enhanced directory navigation
- File commenting
- Directly parsed system metacharacters, like "$p" for Path

if you work outside your programming IDE much, give 4DOS a run. It is one of shareware's most remarkable, absolutely best programs.

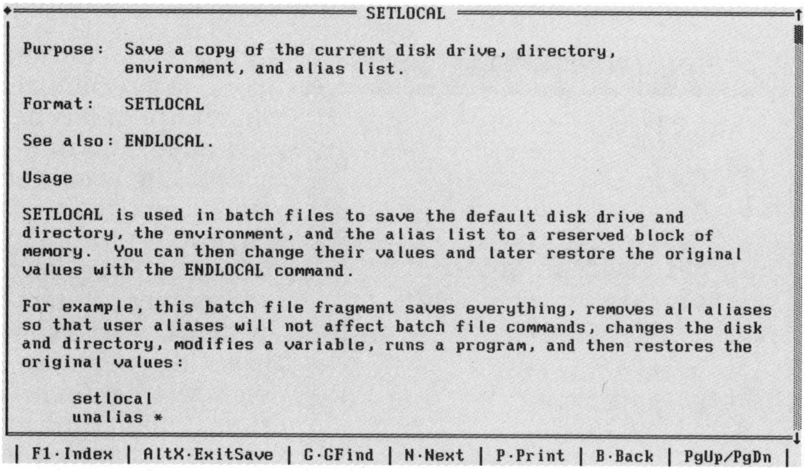
SETLOCAL
Purpose: Save a copy of the current disk drive, directory, environment, and alias list.
Format: SETLOCAL
See also: ENDLOCAL.
Usage
SETLOCAL is used in batch files to save the default disk drive and directory, the environment, and the alias list to a reserved block of memory. You can then change their values and later restore the original values with the ENDLOCAL command.
For example, this batch file fragment saves everything, removes all aliases so that user aliases will not affect batch file commands, changes the disk and directory, modifies a variable, runs a program, and then restores the original values:
setlocal
unalias *
| F1·Index | AltX·ExitSave | G·GFind | N·Next | P·Print | B·Back | PgUp/PgDn |

Figure 10-2. *The context-sensitive Help screen in 4DOS*

Hack Facts

CLIkit
Version 2.1
Keith E. Robbins
444 Saratoga Ave. #1L
Santa Clara, CA 95050
408-248-0838
CIS: 71121,2426
Shareware: $20 requested
244,178 bytes
CLIKIT.ZIP

If you're reluctant to change command interpreters, or you can't for some reason (like you have a no-soul droid for a boss), CLIkit (for Command Line Interface [tool]kit) provides most of the same services. For that matter, you can use it to enhance 4DOS too. CLIkit is an extremely good utility suite for power users, and no registration is required. (But if you use these tools a lot, do send author Keith Robbins his requested $20. He put a lot of nights and weekends into this gem.)

Incidentally, the distribution file (CLIKIT.ZIP) contains some sample DOS command remapping to the CLIkit utilities for both XDOS aliasing and PCED synonyms. That makes it easy to give these terrific utilities a try even in one of those custom environments. Or you can run the CLIkit aliasing program, which comes with its own set of fully commented sample aliases.

Our favorite among these utilities is EE.EXE, for Environment Editor. It has more and better options than any other DOS environment manipulation tool we've seen. If you try no other utility in this set, do give EE.EXE a try. But if you spend much time at the command line, take it from us, it's worth investing a few minutes to learn how to use this set of well wrought tools.

Hack Facts

Grab Plus
Version 6.5
Paul Mayer
ZPAY Payroll Systems
2526 69th Avenue South
St. Petersburg, FL 33712
Voice: 813-866-8233
CIS: GO ZPAY
Shareware: $39.95
419,747 bytes
GRAB65.ZIP

Grab Plus, an envelope addresser and more, is a recognized classic of shareware. It has never stopped being upgraded, and now where envelope addressing is concerned, it pretty much owns the territory. This is good territory to own, too, because—aside from a few specialized envelope-addressing printers—computer systems have just never been terrific at handling envelopes. No two printers seem to treat them the same, and it's almost impossible, with some word processors and editors, to produce a neat, properly printed envelope. This is why you'll see little typewriters off to the side in many small offices, often used almost exclusively to address envelopes.

Pardon us, but that's like owning a car and yet keeping a horse for trips to the neighborhood store because the horse can go slower than 5 MPH. It just doesn't make a whole lot of sense.

Edit
Tip
Quote

The difference between genius and stupidity is that genius has its limits.
—Anonymous

Grab solves the problem on most printers. This fine utility—which also comes with a very good name-and-address database and a label-printing program—can be loaded as a TSR, and used to pluck names and addresses right off the screen while inside your editor or text-based word processor. Or you can pull a name and address from GrabDB (also in the distribution file) to print an envelope, then paste the same name and address into the letter or other document loaded in your editor. Grab also will print graphic logos and postal bar codes, and can use style sheets for different formats on different types of mailings. GrabDB comes with downloadable fonts and effects to spiff up your Avery-type labels, in various standard sizes.

Grab Plus is the envelope-addressing standard by which other envelope addressers are measured, and is the classic we referred to in Chapter 2 as "the one that shareware newsletters review and love."

10

Hack Facts

PC Catalog
Version 3.2
Dale R. Andrews
44 Ridgelane Dr.
Decatur, Illinois 62521
CIS: 71521.3274
Shareware: $19.95 to $39.95
132,592 bytes
PCAT3B.ZIP

Unlike many disk catalog programs, PC Catalog keeps track of your files in a very clean, straightforward way. Is your 500+ MB hard drive stuffed with utilities, applications, and data files that you can't remember how to use—or even how to find when you need them? You'll love this cataloging program for taking the guesswork out of file control. It optionally lists files inside compressed archives of the ARC, LBR, LZH, PAK, ZIP, ZOO, and SFX persuasions. It extracts comment lines from PAK, ZIP, and ZOO archives. You can search for names, keywords, descriptions, times, sizes, and duplicates. PC catalog also works with CD-ROM drives, and is network compatible. Use it to catalog your collection of floppies, too. When you register, you'll get a fully enabled version of the program, plus additional utilities for creating and maintaining a master file of descriptions, other programs the author has written, and an upgrade to the most recent registered version. This is a well-designed cataloging system.

Hack Facts

RView
Version 2.51
Raymond T. Kaya
P.O. Box 1436
Honolulu, HI 96806
CIS: 71230,2500
Free
24,293 bytes
RV251.ZIP

This free program by Raymond T. Kaya looks inside any popular form of compressed file (ZIP, ARJ, and so on) and reports the files it finds there. What makes RView special is that it offers a variety of options, including sort order and display format. We frequently use the /U option to return a self-extracting (SFX) file to its original format and the /R option to reset a compressed file's date to that of the most recent filedate inside the archive. An optional ASCII configuration file can set default switches, such as /P for "pause" or /R for "reset date" if you wish. It's one of our favorite small utilities.

While we're at it, here are three more free Kaya utility programs, all included on the CD-ROM:

RViewShell
Here's a shell for viewing and extracting the contents of the popular archive types. It's done with the clean approach of all of his utilities. For those who don't want or need the full, do-everything approach of the SHEZ powerhouse archiving shell. (In RVS.ZIP. See Figure 10-3.)

DIRX
Another shell, this one for detecting executable compressed files. Calls on user-selectable external programs to transparently compress and uncompress files. Supports the popular formats. (In DIRX.ZIP.)

RCALC
A non-TSR dec/hex/bin/oct expression calculator. Does decimal floating-point. Supports modulus (%) and exponentiation (^), plus the four basic arithmetic operations, plus nested parentheses, extra space characters, etc. It's there when you need it, and carries with it a useful, programmer slant. (In RCALC.ZIP.)

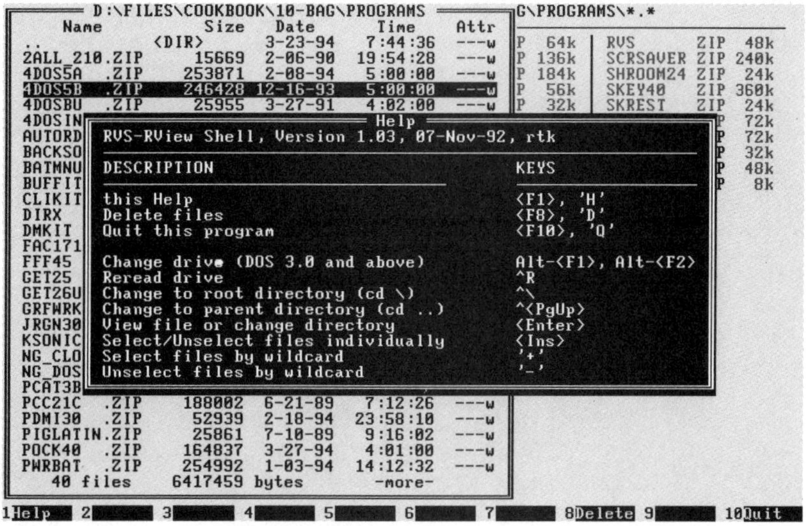
D:\FILES\COOKBOOK\10-BAG\PROGRAMS
Name Size Date Time Attr
.. <DIR> 3-23-94 7:44:36 ---w
2ALL_210.ZIP 15669 2-06-90 19:54:28 ---w
4DOS5A .ZIP 253871 2-08-94 5:00:00 ---w
4DOS5B .ZIP 246428 12-16-93 5:00:00 ---w
4DOSBU .ZIP 25955 3-27-91 4:02:00 ---w
G\PROGRAMS*.*
RVS ZIP 48k
SCRSAVER ZIP 240k
SHROOM24 ZIP 24k
SKEY40 ZIP 360k
SKREST ZIP 24k
Help
RVS-RView Shell, Version 1.03, 07-Nov-92, rtk
DESCRIPTION KEYS
this Help <F1>, 'H'
Delete files <F8>, 'D'
Quit this program <F10>, 'Q'
Change drive (DOS 3.0 and above) Alt-<F1>, Alt-<F2>
Reread drive ^R
Change to root directory (cd \) ^\
Change to parent directory (cd ..) ^<PgUp>
View file or change directory <Enter>
Select/Unselect files individually <Ins>
Select files by wildcard '+'
Unselect files by wildcard '-'
PCC21C .ZIP 188002 6-21-89 7:12:26 ---w
PDMI30 .ZIP 52939 2-18-94 23:58:10 ---w
PIGLATIN.ZIP 25861 7-10-89 9:16:02 ---w
POCK40 .ZIP 164837 3-27-94 4:01:00 ---w
PWRBAT .ZIP 254992 1-03-94 14:12:32 ---w
40 files 6417459 bytes -more-
1Help 2 3 4 5 6 7 8Delete 9 10Quit

Figure 10-3. *RVS (the RView Shell), showing a list of ZIP files along with its Help screen*

10

these utilities are all well-designed, useful and free. If you like them, message a thank you to Kaya on CompuServe at 71230,2500. It's all the pay he expects.

More Useful Utilities

Here are three more utilities that we find useful. The first lets you shell out of programs with plenty of operating room to run other large programs. The second does quick, clean archive format conversions. The last program in this section lets you record commands and error messages in a file even while they appear on the screen.

SHROOM: Shell Room

Back in Chapter 7 we described LegRoom, a very good TSR that makes any program "shellable." SHROOM (for SHell ROOM, kids, not for anything exciting that grows in pastures) provides similar service from the command line for programs that already have a shell-out capability. We love this program (in SHROOM24.ZIP), because not only does it provide room for a secondary program to run (only about 6K less lower memory than with a full exit)—it also sets any amount of DOS environment space your batch files or other programs may require. Oh, and it'll swap the shelled program's code out to disk, EMS, or XMS, as you wish. A superior little utility. Look for SHROOM24.ZIP on the CD-ROM.

2ALL Archive Converter

The simple 2ALL utility (in 2ALL_210.ZIP) quickly and painlessly converts archived files from one format to another. You tell it in an ASCII configuration file what programs to use with what switches, and 2ALL does the rest. It's a fine no-bells, no-whistles hack. We also admire author Doug Martin's attitude: "2ALL can be registered for the modest fee of $10,000.00 for which you'll get the latest version on disk...or you can just download it from your favorite BBS and use it for free. Whatever's easiest for you." We urge you to apply to the Chief Cybermuffin for funding to register this program.

TEE: Making a Record

This little utility (in TEE.ZIP) pipes the output of any command to a specified file as well as to the console. We include TEE mostly because it includes C source code and can be handy for cleaning up debugging processes that have gone awry, or for doing other kinds of logging.

Text Files and Readers

The next section contains text files, database readers, and lookup engines. These choices had to be somewhat arbitrary, since there are so many of these programs out there. The ones we selected for the CD-ROM all stand out from the herd in one way or another. Or we just like them. If you don't find what you need here, see Chapter 2, "The Art of the Gem," or Chapter 3, "Walking the Wires," for tips on fishing the shareware stream. There's a ton of very good alternatives as close as your telephone.

Hack Facts

The Jargon File
Version 3.0.0
Eric Raymond, Ed.
215-296-5718
Internet:
esr@snark.thyrsus.com
Free
477,345 bytes
JRGN300.ZIP

The Jargon File is a labor of love maintained at MIT that occasionally finds its way between book covers. Its chief volunteer editor is Eric Raymond. Sort of a Hackish crib sheet, The Jargon File constitutes the closest thing available to a comprehensive view of Hackish culture. This is a rather long but entertaining text file; we include it for those of you who might like the amusement or who have something (maybe gleaned off the Internet) to look up.

The Jargon File

The following excerpts were taken from The Jargon File, which is included on this book's CD-ROM as JRGN300.ZIP. The bracketed terms are cross references to other entries. To find actual entries, search for a term preceded by a colon, e.g., ***:fall through***.

Duff's Device: A New C Device

Duff's device: n. The most dramatic use yet seen of {fall through} in C, invented by Tom Duff when he was at Lucasfilm. Trying to {bum} all the instructions he could out of an inner loop that copied data serially onto an output port, he decided to {unroll} it. He then realized that the unrolled version could be implemented by *interlacing* the structures of a switch and a loop, as shown here:

```
register n = (count + 7) / 8;          /* count > 0
                                          assumed */
switch (count % 8)
{
case 0: do {    *to = *from++;
case 7:         *to = *from++;
case 6:         *to = *from++;
case 5:         *to = *from++;
case 4:         *to = *from++;
case 3:         *to = *from++;
case 2:         *to = *from++;
case 1:         *to = *from++;
     } while (--n > 0);
}
```

Having verified that the device is valid portable C, Duff announced it. C's default {fall through} in case statements has long been its most controversial single feature; Duff observed that "This code forms some sort of argument in that debate, but I'm not sure whether it's for or against."

Droids

Droid: n. A person (esp. a low-level bureaucrat or service-business employee) exhibiting most of the following characteristics: (a) naive trust in the wisdom of the parent organization or 'the system'; (b) a propensity to believe obvious nonsense emitted by authority figures (or computers!); blind faith; (c) a rule-governed mentality, one unwilling or unable to look beyond the 'letter of the law' in exceptional situations; and (d) no interest in fixing that which is broken; an "It's not my job, man" attitude.

Typical droid positions include supermarket checkout assistant and bank clerk; the syndrome is also endemic in low-level government employees. The implication is that the rules and official procedures constitute software that the droid is executing. This becomes a problem when the software has not been properly debugged. The term 'droid mentality' is also used to describe the mindset behind this behavior. Compare {suit}, {marketroid}.

Hack Facts

FAC
Version 1.71
Michael K. Molloy
Mountain Data Systems
8531 East Dry Creek Place
Englewood, CO 80112-2701
Orders: 800-242-4775
CIS: 72737,3237
Shareware: $17.95
120,861 bytes
FAC171.ZIP

FAC (for Find Area Code) is an uncommonly fine text search engine that, as it happens, has been put to use by author Michael Molloy to pop up data on telephone area codes. You can search by area code, state, town, country, or terms you've inserted into the ASCII data file such as "Rich Uncle Bill in Seattle." Very handy, but don't stop there. You can also use this engine to race through any specified ASCII database, using its outstanding "fuzzy" search option to specify sound-alike, phonetic spellings to pin down names, places, or other tip-of-the-tongue, "I can *almost* remember" types of data.

FAC is both very fast and very flexible. It can examine 800 lines per second on a slow XT and up to 40,000 lines per second on a 486. It can run either from the DOS prompt or as a 7K TSR that uses EMS or a specified disk for swapping. And when you register, the author sends you a bonus data file of 43,000 U.S. ZIP codes, cities, states, and counties. Terrific deal.

Hack Facts

AutoRead
Version 2.01
David R. Grigg
Rightword Enterprises
1556 Main Road
Research
Victoria 3095, AUSTRALIA.
CIS: 76264,2530
CIS: GO SWREG (orders)
Shareware: $35
154,277 bytes
AUTORD2.ZIP

AutoRead is a terrific text file reader with a host of features. Author David Grigg wrote it because he tended to accumulate large text files, often shareware manuals or long BBS listings, and he didn't want to waste trees by printing them. AutoRead makes reading text files a breeze by automatically popping up movable and resizable windows with chapter headings and keywords that you select with a mouse cursor or lightbar. It's a super fast, automatic text indexing and lookup system coupled with a serviceable text file lister.

You can set AutoRead to automagically return to the last section read when you reopen a file. We use it to take the annoyance out of those occasional convoluted command strings that we can't quite get right. Just takes a moment to pull up the docs and view the same screen we last looked up—usually the one that covers the command string we can't remember. If there are more than one, AutoRead lets you set bookmarks which you can save from one session to the next. (Figure 10-4 shows a bookmark being set in the AutoRead manual.) You also can index up to 250 keywords and skip rapidly from one occurrence to the next. Give this jewel a try if you want to think green and save paper, or if you simply prefer to use your software manuals online.

Brief Mentions

Here are two more file reading programs that you may find useful. The first provides a way to peek into Norton Guides (.NG) reference datafiles, and the second is a fine database system for modem commands.

NG_Clone: TSR Reference Engine

Some very good guides to programs, programming languages, and the like come in the form of .NG files, a type of hypertext system designed to be read by Norton Guides, an excellent retail TSR hypertext engine. If you've run across

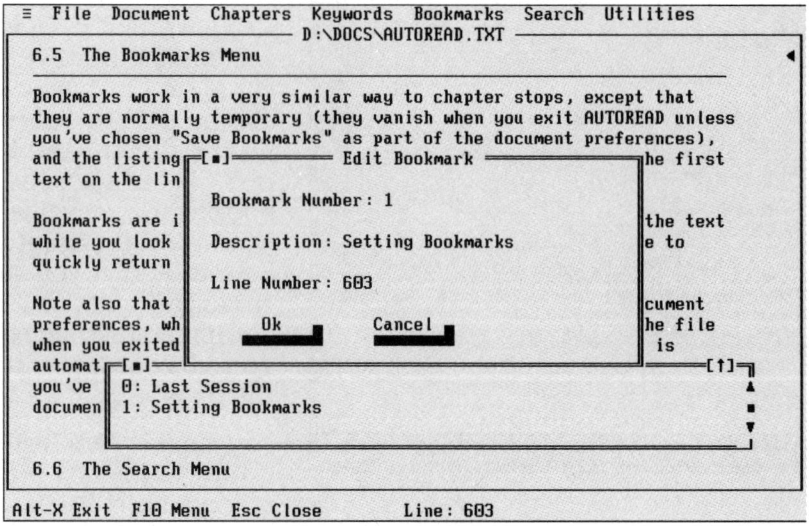
≡ File Document Chapters Keywords Bookmarks Search Utilities
D:\DOCS\AUTOREAD.TXT
6.5 The Bookmarks Menu
Bookmarks work in a very similar way to chapter stops, except that
they are normally temporary (they vanish when you exit AUTOREAD unless
you've chosen "Save Bookmarks" as part of the document preferences),
and the listing
he first
text on the lin
Bookmarks are i
the text
while you look
e to
quickly return
Note also that
cument
preferences, wh
he file
when you exited
is
automat
you've
documen
Edit Bookmark
Bookmark Number: 1
Description: Setting Bookmarks
Line Number: 603
Ok
Cancel
0: Last Session
1: Setting Bookmarks
6.6 The Search Menu
Alt-X Exit F10 Menu Esc Close Line: 603

Figure 10-4. *AutoRead setting a bookmark*

some Norton Guides files (they all end with the extension .NG) but do not have the engine, the rather bare-bones program NG_CLONE (in NG_CLONE.ZIP on the CD-ROM) does the job. If you don't have any data files handy to read with it, try it on CBRIEF (the Brief macro system described in Chapter 4) or on DH.NG, a DOS Help database contained in NG_DOS.ZIP, also on the CD-ROM.

PDMI: Put Away Your Modem Book

The Pull Down Modem Information (in PDMI30.ZIP) database is a great tool for troubleshooting recalcitrant modems. It holds information on 120 S-registers and 52 AT and ampersand-class AT commands, along with a calendar and date search and digital clock with chimes (we guess those are there because the author felt like it). It's a very easy database for fast modem reference, much better than poring over a badly organized modem handbook. The docs are included as a pull-down menu option.

Extra Compilers

The next couple of files are specialized programmer's tools, one for use with C and the other for use with a hybrid, batch file-like language.

Hack Facts

PCC
Version 2.1
Kevin Dahl
SimpleSoft
1209 Poplar Street
La Crescent, MN 55947
Shareware: $50
477K bytes
FPCLIB36.ZIP

PCC (in PCC21C.ZIP) stands for Personal C Compiler and is a fully operational, well tested earlier version of the DeSmet C developer system. It is also one of the fastest compilers around. The publisher, C Ware Corporation, put this outstanding compiler out on the wires strictly for personal use by students and programmers. If you market a program compiled by this program, do follow the instructions in the docs to get the C Ware Corporation letter of permission.

PCC may be all the compiler some programmers need, but be aware that it does not adhere to the ANSI standard for C. Also, it is not all gussied up with features. From the docs: "This compiler is NOT full of bells and whistles, it just makes fast tight compact programs." It does come with spare but complete docs, and the low registration fee of $30 brings a C source file reader with cross-referencing, an object code librarian, a profiler, and a library (with source) of memory access functions. A good, no-frills hacking tool.

Hack Facts

PowerBatch
Version 2.0
Computing Systems Design, Inc.
4437 Ormond Trace
Marietta, GA 30066
CIS: 72701,155
Shareware: $30-$45
254,992 bytes
PWRBAT.ZIP

The PowerBatch compiler is "for a very high-level language," as the docs put it, that supports more than 100 commands plus all DOS and most 4DOS and NDOS commands. We like it because it uses easy-to-write source files that in some ways resemble batch files and that compile quickly into stand-alone EXE programs.

If you prefer COM files based on "real" batch file source, try TurboBat (described earlier). PowerBatch does, however, support the standard DOS commands, the 4DOS enhancements if 4DOS is the running command interpreter, and normal external executables. So it can stand in for batch files if that's all you need.

PowerBatch can check source for errors when compiling, can create a map of program flow, and can support pre-DOS 3.0 systems if you tell it to. It's a compiler for fast, easy, on-the-fly programs in a high-level language more powerful than batch but (we're lazy) easier than C or ASM.

Screens and Multimedia

The utilities in this section all work with screens or sound cards. We'll lead off with Screen Thief, one of the best, most flexible screen capture utilities available.

Hack Facts

```
Screen Thief
Version 1.01
Nildram Software
82 Akeman Street
Tring. Herts HP23 6AF
United Kingdom
+44 (0)442 891331
CIS: 76004,3436
Shareware: $39
67,350 bytes
ST101.ZIP
```

Screen Thief, by Nildram Software, is a remarkable screen capture program. It handles both VGA text and VGA standard graphics modes, as well as SVGA modes with cards that use either the Trident or Paradise chip sets. Save your screen dumps in PCX, TIFF, Windows BMP, or CompuServe GIF formats. Screen Thief is unique among screen capture programs that we know of in letting the user pick the interrupt vector and hotkeys. Having trouble grabbing screens for your docs using one combination? Try another. The program only takes 2K-10K of lower memory (a very modest number for utilities of this sort) because it can use UMB or EMS memory, leaving only a small resident stub in the lower 640.

Additional bells and whistles abound. It has a monochrome filter and switches to specify a screen storage directory, and it can toggle between EGA and VGA fonts for text-screen captures or automatically number a series of screen shots. Screen Thief can capture Windows screens or run in a DOS box within Windows—and those are tricky territories for video utilities. It can be unloaded from memory on the fly, and it comes with an extensive online Help guide (see Figure 10-5). This is the best shareware capture utility we've seen for general use.

Hack Facts

```
Graphics Workshop
Version 7.0b
Alchemy Mindworks Inc.
P.O. Box 500
Beeton, Ontario
LOG 1A0, Canada
800-263-1138 (orders)
Shareware: $40
533,826 bytes
GRFWRK70.ZIP
```

Graphics Workshop is the ultimate shareware bitmap utility for DOS. This file viewer-converter-editor-printer by Alchemy Mindworks, Inc. can handle more than 20 DOS bitmapped formats and several Macintosh formats as well. Like 4DOS (described earlier), Graphics Workshop stands so far above its competition that there's not much point in comparing them. It is also one of those happy fusions of work and play that results in a powerful tool that is also a thoroughly habit-forming toy. It is, simply, a great program.

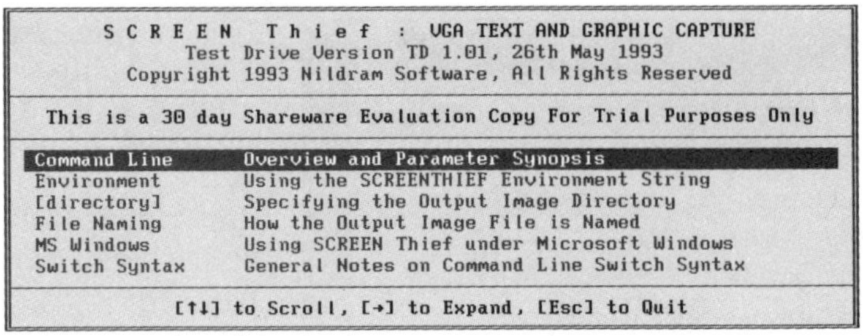

S C R E E N T h i e f : VGA TEXT AND GRAPHIC CAPTURE
Test Drive Version TD 1.01, 26th May 1993
Copyright 1993 Nildram Software, All Rights Reserved
This is a 30 day Shareware Evaluation Copy For Trial Purposes Only
Command Line Overview and Parameter Synopsis
Environment Using the SCREENTHIEF Environment String
[directory] Specifying the Output Image Directory
File Naming How the Output Image File is Named
MS Windows Using SCREEN Thief under Microsoft Windows
Switch Syntax General Notes on Command Line Switch Syntax
[↑↓] to Scroll, [→] to Expand, [Esc] to Quit

Figure 10-5. *Screen Thief's menued Help screen*

Graphics Workshop has been around since the early days of the IBM PC. Originally, it was a free utility distributed to fans of author Steve Rimmer's novels. It has grown in power and scope since then, and now it handles graphics files of any size, using XMS/EMS memory or creating virtual space on a hard disk. It supports almost all known video cards and includes algorithms to let you clean up bitmapped graphic files or add numerous special visual effects.

Award for the Mightiest Registration Plea

We can't say for sure that stranger pleas for registration haven't been put out on the wires, but the following paragraph in the Graphics Workshop registration doc has got to be the most compelling reason to register that we've seen:

> Oh yes, should you fail to support this program and continue to use it, a leather winged demon of the night will tear itself, shrieking blood and fury, from the endless caverns of the nether world, hurl itself into the darkness with a thirst for blood on its slavering fangs and search the very threads of time for the throbbing of your heartbeat. Just thought you'd want to know that.

Then they post a free 800 number to call for registration. We beg you to use it.

Edit Tip Quote

Use Graphics Workshop to create image catalogs by adding text descriptions to bitmapped snapshots.

The package performs all standard image-editing stunts such as right-left reversal, rotate-and-flip, resizing, cropping, and pixel inversion. You can also enhance or decrease a graphic's color depth, adjust the brightness, contrast, and color balance, dither colors with four different algorithms, and print to Postscript, HP-compatible, and most dot matrix printers.

Use Graphics Workshop to convert digitized color photographs for use as black-and-white clip art. If you pull documentation off the Internet in EPS form, GWS lets you preview it without loading a DTP package. The program also triples as a GIF viewer, image converter, and graphics compressor. It supports JPEG displays as well as some of the more exotic compression formats.

Registration gets you a capture utility that can grab screens in most popular VGA and super-VGA text and graphics modes. The authors have also written a Windows version of Graphics Workshop for those who prefer GUI-flavored image manipulation. Figure 10-6 shows part of the program's long list of supported file formats.

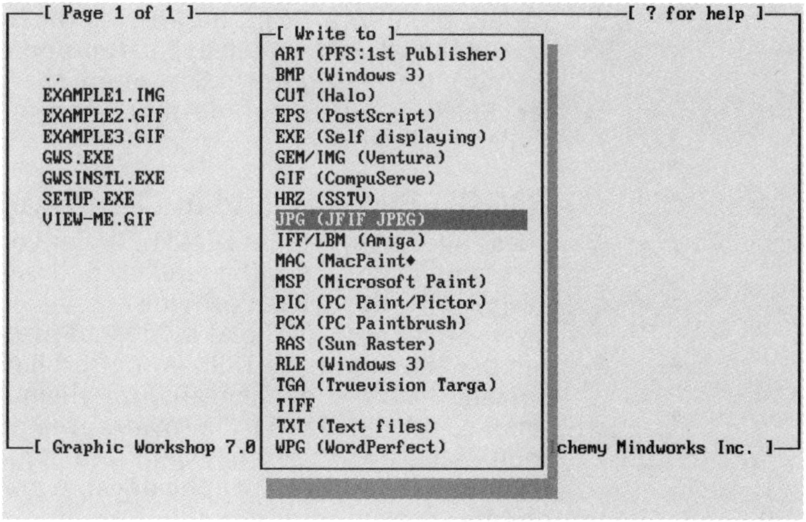
[Page 1 of 1]
[? for help]
[Write to]
..
EXAMPLE1.IMG
EXAMPLE2.GIF
EXAMPLE3.GIF
GWS.EXE
GWSINSTL.EXE
SETUP.EXE
VIEW-ME.GIF
ART (PFS:1st Publisher)
BMP (Windows 3)
CUT (Halo)
EPS (PostScript)
EXE (Self displaying)
GEM/IMG (Ventura)
GIF (CompuServe)
HRZ (SSTV)
JPG (JFIF JPEG)
IFF/LBM (Amiga)
MAC (MacPaint♦
MSP (Microsoft Paint)
PIC (PC Paint/Pictor)
PCX (PC Paintbrush)
RAS (Sun Raster)
RLE (Windows 3)
TGA (Truevision Targa)
TIFF
TXT (Text files)
WPG (WordPerfect)
[Graphic Workshop 7.0
chemy Mindworks Inc.]

Figure 10-6. *Pick a format, any format, in Graphics Workshop*

Brief Mentions

The following utilities and programs are of special interest either because they can enhance your time at the console or because they demonstrate what can be done with resources included on the CD-ROM.

RollBack and Buffit: Video Recall Utilities

The RollBack TSR program (in ROLLBACK.ZIP) captures both standard DOS and BIOS video calls, rolling back the screen image on demand with ALT-PGUP as the default hot key. The shareware version is very limited (about two screens of text) but the registered version supports up to 60 full screens. That's a serious hobble, but we include the program here because it can capture graphics modes up to 640 by 350 resolution, as well as all DOS text modes. Commented Assembly and Pascal source code are also available, which makes it potentially twice as interesting for working programmers.

If you only need to capture text mode screens, try David Hamilton's Buffit screen scroller (in BUFFIT.ZIP). With this one, you can set the buffer size yourself. When you recall a screen, you can pick from a variety of options including writing the buffer to screen or saving the current screen even after you exit back to DOS to do more text-based work. Best of all, there's no registration fee. Buffit is quite a well-designed program, and you just can't beat the price.

DMKIT: Super Sound in C and ASM

These sound drivers (in DMKIT.ZIP) let your programs drive any major current sound card directly from DOS. Technically, the drivers provide a device-independent API layer, under both DOS real mode and protected mode. You can use the drivers as TSRs or (better) have your program demand-load and dynamically link them. Registration is at a retail cost level ($500 for a royalty-free license) but author John Ratcliff will defer payment under conditions favorable to shareware authors (see the docs). A great set of sound drivers, done all in C and ASM.

KaleidoSonic: Kaleidoscope to Music

Masque Publishing president James Wisler describes KaleidoSonic as a "toy," and in that spirit let us warn you—when you start playing with this program, set aside plenty of time. It's relaxing, true, but it's also very hard to stop.

We could have put this wonderful program (in KSONIC.EXE) in with the screen savers. That's how a lot of people use KaleidoSonic, even though it lacks a TSR to invoke it after *n* minutes of keyboard inactivity. We also could have tucked it into the "Just for Fun" section following. But we put it here instead because it uses John Ratcliff's DMKIT sound drivers. In fact, Ratcliff himself produced this multimedia program. The retail CD-ROM version may be the first music CD-ROM produced and mastered in a 100 percent MIDI studio. It features some impressive synthesizer music by well-known new-age/jazz composer Rob Wallace, set to some stunning graphics that you can manipulate in a huge variety of ways while the music plays. If Wallace's music doesn't strike your fancy, put something industrial or heavy-metal into your CD-ROM drive. KaleidoSonic will play it, though it will no doubt alter the total experience.

But here's our favorite trick. Use SCRSAVER (described in the "Just for Fun" section following) to invoke the included fully functional demo version of KaleidoSonic, and you have a captivating screen saver within DOS. If you like the results, the retail version has many more modules.

Just for Fun

We'll start out this section by describing two screen savers that do their jobs in ways that make them stand out from their normal, run-of-the-mill competition. These are nice little hacks, both of them. And, finally, we include an example of an AI language filter—a program that uses artificial intelligence (well...in this case, artificial *something*) to change the form, but not the content, of the written word. Such language filters are common on the Internet, where they are used for such solemn purposes as translating the Book of Genesis into "Swedish Sea Captain" speech, to cite just one example. We chose Pig Latin for no very good reason...it was just there, and relatively inoffensive.

Screen Savers

The following screen savers stand out from the crowd. The first runs any program you tell it to (not a common flexibility in screen savers), while the second takes messages from passers-by and sometimes, as you'll see, from... *Somewhere Beyond.*

SCRSAVER: Run Anything, Anywhere

This well-designed utility (in SCRSAVER.ZIP) does something we had long included on our wish list but had given up finding. Then someone on the Internet pointed it out to us. We pass it on to you.

the Screen Saver, by Andrew Cramer, executes *any specified* program, instead of insisting on starting its own display when it kicks in. That's the first thing we liked about it, but it's not the whole story. Screen Saver works equally well in DOS, Windows, or OS/2. In DOS, it's a TSR that takes only 7K of memory (load it high if you want). In Windows it runs as a standard .SCR file that invokes a .PIF file that invokes...any full-screen DOS program you want. And it comes with a selection of animation using GLs, GIFs, and FLIs, just to show some of what this program can do. Very slick!

Back Soon: Animated Message Taker

Like the Screen Saver, Chuck Steenburgh's excellent Back Soon! utility (in BACKSOON.ZIP) does double duty. In this case, it's a message taker as well as a screen saver. The saver part shows a dressy looking, moving window that displays (in VGA graphics format) any simple ASCII message you specify, such as "Out to lunch—leave a message and I'll get back to you." If someone presses a key, the program asks their name and invites them to leave a message. When you get back, you exit to a menu and check your messages. Figure 10-7 shows a message left on one of our machines during a brief meal break.

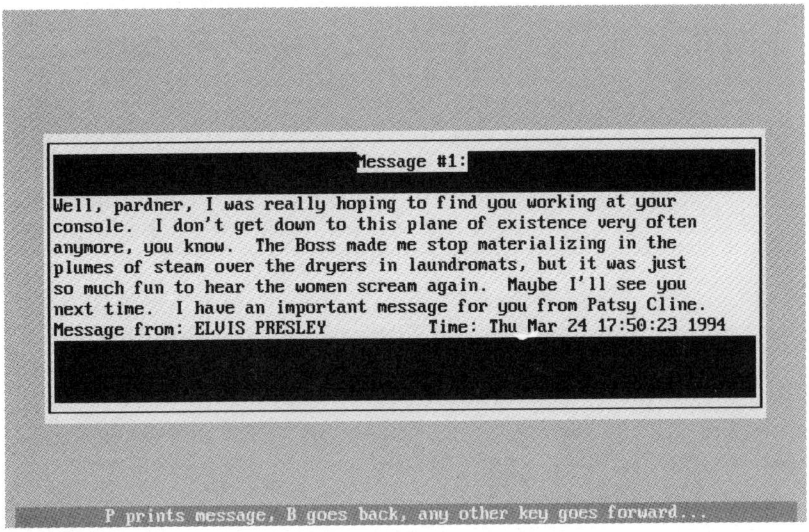
Message #1:
Well, pardner, I was really hoping to find you working at your console. I don't get down to this plane of existence very often anymore, you know. The Boss made me stop materializing in the plumes of steam over the dryers in laundromats, but it was just so much fun to hear the women scream again. Maybe I'll see you next time. I have an important message for you from Patsy Cline.
Message from: ELVIS PRESLEY Time: Thu Mar 24 17:50:23 1994
P prints message, B goes back, any other key goes forward...

Figure 10-7. *A Back Soon message from Elvis*

PIGLATIN: Osay Osay Illysay

Quote

Ityay asway inevitableyay. Ethay ighhay choolsay idskay, ethay rammargay choolsay idskay, andyay ethay overnmentgay ypestay otgay intoyay ethay actyay. Oneyay ofyay osethay—ethay oneyay ithway ethay trongestsay esireday otay ebay unintelligibleyay, eway ouldn'tway arecay otay uessgay ichwhay oneyay—reatedcay ethay Igpay Atinlay ranslationtay rogrampay. A isgracefulday abuseyay ofyay umanhay intelligenceyay. Utbay hatway ancay ouyay expectyay omfray ackershay?

This little hack is best used to help people who take themselves too seriously. For example, if you find yourself working for some mindless corporate droid, let us suggest that you write a solemn memo about, say, the impending world-wide shortage of No. 3 pencils. Run the text through the Pig Latin language translation program (in PIGLATIN.ZIP), and print it out on the droid's memo letterhead. Then sneak it into the interoffice mail to the Big Boss and stand back with an innocent look.

On second thought, maybe you'd better not do that...it's best to be, um...responsible—yeah, that's it, be *responsible* in your workplace. Otherwise—well, just don't blame us if you get caught.

Next Up

The next chapter starts Part III of the book, where we'll get seriously technical in places. We'll cover fine points of video control, use of interrupts, and low-level programming. You'll find some great programs and other resources here.

011010 11000110 0011010 11001001 100010001

011010 11000110 0011010 11001001 100010001

0011010 11001001 100010001

part 3

Do Not Disturb: Gone Hacking

11

We Interrupt This Program...

Human beings often function somewhat like a multitasking computer: We get into heavy duty task switching (watching TV and reading a magazine, playing catch with the kids and thinking out a difficult algorithm, chewing gum and walking). We draw on resources of memory (even if, for some of us, the bits get scrambled a little too often). We process data (often slower than we would like, but with a creative flexibility that computers might envy, if they could envy at all).

And, of course, we all get interrupts. No matter what we are doing, there is always a time when we really don't want to be disturbed, and that's when the interrupts occur. The phone rings, the UPS man arrives with a delivery, a daughter scrapes her knee, a son wants to use the computer (or the car), and so on, and so on and on.

how do we humans handle interrupts? Well, certainly, we stop our primary task, turn our attention aside, and do whatever is needed to take care of, or service, the interruption. What does this have to do with DOS programming? Not much, maybe, but we can stretch our human behavior into an analogy about PCs and their interrupts. After all, PCs do their best "thinking" in response to interrupts that we—or our programs—send them. Let's follow the analogy for awhile.

The Nature of an Interrupt

Many things difficult to design prove easy to perform.
—Samuel Johnson

An *interrupt* is an actual interruption of the work the processor on your computer is doing at the time it receives the interrupt signal. The interrupt is, however, managed so that processing can continue at a later time. For instance, the PC may save the current values of all the registers, or the precise location where it is working in memory, and so on, before handling (or *servicing*) the interrupt call.

The type of handling that occurs depends on the values you pass to an interrupt. You can actually think of an interrupt as another type of function call that you can use in your programs. You pass the information into the interrupt and receive information back from it through *registers*, a group of memory locations that the processor can always view. In C, for instance, the registers are defined like this:

```
struct WORDREGS {
  unsigned int    ax, bx, cx, dx, si, di, cflag, flags;
};

struct BYTEREGS {
  unsigned char   al, ah, bl, bh, cl, ch, dl, dh;
};

union  REGS    {
  struct  WORDREGS x;
  struct  BYTEREGS h;
};
```

Notice the several types of registers. *Byte-size registers* (defined with the BYTEREGS structure) are named al, ah, bl, bh, cl, ch, dl, and dh, both in the structure definition and in most discussions of PC hardware in general. The *double byte-size registers* (defined in WORDREGS) are named ax, bx, cx, dx, si, di, cflag, and flags; some of these registers are made up of two of the byte-size registers (for example, the ax register contains both the al and ah registers). This is required, since some interrupts use byte-size information, and others require *integer* (double-byte) sized data.

The *union* is like a structure, telling the compiler that WORDREGS and BYTEREGS share the same location in memory, so you can view either bytes or words when required.

To use an interrupt call, you need to put the correct information into the appropriate registers, pass this information to the interrupt call, and then check the registers for any returned information. "Are there many interrupt calls I can use," you ask? Just sit back, children, and we'll tell you a fine story of *programmus interruptus.*

Interrupts in a List

You can choose from among many hundreds of interrupt calls. They are broken down into several groups, the more common of which are shown in Table 11-1.

HEX INTERRUPT CODE	GENERAL DESCRIPTION OF USE
00	Divide-by-zero interrupt
01	Single step interrupt
02	Non-maskable interrupt
03	Breakpoint interrupt
04	Arithmetic Overflow interrupt
05	Print Screen interrupt
08	System Timer interrupt
09	Keyboard interrupt
0B	Communications interrupt
0C	Communications interrupt
0D	Hard Disk Controller interrupt
0E	Floppy Disk Controller interrupt
0F	Printer Management interrupt
10	Video interrupt
11	Equipment Status interrupt
12	Memory Size interrupt

Table 11-1. *General Interrupt Groupings*

HEX INTERRUPT CODE	GENERAL DESCRIPTION OF USE
13	Diskette Management interrupt
14	Asynchronous Communications interrupt
15	System Services interrupt
16	Keyboard interrupt
17	Printer interrupt
19	System Warm Boot interrupt
1A	System Timer Services interrupt
1B	Control-Break Address interrupt
1C	Timer Tick interrupt
70	Real Time Clock interrupt

Table 11-1. *General Interrupt Groupings* (continued)

Tip

Other interrupt groups exist as well; the table only has the most common ones. Read on to find out how to get the actual information you need.

Every hardware device connected to your computer is likely to use interrupts to communicate with the processor. The BIOS and DOS on your machine both use interrupts for communications. So how do you find out about all of these calls that are possible, especially if there are so many? Most people start with Ralf Brown's Interrupt List, a classic hacker resource.

Hack Facts

Interrupt List

Version 39
Ralf Brown
Free
3.5MB
INTER39A.ZIP
INTER39B.ZIP
INTER39C.ZIP

Ralf Brown, the author of several books dealing with programming with interrupts, has put much of his accumulated knowledge into a set of free documents available on lots of BBSs and electronic services. We include it on this book's CD-ROM for your convenience.

Is Brown's list complete, got 'em all, missed nothing? We're not sure, but if it's not, it's probably as close as you'll ever come to getting them all down in one place. The list is never stagnant, and updates continue to come forth at regular intervals.

this list has many contributors. Although Ralf has become a sort of hackish central repository for all this information, he lists about a thousand lines in one of his files of the names and companies of those who have contributed. Think of that—hundreds of people from all walks of life, all companies, all backgrounds, working on the same project for no reason other than to disseminate the knowledge. It's more than free—it's a reflection of the very best in the hackish subculture.

If you want to print this list out, you have several options. First, you can just print the files. Ralf says in the documentation that the list runs about 1450 pages at 60 lines per page. Because the list doesn't have page numbers, it might be hard to build any type of index for yourself. Or you could use the DocSmash printer utility described in Chapter 9, "Taming the Wild Printer," and cut the pages by a quarter or less (but maybe drive yourself blind). Again, indexing would be a problem.

Another option is to use the INTPRINT program included in the INTER*xxx* archives. Using this program, you will print about 1553 pages, but the list will include headers with page numbers so it'll be easier to move around. Or you can buy Ralf's book, an advertisement for which is also included in the archive. Remember, though, that although this may be the simplest way to get a printed image, it is by no means the most up-to-date list. Tradeoffs are a hacker's middle name, though, so we'll let you decide.

Edit
Tip
Quote

A little experience often upsets a lot of theory.
—*Cadman*

Perhaps the best option is to use the list as an online database, and simply look up what you need when you need it, using the speed of a computer instead of thumbing through pages manually. That makes Brown's own lookup program, InterVue, a very good choice.

Hack Facts

InterVue
Version 1.5
Ralf Brown
Free
17K bytes
INTVUE15.ZIP

InterVue, also by Ralf Brown, provides an easy way to peruse the Interrupt List while you work. This program (see Figure 11-1) lets you quickly look at a listing of available interrupts and select the ones for which you need moreinformation.

The main screen of the InterVue program shows a simple listing of interrupts, along with the register information for AL and AH that you need to make the call. This resource is extremely handy when you are reading assembly code and aren't sure what a specific interrupt call will do.

If you're considering a specific call, just highlight it and press ENTER to have InterVue jump immediately to the right place to read about it. Placing you in the actual documentation instead of just showing a summary is a nice feature. This allows you to scroll around to other, similar calls, looking for alternatives to the one you might have originally chosen.

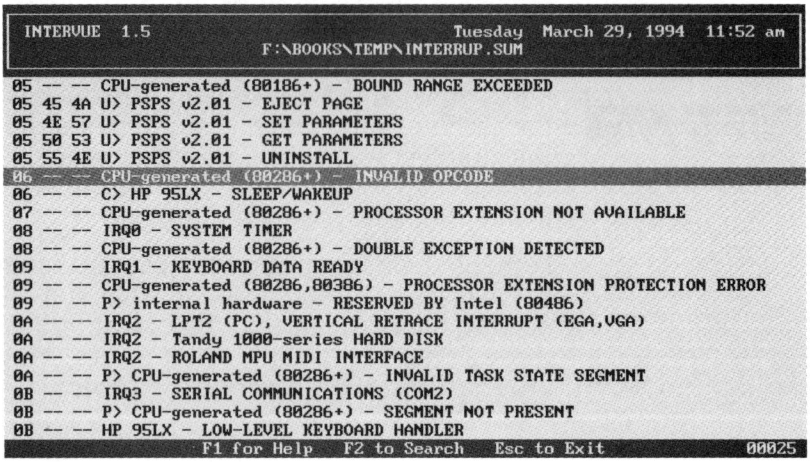
INTERVUE 1.5
Tuesday March 29, 1994 11:52 am
F:\BOOKS\TEMP\INTERRUP.SUM
05 -- -- CPU-generated (80186+) - BOUND RANGE EXCEEDED
05 45 4A U> PSPS v2.01 - EJECT PAGE
05 4E 57 U> PSPS v2.01 - SET PARAMETERS
05 50 53 U> PSPS v2.01 - GET PARAMETERS
05 55 4E U> PSPS v2.01 - UNINSTALL
06 -- -- CPU-generated (80286+) - INVALID OPCODE
06 -- -- C> HP 95LX - SLEEP/WAKEUP
07 -- -- CPU-generated (80286+) - PROCESSOR EXTENSION NOT AVAILABLE
08 -- -- IRQ0 - SYSTEM TIMER
08 -- -- CPU-generated (80286+) - DOUBLE EXCEPTION DETECTED
09 -- -- IRQ1 - KEYBOARD DATA READY
09 -- -- CPU-generated (80286,80386) - PROCESSOR EXTENSION PROTECTION ERROR
09 -- -- P> internal hardware - RESERVED BY Intel (80486)
0A -- -- IRQ2 - LPT2 (PC), VERTICAL RETRACE INTERRUPT (EGA,VGA)
0A -- -- IRQ2 - Tandy 1000-series HARD DISK
0A -- -- IRQ2 - ROLAND MPU MIDI INTERFACE
0A -- -- P> CPU-generated (80286+) - INVALID TASK STATE SEGMENT
0B -- -- IRQ3 - SERIAL COMMUNICATIONS (COM2)
0B -- -- P> CPU-generated (80286+) - SEGMENT NOT PRESENT
0B -- -- HP 95LX - LOW-LEVEL KEYBOARD HANDLER
F1 for Help F2 to Search Esc to Exit 00025

Figure 11-1. *InterVue turns Ralf Brown's 1500-page Interrupt List into a database*

once in place, you see a complete display of all the registers that are used on entry to the interrupt (information passed into the function) as well as their use upon exit from the function (the return values).

By the way, Ralf doesn't just present the interrupt listings in InterVue. He also includes reference files that deal with bugs in the 8086 processor line, how to access the data stored in CMOS, memory and port locations of interest to programmers, and even a complete glossary of terms to bring you up to speed in any areas where you might feel a bit rusty.

Hack Facts

DOSREF
Version 3.3
Dave Williams
P.O. Box 181
Jacksonville, AR 72078-0181
Shareware: $20
1MB
DOSREF33.ZIP

Before we close this chapter, here's one more entry you should know about. DOSREF is subtitled "The Programmer's Technical Reference for MSDOS and the IBM PC." This program is not free, but it has a lot of good information and is just as up-to-date as the Interrupt List.

DOSREF is presented in a format different from Ralf Brown's listing. Ralf lists every single possible interrupt that might be available and draws from hundreds of sources to build a complete list. If you are a more advanced programmer, looking for a reference listing, then Ralf Brown's list is ideal. In fact, everyone should keep a copy handy for reference. However, it is just a list.

DOSREF, on the other hand, has a lot more background and tutorial information, along with helpful hints and tips for use with specific interrupts. It's a good reading source when you need more than just the reference material (for instance, when you have several interrupts that perform in a similar fashion, but you aren't quite sure which one to use.) Ralf will help you use the interrupts correctly, but DOSREF is more likely to help you choose the right one. We think having both of these references handy is worth the DOSREF twenty-bucks registration fee.

Next Up

In the next chapter, we'll deal with an area that programmers always seem to either love or hate—putting a program's messages out effectively on the monitor. What a user sees is what a user responds to, and if you want a positive response, you'll ignore the video maze at your own peril. If you're among the huge group of programmers who feel stymied by the lack of standard VGA and SVGA graphics modes, read on. We may be able to help.

12

Video Wizardry

Like it or not, the thing that the user sees most in your programs is what you put on the monitor. Video programming, therefore, should play an important part in your program design. Will you program in Windows (a whole other nightmare), use a fancy, high-resolution graphics mode, or use simple text? You have lots of options. How will you know what type of monitor the user has? Should your program work differently on different types of monitors? This chapter will help you answer some of these questions.

Video Modes

That's enough, Moon Master! Earth will tolerate no more of your evil schemes!
—Captain Video (Saturday matinee serial, ca. 1951)

All the different text and graphics capabilities that abound in the IBM PC world are based on the concept of video modes. Literally dozens of video modes are available in the current generation of personal computers. Determining which one a user has can be somewhat bewildering, but this chapter will help you through the mire. Table 12-1 lists the most common modes available in the PC family. (For a more complete list of over 100 modes, and hundreds of specific video adapter notes, look at Ralf Brown's interrupt list, which is discussed in Chapter 11.)

MODE NUMBER	DESCRIPTION	ADAPTORS
0	40 × 25 monochrome text	CGA, EGA
1	40 × 25 color text	CGA, EGA
2	80 × 25 monochrome text	CGA, EGA
3	80 × 25 color text	CGA, EGA
4	320 × 200 4-color graphics	CGA, EGA
5	320 × 200 monochrome graphics	CGA, EGA
6	640 × 200 monochrome graphics	CGA, EGA
7	80 × 25 (720x350) monochrome text	Monochrome, EGA
D	320 × 200 16-color graphics	EGA
E	640 × 200 16-color graphics	EGA
F	640 × 350 4-color graphics on mono display	EGA
10	640 × 350 4- or 16-color graphics	EGA
11	640 × 480 monochrome graphics	VGA
12	640 × 480 16-color graphics	VGA
13	320 × 200 265-color graphics	VGA

Table 12-1. *Standard Video Modes Available for the PC*

Of course, with the advent of VGA, SVGA, and VESA (which we'll discuss shortly), you also need to know about a lot more combinations. In common use are 640 × 480 VGA, Super VGA resolutions of 800 × 600, 1024 × 768, 1280 × 1024, and even higher. Add to this the choice of 16 colors, 256 colors, or 16 million colors.

Let's look back for a minute.

A Little History

IBM came out with the Color Graphics Adapter (CGA) not long after the original IBM PC. At best, the CGA card gave a little rudimentary support for four-color graphics and something (we laugh now) called high-resolution graphics.

These modes were useful for displaying a small amount of graphical information. The "medium resolution" could put 320 × 200 dots on the screen in four pre-selected colors. The "high resolution" could put 640 × 200 dots on the screen, but it could only use two colors, usually black and white.

Almost immediately Hercules and Plantronics came out with alternatives with more colors and higher resolution. But real color graphics capability did not come to the PC world until IBM released the EGA (Enhanced Graphics Adapter) card.

The EGA standard allowed for a higher resolution of graphics information, normally 640 × 350 dots in up to 16 colors. It was extensible in the sense that vendors could support the EGA standard and create extended EGA modes of up to 640 × 480 dots of 16 colors at a time on the screen. With the cheap EGA boards and the arrival of high-resolution graphics files (available on BBSs, in computer shops, and elsewhere), the demand for color graphics boomed.

> *If you want to contact your video manufacturer, look them up in VFAQ1.ZIP, a listing of all the major players.*

About this time, CompuServe was developing its GIF standard for graphic images. GIF, which stands for *G*raphics *I*nterchange *F*ormat, was designed as a standard to allow people with all sorts of computers to share graphic images. This was necessary for CompuServe, because their users operate on PCs, Macintoshes, Apple IIs, Commodore 64s, and everything in between.

Meanwhile, IBM made the VGA (Video Graphics Adapter) mode very complicated but allowed a fairly simple programming interface, trying, one might assume, to corner the market in graphics. A number of VGA clone cards appeared almost immediately.

The VGA, showing a standard resolution of 640 × 480 dots, was a little graphics computer on a card that could be programmed. With small hardware extensions the VGA could display millions of colors at huge resolutions. When cheap sound cards and inexpensive CD-ROM titles were added, multimedia for the home took off, and a number of SVGA (Super VGA) modes sprung up all over the place. SVGA is now a must, and not even IBM tries to sell standard VGA modes anymore.

Hack Facts

```
Super VGA Test Library
Version 4.2
Kendall Bennett
SciTech Software
G.P.O. 4216NN
Melbourne 3001
Australia
Freeware
380K bytes
SVGKT4.ZIP
```

What is SVGA? This is a hard question. Super VGA is simply more than VGA, but is it 800 × 600, 1024 × 768, 1280 × 1024, or even higher? Is it 16 colors, 256, or a gazillion? The answer is yes.

SVGA is not currently standardized, and a card that advertises itself as Super VGA must only be little more than a VGA to be telling the truth. Figuring out how to determine the video modes available on a specific computer takes a bit of work. Rather than starting from scratch, you should look at the Super VGA Test Library, which does much of the detection and mode changing for you.

Enter VESA

VESA (the Video Electronics Standards Association) was created by a consortium of graphics card manufacturers and other interested parties in order to develop a standard for expanding VGA features. VESA is not a particular set of video modes; rather, it is a standard method for asking a card what resolutions it supports, and then accessing those modes. Technically, it would be possible to have a VESA driver for CGA, Hercules, or EGA: A program would ask the driver what modes it supports, and the answer would only be the lower resolutions. Table 12-2 lists some of the video modes provided by the VESA standard.

Tip

VESAMO.ZIP contains a utility (with C++ source code) that allows you to set VESA modes from the command line. VESAKB.ZIP contains C-language routines for setting modes, checking the VESA information, and testing your video board.

It is a good idea for the hacker to write code to the VESA standard in addition to standard VGA. A user will have a machine that supports VGA and might have a VESA supported card as well. On the companion CD are two "universal" VESA drivers (VESA32.ZIP and UVBE43.ZIP). They are not entirely universal, but they can ensure that you and

VESA MODE NUMBER	DESCRIPTION
100	640 × 400 256-color graphics
101	640 × 480 256-color graphics
102	800 × 600 16-color graphics
103	800 × 600 256-color graphics
104	1024 × 768 16-color graphics
105	1024 × 768 256-color graphics
106	1280 × 1024 16-color graphics
107	1280 × 1024 256-color graphics
10D	320 × 200 32K-color graphics
10E	320 × 200 64K-color graphics
10F	320 × 200 16M-color graphics
110	640 × 480 32K-color graphics
111	640 × 480 64K-color graphics
112	640 × 480 16M-color graphics
113	800 × 600 32K-color graphics
114	800 × 600 64K-color graphics
115	800 × 600 16M-color graphics
116	1024 × 768 32K-color graphics
117	1024 × 768 64K-color graphics
118	1024 × 768 16M-color graphics
119	1280 × 1024 32K-color graphics
11C	640 × 350 256-color graphics
11D	640 × 350 32K-color graphics
11E	640 × 400 32K-color graphics
11F	640 × 350 64K-color graphics
11A	1280 × 1024 64K-color graphics
11B	1280 × 1024 16M-color graphics
120	640 × 400 64K-color graphics
121	640 × 350 16M-color graphics
122	640 × 400 16M-color graphics

Table 12-2. *Video Modes Provided by the VESA Standard*

most of your users will be able to make use of the SVGA modes on their cards. Most card manufacturers support VESA now and supply a VESA.COM or other program to support the standard. In fact, Video-7 supports VESA in its BIOS (Video-7 was instrumental in creating VESA).

Detecting Video Cards

Detecting video modes is simply a process of elimination. The code for a simple video detect program is on the companion disk in several files. The file contained in the DETMODE.ZIP archive describes a simple method, written by Borland Technical Support professionals, to determine the major video modes. The process you should follow is very straightforward.

Tip

DETMODE.ZIP contains some example C code from Borland Technical Support that implements a video detection scheme, as described in this chapter. PHIRES.ZIP contains C code that lets you use the 640 x 400 graphics mode for programming games. SV.ZIP contains Pascal source code for setting video modes. VIDID.ZIP contains assembler code that determines the video adapter (VGA, EGA, CGA, etc.) and monitor type that your system is using.

do the hardest one first—try to eliminate VGA. This is done by calling an interrupt that only VGA (or better) supports. If you find a VGA card, then you can go and check if it supports VESA. If you don't find VGA, then eliminate EGA by doing an EGA-only function interrupt. If the EGA answers, then the system has EGA. Detecting CGA is easy. If you start up in any text mode other than mode 7 (monochrome text), then you have a CGA.

However, detecting Hercules is nearly impossible. If you start up in mode 7 and it doesn't detect anything else, the system might have a Hercules card. Or, it might have any one of hundreds of Hercules clones, some of which act much differently than a real Hercules card. It might even have the original IBM monochrome card, which does not support any graphics. There are times when your best bet is to assume that your user knows what kind of card he or she has, and simply ask.

Monochrome?!?

Of course, VGA is almost universally affordable these days, and SVGA is all but a necessity for an increasing number of sophisticated video applications. If you run across a user who still has one of the older modes discussed here, you might do him or her a big favor by suggesting a trip to the local computer store.

Since you are a DOS hacker, however, consider this: DOS text mode is supported very well by EGA, CGA, and yes, even monochrome. There are still folks out there using text-based applications exclusively, along with a number of BBS operators and other perfectly sensible folks, who would just as soon stick with their trusty old monitors and spend their money on other neat stuff—like maybe the slick new screen saver you've designed just for them.

Writing to the Screen, Real Fast!

If you aren't going to use graphics and you're planning a really killer text-mode application, then you might like to use direct video writing. Direct video writing places your information directly into the video adapter memory, without using DOS, BIOS, or any other intermediate means.

Hack Facts

FlashPac C
Version 3.6
Kevin Dahl
SimpleSoft
1209 Poplar Street
La Crescent, MN 55947
Shareware: $50
477K bytes
FPCLIB36.ZIP

If you want a full library that performs all the direct video work as well as adding other tools that you can undoubtably use, check out the FlashPac C library. It has a base message-handling library that lets your programs respond to any event, kind of like Windows. A lot of good software for a low registration fee, and you can try it here first for free!

FlashPac provides lots and lots of functions beyond just screen management. The library is written in assembler, and provides over 40 direct video routines that save and restore screen data, draw window frames, display strings, change attributes, edit data fields, and more. BIOS video support is included for cursor control, hardware detection, font selection, font definition, and more. Several mouse support functions are also included, such as getting and setting the mouse cursor position, setting the mouse x and y range, and creating your own mouse interrupt handler for queuing mouse events. BIOS and DOS keyboard support are provided for total keyboard control, along with a critical interrupt handler, and DOS support functions for getting and setting file times and dates, clock times and dates, and the DTA. Finally, the FPWin library includes a set of C and assembler functions that implement the basic elements needed for creating message-based applications.

Speed and Spice for Text Mode

If you'd rather learn the innards on your own, there are several other places you can start. Look at the files DIR_SVID.ZIP, DIR_RVID.ZIP, and DIR_WRIT.ZIP on the CD-ROM. These files, respectively, save a portion of the screen, restore a portion of the screen, and write characters directly to the screen. These could form the basis of a very fast windowing library, if you have the time. These are all provided with C source code, and each of them are about half a page long. This can be a nice, quick introduction for you.

If you want an assembly language introduction, look at TAVID12.ZIP. This archive contains direct screen

Edit
Tip
Quote

I should have stayed home and played with my computer games.
—Attributed to Peewee Herman, video trailblazer

manipulation routines in Turbo Assembler. Much of this can also be called from other languages or converted to interrupt calls in your favorite code with little trouble.

If you want to add some spice to your programs, you should also look into SMOOTH.ZIP. This archive contains an assembly language program to scroll text smoothly on your screen. Of course, you need an application to use this, but it beats using the normal TYPE statement from DOS when you want to look at a text file.

Graphics for Hackers

Once you roll up your shirtsleeves and tackle graphics, it's a lot easier than you might think. The hard part about graphics is putting a dot on the screen. Figuring out how to do this and do it fast is the only trick to graphics programming.

Plane Versus Chunky

12

Putting a dot on a screen is a simple matter of poking a byte into the correct location. This requires a little knowledge of the video card and some arithmetic. It also requires an understanding of the type of dots you want to write. EGA and VGA 16-color modes are known as *plane mode.* This means that you write to the screen in planes. The screen is located in real memory at 0xa000 to 0xafff. Sixteen colors require four bits per color, and a little simple arithmetic shows you that there isn't room on 64K of video memory for much in the way of dots.

But wait, you say. My old EGA had 256K on it and my SVGA has 1MB of RAM on it. That's a lot of dots, but the window that you can write to is only 64K. If you want to write to the whole 1MB of RAM on the video card, then you have to use page planes of memory. You page in 64K, write your dots, and then page in another 64K. In plane video modes, each plane is a different piece of the final color. If you want to write a red dot, you page in the red plane and type **1** on the place where you want the dot to appear. You then write zeroes to the other planes at the same place. Like magic, a red dot appears.

EGA and simple VGA use four page planes. Each plane contributes to the color. Four bits make 16 combinations, and in EGA that's what you've got—16 colors. VGA makes it more complicated (and more flexible) by making the 16 possible values offsets into a color table, where the actual colors are stored. The result is that you still have a limit of 16 colors, but they are 16 colors that *you* choose.

It's a Zen Thing...

The archive PLSMA3.ZIP contains a program you may enjoy at this point. (It contains full C source code, too, so you can see some intense graphics programming at work.) This program simply places a plasma cloud on your screen. You may have seen something like this before (they show up on Star Trek now and then); it's simply a moving color scheme that twists and blends continuously. Check it out—after all this technical fare, you may need a short break.

plane graphics is complicated, because you have to juggle the page planes. You can set a mask on the card and write to all planes at the same time, or you can set each plane on one at a time and do four writes to memory. It's actually faster to do the four writes than to keep fiddling with the color mask. The EGA/VGA doesn't respond very fast because it has to keep in synch with the computer.

Chunky graphics is by far the easier mode to support. All of the VGA and SVGA modes with 256 colors are chunky, meaning that you write a chunk, which is a single byte, for each dot. Since this value is a byte, you are allowed 256 different values. This number (your chunk) is an offset into a color lookup table. You can use any of 64K possible colors, but only 256 different ones at a time.

You still have to page in chunky modes. The simplest mode 0x13 is 320 × 200 × 256 colors, which is 64K and requires no paging. For higher resolutions, you can fix it so that the top 50 lines of the screen is one page and the next 50 is another page, and so on. This method is much easier than worrying about four planes for each dot.

Mode X

A mode we haven't discussed is called mode X. This is a special mode that is often used for games programming because of the speed that is available. However, mode X is not always available on all machines. If you'd like to experiment with mode X (perhaps to write that game you've always wanted), look at XLIB, the Mode X Graphics Library, from Themie Gouthas. It is freeware, found in XLIB06.ZIP. It will take about 800K on your drive, but you can have lots of fun with what you find!

Where Am I?

The arithmetic is easy for deciding which dot to write. The video buffers for EGA and VGA modes is at 0xa000. In Assembler, set this to a segment register and then calculate an offset into the space. The offset is the width of the screen in bytes multiplied by the line number plus the horizontal location in bytes. It's a no-brainer. When pages are involved, chunky mode gets a little more complicated. You divide by the number of bytes per page to get a page number and then calculate the offset into that page. There are a few chunky style graphics modes that use interlacing pages; page 1 is line 1, page 2 is line 2, and so on. It's even possible to interlace the pixels so that page 1 is pixel 1, and page 2 is pixel 2...however, interlacing slows down the program. Ideally you want to calculate a page and switch to it at the beginning of each line. Each page swap requires the VGA card to take some time, which may slow your graphics down to turtle speed.

Using VESA

VESA graphics allow you not only to identify which graphics modes are available, but also to access the pages in an orderly manner. The strategy for using VESA is first to detect it. Then do a VESA-only call to determine the possible video modes, and inspect the modes to determine which one to use. Next check again with the VESA driver to make sure that the combination of card and monitor supports the mode.

To put a dot on the screen, you must calculate the line number of the dot and then instruct VESA to shift to that page. VESA provides you with the segment and offset values for that dot. Move a byte of color information and then do the next dot. It is better to paint one line at a time, from top to bottom, to get the best speed. Ask VESA for a location only at the beginning of each line. This limits the page swaps and the overhead that a VESA driver can add to the program. You should be able to paint a screen so fast that the user is not aware of the process. On a fast machine with a fast card, you should be able to do 32 screen paints per second at 1024 × 768, 256-color mode. This is fast enough for full-motion video. You can only do this in assembly language now, but faster machines in the future will make it possible in C or even Basic.

Graphics File Formats

There are literally thousands of graphics file formats. They are split roughly between bitmaps and vector graphics files. *Bitmap* files are just lots of pixels, sometimes with color information. Bitmaps are huge, so they are often compressed for storage and transfer. Compressed bitmaps include CompuServe GIF and JPEG images. Uncompressed bitmaps include Windows BMP files and First Publisher ART files. *Vector* files contain shorthand commands for drawing circles and lines and other shapes. Examples are CGM files and Adobe Illustrator files. CAD packages store their drawings in vector graphics files.

Bitmaps

The hacker doesn't have to support many graphics files formats. Basically you have TIFF, GIF, and JPEG. TIFF is a popular extensible format. It supports black-and-white images very well, and also has decent support for color. The main advantage of using TIFF is that it is platform-independent. TIFFs can be written and read by Apple, PC,

Edit
Tip
Quote

Video games have graduated from Pac-man, where a little ball eats grapes, to Mortal Kombat, a game with a warrior who rips out his opponent's heart and thrusts it skyward.
—Diane Martinez, California State Assemblywoman

Amiga, and STs. GIF files are also very popular. They use a compression scheme that was great at the time but now (just a few years later) is old technology. GIF files have limits on the number of colors they can store. JPEG is more highly compressed than GIF, and offers a greater variety of color and compression options. JPEG is a bear to decompress, however, and most JPEG viewers are slower than their GIF equivalents. Zsoft's PCX format should also be considered, because it was an early standard and nearly everyone supports the old flavors of PCX. The newer versions of PCX require external palette files, and are not as easy to support.

On the companion CD is an archive called TIFF_11B.ZIP that presents tools for displaying TIFF images.

Vector Graphics

Vector graphics are hard to support because you have to support the drawing ability that each file format might use. You have to be able to draw lines, circles, and fills and use fonts. To be able to support PostScript you need an entire PostScript interpreter. To support AutoCAD DWG files properly you would need AutoCAD. There are, however, a few vector graphics file formats that you might want to try.

CGM: Computer Graphics Metafiles

These files are supported by a variety of products. They are very simple graphics drawing commands, and, with a decent library of draw routines, you could knock off an interpreter in a week. It is simple enough to code and powerful enough to do fairly complex drawings. On the companion CD is the CGM specs and some sample code.

DXF-DXB: AutoCAD Drawing Interchange Files

This spec is in the AutoCAD documentation. It is fairly large but it is very easy to code a subset of these files. Every CAD package makes an attempt at using these files.

HPGL: Hewlett-Packard Graphics Language

This is not really a file format so much as a dump of data that would go to a Hewlett-Packard plotter. It uses plot commands such as "Lift pen" and "Goto x,y". It is easy to code a basic set of commands, and many graphics programs support the language. You may want to get a copy of a plotter technical reference from HP.

Other Types of Graphics Files

Font files are essentially little graphics files. Microsoft publishes the TrueType specifications. Adobe now publishes the internal specs to its files. The Hewlett-Packard LaserJet series is so popular that its soft fonts are a kind of standard.

Animation files such as GRASP and other slideshow files can be very complex, but their hearts are often simple graphics file formats. These allow you to view AutoDesk Animator files.

Next Up

The next chapter provides an assortment of power tools for the hardcore hacker. Check it out...you'll find compilers and debuggers, a righteous disassembler, a handful of code libraries, and a couple of additional utilities to help make your programs run fast and smooth.

13

Down in the Bits

Quote

- *Real programmers don't write in Pascal, or Bliss, or Ada, or any of those pinko computer science languages. Strong typing is for people with weak memories.*
- *Real programmers know better than the users what they need.*
- *Real programmers think structured programming is a communist plot.*

—Ed Post

If a phrase like "down in the bits" breaks you into those "more power!" guttural sounds made famous by comedian Tim Allen, don't worry. You're not alone. This is where the essence of computing takes place, where you discover *exactly* which registers a program modifies or what values reside in which memory locations. Extremists may want in their hearts to program only in machine language. Purists may stick with assembly language, for aesthetic or—in the case of utilities—for practical reasons. The lower you delve, the closer you are to the ever changing, dynamic flow of the data.

But immersion in the data stream does not make you cleaner or, necessarily, closer to Godliness. Not everyone of hackish spirit ever used a machine that could be programmed by changing switches inside the front panels. In fact, only a minority of skilled programmers and hackers—don't cringe—even *remember* machines with front panels. You may prefer higher-order languages and refuse to dwell, nostalgically or otherwise, on assembly language or machine code. If you're into the latest OO techniques and the most productive programming environments, lower-order languages may seem like dinosaurs.

You get it 'til it's perfect, then you cut two minutes.
—Fred Astaire

Somewhere comfortably in the middle you'll find programmers who are at ease with C and assembly language and, maybe, one or two other languages such as BASIC or Pascal, or who just try to stay open to any technique that can get the job done.

Wherever you may locate yourself in this multidimensional universe of skills (the flaming arguments between camps sometimes make the Internet wires smoke), the bottom line is that a good hack is not language-specific but simply gets a lot done with as little code as possible. Well hacked code is spare in any language. Elegance is lean, not fat.

SO although the chapter title may imply that we'll be wallowing in machine code at every turn, the information here is actually divided pretty evenly between assembler tools and C, with some additional tools thrown in for other, higher-level languages. Settling on a favorite programming language doesn't have to be a religious issue. Pick and choose what you like in this chapter, and ignore the rest.

Quote

- *Assembler - A Formula I race car. Very fast, but difficult to drive and expensive to maintain.*
- *BASIC - A second-hand Rambler with a rebuilt engine and patched upholstery. Your dad bought it for you to learn to drive. You'll ditch the car as soon as you can afford a new one.*
- *C - A black Firebird, the all-macho car. Comes with optional seat belts (lint) and optional fuzz buster (escape to assembler).*
- *Pascal - A Volkswagon Beetle. It's small but sturdy. Was once popular with intellectuals.*

—Solomon and Rosenbluth,
"Selecting a Programming Language Made Easy"

Assemblers and Compilers (Making It Executable)

Certain languages excel at low-level programming, down in the bits. Assembler is by far the best, with C close behind. This section describes a few of the assemblers and other tools available in those languages.

Hack Facts

A86 Macro Assembler
Version 3.70
Eric Isaacson
416 E. University Avenue
Bloomington, IN 47401
812-339-1811
CIS: 71520,74
177,145 bytes
Shareware: $50
A86V370.ZIP

A86 is a worthy standard in shareware assemblers, undoubtedly one of the best programming tools ever, well, assembled as shareware. According to author Eric Isaacson's own description, A86 is the "finest assembler available, at any cost under any terms." A lot of programmers agree. Here are some key A86 features:

- The assembler itself works at lightning speed— thousands of lines of code every second, even on the slowest 286 dinosaur.
- It can generate either OBJ files, which can be linked into an executable, or an immediately executable COM file.
- The documentation that comes standard with the ZIP file is comprehensive.
- It's programs can be debugged using another Isaacson shareware product, D86 (covered later in this chapter).

Edit
Tip
Quote

A programming language is low-level when its programs require attention to the irrelevant.
—from BLURBS, a quote-of-the-day program

Once you decide to keep using this classic, Isaacson offers some good reasons to register. For one, you get a printed manual, formatted and bound much more nicely than you would likely be able to manage if you just printed out the on-disk shareware manual. For another, you'll get A86LIB.COM, a tool that lets you create libraries of your own source files. Once they're libraried, A86 will search them automatically whenever your program has an undefined symbol. In effect, A86LIB.COM lets you add powerful new features to the A86 assembler program.

Quote

Real programmers scorn floating point arithmetic. The decimal point was invented for...[those] who are unable to "think big."

—*Ed Post*

Hack Facts

Micro-C Compiler
Version 1.41
Dave Dunfield
56 Burnetts Grove Circle
Nepean, Ontario, Canada
K2J 1N6
259,328 bytes
Free
MC141.ZIP

If you want to start tinkering in C but you don't feel like shelling out any shillings at all, or if you need an extremely portable C compiler that you can easily move between processors and systems, then try Micro-C. This subset of ANSI C does not support floating-point variables or structures, so creating the world's next megabuck super success 45MB application might best be done elsewhere. But if you don't need floating-point capability, this is a fine, portable, small, fast compiler for C hackers.

Micro-C's excellent documentation includes an introduction to C programming, so it's great if you are just starting out in the programming world or you feel a bit rusty with C. The documentation for the compiler itself is also very complete. And if your wallet is as flat as last night's beer, no problem—this compiler is free.

Edit
Tip
Quote

Intelligence is the faculty of making artificial objects, especially tools to make tools.

—*Henri-Louis Bergson*

Micro-C includes its own source code, so you can recompile the compiler itself, with different characteristics if you like. You can even use the Micro-C compiler (MCC.COM) to do it. The version included with the distribution file was compiled using Turbo-C 2.0 with full optimization enabled and all code-producing options (stack checking, debugging aids, and so forth) turned off. The result is very small and fast.

Hack Facts

Small-C Compiler
James E. Hendrix
Box 1435
Oxford, MS 38655
133,062 bytes
Free
SMALLC22.ZIP

There is relatively little difference in the amount of C implemented by the Micro-C and Small-C compilers. They're both pint-sized and useful for on-the-fly programming, and their simplicity makes them both popular with novices in C programming as well as with traveling hackers. Small-C, however, also includes Small Assembler—a nice feature if you like to carry both languages around in your head and you want to work in both—using, for example, your laptop. In effect, you have access to two languages for the price of learning one compiler. More interestingly, if you're curious about the relationships between the two languages, Small-C lets you see the assembly language it creates from C code that you write. This is a great educational tool if you're conversant with C but rusty with, or just learning, assembler.

When It IS Broke, Fix It!

Edit
Tip
Quote

BUG: What your eyes do after you stare at the tiny green computer screen for more than 15 minutes. Also: what computer magazine companies do to you after they get your name on their mailing list.
—Author unknown

"If it ain't broke, don't fix it," is an old saw every hacker hears eventually from a spouse, employer, or some other impatient observer. We won't philosophize about hacking here other than to observe that if God didn't want hackers to putter, s/he wouldn't have built such a high fiddle factor into computers and programming. For many (we plead guilty here), fiddling is often its own reward.

But sometimes things do break and the puttering takes on a serious cast. The best laid code falls prey to Murphy. For those challenging moments, a great compiler isn't enough. A program that compiles fast and runs fast into a brick wall lacks something critical, like functionality. This problem is seen from time to time in all computer languages, on every platform.

Quote

- *Ada - An army-green Mercedes-Benz staff car. Power steering, power brakes, and automatic transmission are all standard. No other colors or options are available. If it's good enough for the generals, it's good enough for you. Manufacturing delays due to difficulties reading the design specification are starting to clear up.*
- *APL - A double-decker bus. It takes rows and columns of passengers to the same place all at the same time. But it drives only in reverse gear and is instrumented in Greek.*
- *COBOL - A delivery van. It's bulky and ugly, but it does the work.*
- *FORTH - A go-cart.*
- *LISP - An electric car. It's simple but slow. Seat belts are not available.*

—Solomon and Rosenbluth,
"Selecting a Programming Language Made Easy"

When you buy a high-order language compiler or a full-bore programming system off the shelf at your local software store, you usually get a fully integrated environment complete with editor, compiler, and debugger. We would be blowing smoke if we tried to convince you that the usual shareware systems are better than the expensive ones retailed by the giants. Shareware authors don't have megabucks to spend on development. But the systems on this book's CD-ROM are good ones, and here we'll toss in two more products (both on the CD-ROM) to complement them. D86, a debugger, helps you fix programs or modules written for the A86 assembler. SOS-ENGINE monitors certain DOS functions that other debuggers can't.

Hack Facts

D86 Debugger

Version 3.70
Eric Isaacson
416 E. University Avenue
Bloomington, IN 47401-4739
Voice: 812-339-1811
CIS: 71520,74
92,955 bytes
Shareware: $50 ($80 for A86 and D86 combined)
D86V370.ZIP

Using the A86 assembler without its D86 companion is like taking the subway in Paris without a map: you get to places quickly, but you have no idea where you are. D86 lets you interactively debug your A86 or any other assembled program. It lets you follow the disassembled execution path, monitor memory locations and registers, explore your computer's machine state, do floating-point debugging, and make patches to your program in real-time. The online help is brief, presumably because the rest of the screen is taken up by displays, but the reference document is well written and comprehensive.

When you register, you'll get a printed manual plus some tools to make D86 even more powerful—for example, MAPD86 will convert a link MAP listing from another language into a SYM file so you can use D86 to do symbolic debugging. Registration also lets you use a D option on 386 machines to set memory breakpoints.

D86 comes with its own copy of A86.COM, because it is needed for D86 to work. However, there is no significant difference between the two copies of A86.COM. Use the one compiled with the A86 compiler in A86V370.ZIP (also on the CD-ROM).

Quote

I programmed three days
And heard no human voices.
But the hard disk sang.

—*The Zen of Programming*
(Haiku from theTinyHost Welcome screen)

Hack Facts

SOS-ENGINE
Solid Oak Software
P.O. Box 6826
Santa Barbara, CA 93160
Voice: 805-967-9853
Orders: 800-388-2761
CIS: 75500,2610
13,509 bytes
Shareware: $25
SOSENG.ZIP

What's the last debugger you used that tracked file input and output for you? Or that tracked changes in file date/time stamps? SOS-ENGINE begins where most debuggers leave off. This well-written tool supports programs written in BASIC, C, Clipper, or Pascal, and comes with examples written in each language. Source code is included for all those languages, so you can cut and paste the debugging code right into your application source before compiling. Or you can use the prepared OBJ file to do the same. It's compatible with both Windows and DOS, so you can use it the way MECA did when they developed the latest version of Andrew Tobias' *Managing Your Money.* Programmers can quickly come to depend on this gem.

Edit
Tip
Quote

If you don't mind adding about 600 bytes to the size of your application, pay a bit extra for a distribution license; then leave the OBJ file linked, and distribute the SOSENGN.EXE TSR with your application. It will let you provide incredibly detailed and accurate support to your customers—by long distance.

Here's how you use SOS-ENGINE:

1. Execute a small memory-resident program named SOSENGN.EXE that monitors DOS file and memory activity.
2. Within your program, call a procedure/function that activates the monitor. You can call it either at the very start of the program or wherever you think a problem is occurring.
3. Programmatically activate and deactivate individual options with other subprogram calls.
4. Compile, link, and re-execute your program.

When you are finished, a log file will indicate all activity in quite some detail, making it easy to find and fix problems.

It's So Big!

Edit
Tip
Quote

At a football game, the Real Programmer is the one comparing the plays against his simulations printed on 11-by-14 fanfold paper.
—from a BBS text file

The trademark of many a hacker is the stacks of program listings and output strewn about the room. As your programs grow from merely enormous to truly gargantuan, you will quickly discover the futility of pawing through printouts in search of a listing that has long since been shredded into nest material by Morris the Mouse or used to mop up coffee spills. Not to mention the fire hazard.

Software problems usually have software solutions. The tools in this section are for C and assembly language programmers. They will help you spend more time programming and debugging and less time breathing paper dust.

Quote

Overrun screw: [C programming] n. A variety of {fandango on core} produced by scribbling past the end of an array (C has no checks for this). This is relatively benign and easy to spot if the array is static; if it is auto, the result may be to {smash the stack}—often resulting in {heisenbug}s of the most diabolical subtlety.

—from "The Jargon File"

13

Hack Facts

```
C xref
Version 3.0a
David Archibald
DA Software
3717 Aldon Lane
Flint, MI 48506
Orders: 800-444-5457
CIS: 71203.1301
72,723 bytes
Shareware: $24.95
CXREF3A.ZIP
```

Programming in C is not for absent-minded professors ("Now where did I put that global variable?"). Even steel-trap-minded programmers can lose track of variables—and functions too—as the program starts to grow. This is where a tool like C xref hits the spot.

When you run C xref on a set of modules, you'll get a report with four sections:

- An alphabetical listing of all global variables and where they are declared

- An alphabetical listing of all functions and where they are declared
- A complete breakdown of each function, showing variables used and functions called
- A tree-like summary of the function call hierarchy

Admittedly this report is longer than the code listings themselves, but it is well-ordered, it makes it easy to find the information you need, and it clearly maps everything in relation to everything else. It's a useful, ordered index to the whole.

Hack Facts

PPT
Version 1.0
Gary L. Levine
GL Software Services
4255 S. Buckley Road, #295
Aurora, CO 80013
BBS: 303-840-2840
CIS: 70152,253
453,336
Shareware: $40
PPT100.ZIP

Have you ever tried to change the name of a global variable that is used in many different modules of the same C program? Or tried to keep track of the calls in a complex C program? These are very tedious and error-prone tasks, to say the least. But they're hard to automate, because macros can either skip a module or accidentally replace text within a string constant.

To keep from flubbing such tasks, it helps if you can see "the big picture," so you have some way to make changes in context, without having to slog through manually. PPT (we assume it's an acronym for something like Programmer Productivity Tools or maybe Perfect Picture Toolkit; author Gary L. Levine doesn't say) is a collection of C utilities to take care of these kinds of thankless tasks. One utility, for example, is "C Identifier Search and Replace," a headache- prone chore which this GREP-like utility does quite handily.

Edit
Tip
Quote

One picture is worth more than a thousand words.
—Chinese proverb

Quote

I forget who it was that recommended men for their soul's good to do each day two things they disliked. It is a precept that I have followed scrupulously; for every day I have got up and I have gone to bed.

—Somerset Maugham, The Moon and Sixpence

PPT also does a call tree. Unlike C xref, however, this tree is interactive, as shown in Figure 13-1. You can traverse from a call to an editor that displays the file containing the call, you can expand or elide branches on the tree, and you can exclude certain modules from the tree altogether. Talk about a perfect picture!

Quote

Real programmers don't draw flowcharts. Cavemen drew flowcharts; look how much good it did them. But you may find a flowchart template beneath the Oreos on a real programmer's windowsill, left there by a previous occupant.

—Anonymous (BBS text file)

Hack Facts

```
ASMFLOW
Version 3.0
Mike Schmit
Quantasm Corporation
19855 Stevens Creek Blvd.
Suite 154
Cupertino, CA 95014
800-765-8086
CIS: 76347,3661
53,883 bytes
Free ASMFLO3.ZIP
```

The term "flowchart" flashes pictures of hippies and the Vietnam war. It's hard to imagine a 20+ year-old concept being of any value in an industry where two-year-old software and hardware are considered archaic. For most cases that may be true, except possibly for a 20+ year-old language called assembler. Flowcharts go well with assembler; they're another way to get a "big picture" of a program.

ASMFLOW reads a file containing assembler and uses graphical text symbols to surround the listing with a flowchart. It draws arrows from jumps and branches to their destination labels, as you can see in Figure 13-2, and it creates diamonds around conditional jumps, showing the "YES" path and the "NO" path. It's not a flowchart you

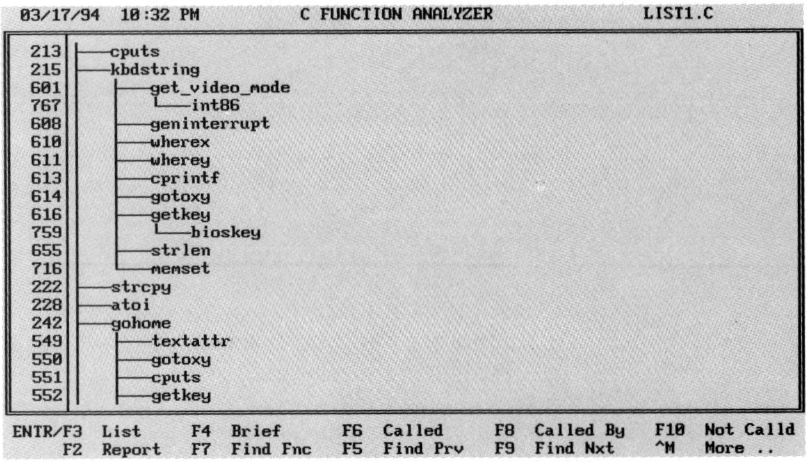
03/17/94 10:32 PM C FUNCTION ANALYZER LIST1.C
213 cputs
215 kbdstring
601 get_video_mode
767 int86
608 geninterrupt
610 wherex
611 wherey
613 cprintf
614 gotoxy
616 getkey
759 bioskey
655 strlen
716 memset
222 strcpy
228 atoi
242 gohome
549 textattr
550 gotoxy
551 cputs
552 getkey
ENTR/F3 List F4 Brief F6 Called F8 Called By F10 Not Calld
F2 Report F7 Find Fnc F5 Find Prv F9 Find Nxt ^M More ..

Figure 13-1. *A call analysis of a simple C program using PPT*

would have found in a 1968 college class...but it sure does help track what's happening in an ASM file. This tool is also terrific for training others on how your programs work.

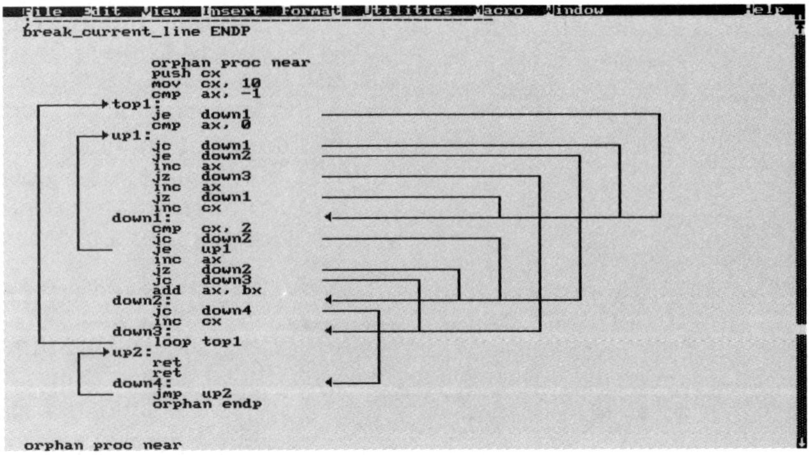
File Edit View Insert Format Utilities Macro Window Help
break_current_line ENDP
orphan proc near
push cx
mov cx, 10
cmp ax, -1
top1:
je down1
cmp ax, 0
up1:
jc down1
je down2
inc ax
jz down3
inc ax
jz down1
inc cx
down1:
cmp cx, 2
jc down2
je up1
inc ax
jz down2
jc down3
add ax, bx
down2:
jc down4
inc cx
down3:
loop top1
up2:
ret
ret
down4:
jmp up2
orphan endp
orphan proc near

Figure 13-2. *A not-so-typical flow of a program, as shown by ASMFLOW*

Tip

If you have arrows going all over the place or going across three or more pages, you probably need to rethink the logic behind your code.

ASMFLOW gives you a real indication of program quality. It also supports Pentium-based machines and data cross-referencing. The demo version is fully functional but limited to code size less than 250 lines of source.

Private Eyes

No! No disassemble!
—Robot Number Five in Short Circuit

One of the earliest images associated with the term "hacker" was that of an unkempt teenage boy like Matthew Broderick's character in the movie *War Games,* breaking into secured computers and wreaking international havoc, changing grades, or transferring money into Swiss bank accounts. Or you might have pictured a guy locked in some basement, surrounded by Oreos and stale Coke, paid by a large corporation to reconstruct a competitor's program from the EXE file back to its original source code. For Joe User, these may be the only people imaginable to have a use for disassemblers.

If penicillin is such a wonder drug, how come it can't cure bread mold?
—Ron Smith

But of course disassemblers are good for all sorts of reverse engineering, most notably reverse engineering of mysterious bugs in programs. No program can fix every bug; no cure is perfect. Still, when bad things happen to good programs, some disassembling can help locate just where the virtual mouse chewed through the virtual wires. On a similar note, peering deeper into existing code can be much easier when you format it to guide the eye properly. So we offer here some tools to help dissect the software frog and see what makes it kick. Enjoy.

Hack Facts

DISASTER
Version 1.1
Feico Nater Shareware
Beukweg 24
7556 DE Hengelo
Netherlands
Voice: 31 74 438373
28,685 bytes
Shareware: $50
DISATR11.ZIP

There is no perfect disassembler, either shareware or retail. If you think about it, very few people wish there were. Developers of expensive retail programs have *no* interest in other people discovering the secrets behind their software. They'll try for the other guy's secrets, but most competitors understand that if they are too successful at uncovering secrets, they can get mixed up in very large lawsuits. The bigger you are, the bigger the judgments (just ask Bill Gates). Anyway, hacker purists would be bored if the Perfect Disassembler made things too easy. However, for those times when you have a valid reason for using a disassembler, DISASTER is a good one to try. It is quite powerful and flexible.

Edit
Tip
Quote

When cryptography is outlawed, bayl bhgynjf jvyy unir cevinpl.
—E-mail message

Pretty, it is not. It also has a terrible personality. Like your worst blind date, DISASTER is very smart and expects a lot of you, but you would never take it proudly home to mom. The program is interactive in nature—it has to be, if you think about it—but the user interface is teletype-compatible. No graphics, no textual boxes, no screen controls; just bone-dry text that tends to scroll off the top of the screen.

Looks and personality aren't everything. The kind of user who needs a nice GUI would have no interest in a disassembler. If you're using this program, you're down in the bits with virtual grease on your face anyway. DISASTER wins its many hacker points for pure functionality. It has automated label generation, automated control generation, and even hints and tips in the text. Give it a try, and if you need to dress up the output, well, tee it to a text file (see TEE.EXE, described in Chapter 10, "A Bag of Other Goodies") and read the results into a DTP program.

Hack Facts

ASMFORM
Version 1.02
Seal-bee Software, Inc.
20786 N.W. Wallula Court
Portland OR 97229
22,357 bytes
Shareware: $20
ASMFORM.ZIP

Why, you might ask, is an assembly language formatter stuck in a section titled "Private Eyes?" Well, it's here because you have two primary reasons for needing such a tool. You either received the code from a fellow hacker, who prefers the e. e. cummings style of writing assembler; or you just disassembled the code and would like to be able to actually read it.

ASMFORM rewrites assembly language files with the following rules:

- It aligns comments at the column location.
- It capitalizes labels and mnemonics consistently.
- It indents opcodes for better readability.
- It removes all blank lines (not our favorite feature, but the good outweighs the bad).

The result is a readable ASM code listing. If you've ever tried working with unformatted ASM files, you'll appreciate the results!

Brief Mentions

The following files, included on the CD-ROM, are assembly language libraries that can help you avoid accidentally wasting time reinventing the wheel.

A86LIB3.ZIP: An A86 Library

This library of ASM routines by Loritec Software is for use with Eric Isaacson's A86 assembler (described earlier). The registered version includes the file A86.LIB, which lets A86 directly assemble code when it finds an undefined symbol. Put this library into your bag of tricks if you're into ASM and you like to use Isaacson's assembler.

ASMLIB.ZIP

ASMLIB, a library of assembly language subroutines, includes a large assortment of well-documented tools to help you avoid tedious and repetive coding chores. See ASMLIB.DOC for a guide to using the library, and to the contents of the many included doc files (which are grouped according to area—disk, EMS/XMS, system, etc.). The distribution file also includes a small, fast, huge-file text editor named E16.COM, constructed from ASMLIB tools. Full source code for E16.COM is available with the $50 level of registration.

ASMWIZ.ZIP

ASMWIZ is another library of ASM subroutines, designed for small programs of the COM persuasion. Most assemblers are supported. Its subroutines include text and graphics, buffered file I/O, kbd, mouse, exception handling, string support, hi-res timers and countdowns, and much more. Tiny model, COM format.

Next Up

In the next (and final) chapter, we'll move to the other end of the spectrum—the programmer/hacker/developer with a product to market. Producing a good hack or a fine application program is terrific, and if it's your hobby, that may be reward enough. But if you need to feed Junior or justify all those 3:00 A.M. sessions to your spouse, you'll need to make a buck or two for the sake of plausibility. If that's your situation, Chapter 14 can help.

14

Hacker Graduation

Quote

The typical Real Programmer lives in front of a computer terminal. Surrounding this terminal are:

- *Listings of all programs the Real Programmer has ever worked on, piled in roughly chronological order on every flat surface in the office...*
- *Taped to the wall is a line-printer Snoopy calendar for the year 1969.*
- *Strewn about the floor are several wrappers for peanut butter filled cheese bars—the type that are made pre-stale at the bakery so they can't get any worse while waiting in the vending machine.*

—Ed Post

We've already talked about the great computer innovations that begin with one or two people hacking away in a garage or basement, tolerating subhuman conditions usually created by their own neuroses. You may be attempting a similar feat, toiling through the wee hours of the night implementing the next Great Tool. Or, having created a program that's way cool, you may want to share it with the universe.

Either way, if you haven't done so already, you may be about to learn the hard way that there is more to a program than functionality—it's got to have class. This chapter will introduce some tools to help you graduate from Hacker to Developer (or perhaps to Hacker First Class, if the other title reminds you of wearing a tie).

We can hear the protests now: "Hey, plenty of great speeches are written on the backs of envelopes." Remember, though, that the majority of great orations were made great by their presentations and not just their content. (For those who believe that "great speech" is an oxymoron, please accept our apologies and try to get with the metaphor.) It's probably true that most programmers prefer more features to ease of use. It's the "More Power!" drive that hackers tend to have. But users who pull out their checkbooks expect us to have already done the hacking for them. If we want to make a buck or two, our programs must be simple to install and use. This is not necessarily an easy goal for a hackmeister to achieve. It's counterintuitive. It *feels* like a waste of time.

The tools in this chapter can help you share your programs more effectively with the rest of the world (but not develop ulcers doing it). We picked these tools because they add a little class to programs without adding a high cost in extra development time, or because they make it easier to maintain a program after it has hit the market. They'll help you create programs for people who march to a diurnal rhythm and who probably eat healthy, too.

Life Beyond "Copy a:*.*"

What do you do when someone hands you a floppy and tells you to try a great new program?

If you're a hacker, you probably throw the disk into your drive and look for a README file or INSTALL.BAT or anything written in plain text that may tell you what the program does and what it needs in order to run. Then you may copy all files to a newly created subdirectory (after checking it thoroughly for viruses, of course). You may uncompress files from the floppy selectively, to avoid littering your hard drive with BBS ads and the like. If you can't avoid using someone else's install routine, you'll probably copy their files from the floppy onto a RAM drive and work from there, because it's faster than a floppy and you won't have any garbage left behind on your hard drive if some bad code locks up your system and makes you reboot.

Whatever your personal try-it procedure may be, you most likely will not simply type **INSTALL** or **SETUP** and blindly allow an unknown author to dictate a "user-friendly" installation. There's just too great a risk that some software engineer has fobbed off a monster that will deface your boot files, the ones you so carefully hacked into a Byzantine masterpiece of loops and branching logic. "Leave the driving to us" does not appeal much to the average hacker.

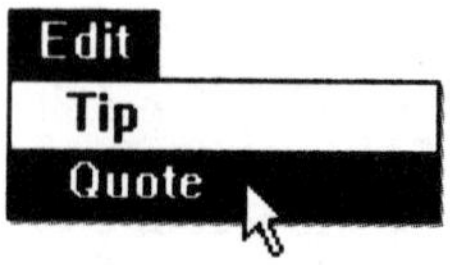
Edit
Tip
Quote

Real programmers don't eat quiche. They can't even spell quiche. But software engineers scarf the stuff up and ask for more.
—E-mail message from a hacker

When preparing your own program, you may be tempted to honor the assumed hacker in others and just set up your program for simple file copying with a "Tip: Read the Help Files" here and a "Press ALT-O, then pick desired options" there. Who needs more?

The average user, that's who. Take a hackish approach and you limit your appeal to the hacker elite. Why do that? Thanks to Windows and the like, most people expect fairly detailed assistance in installation, if not complete hand-holding. Granted, most DOS users adventurous enough to try new programs are not terrified of directories with more than three files in them. But if you make them work less to get to the meat of your program, they'll have more time to try the ALT-O options and decide they want to register your program. Easier installation translates into more open checkbooks.

The right installation routine will walk the line between helpfulness and treating users as the certifiable idiots that your experience probably tells you they are. It also will never, *never* step on a user's elaborate boot routines without first asking permission.

In this section you'll find three programs that make installation from the user's point of view pretty simple, without necessarily offending their sense of control over their own machines. That's the balance to seek in your installation routines.

Hack Facts

QUIK-INSTALL
Version 2.0
Michael L. Wester
Route #6 Box 34
Fuquay-Varina, NC 27526
919-552-0767
115,659 bytes
Single program license: $15
QINST2.ZIP

The name of this program, QUIK-INSTALL, is not a misnomer. The program that creates your program's INSTALL.EXE file is menu-driven and easy to understand. In a matter of minutes you can create a customized installation program that is an unbelievably small 6K in size. The distribution file includes an impressive demo called INSTALL.EXE, which shows you many of the available features. The registration price (only $15) makes it even more attractive, and the license is royalty-free, a plus for developers. Try QUIK-INSTALL if your program doesn't require intricate tuning or complex operations to install. Figure 14-1 shows the simple but flexible QUIK-INSTALL installation option screen.

QUIK-INSTALL can do the installation from floppy or CD-ROM, install from self-extracting archives, create target directories, check for sufficient space on the target drive, and execute the installed application on closing. It also has full mouse support and context-sensitive help. An elegantly simple time-saver.

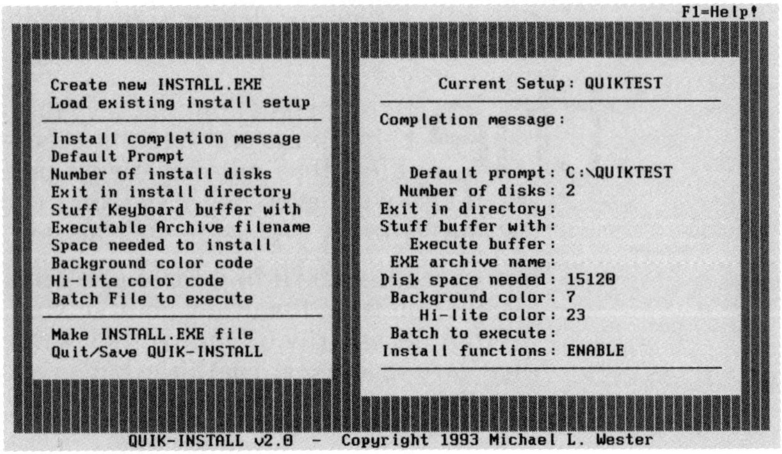
F1=Help!
Create new INSTALL.EXE
Load existing install setup
Install completion message
Default Prompt
Number of install disks
Exit in install directory
Stuff Keyboard buffer with
Executable Archive filename
Space needed to install
Background color code
Hi-lite color code
Batch File to execute
Make INSTALL.EXE file
Quit/Save QUIK-INSTALL
Current Setup: QUIKTEST
Completion message:
Default prompt: C:\QUIKTEST
Number of disks: 2
Exit in directory:
Stuff buffer with:
Execute buffer:
EXE archive name:
Disk space needed: 15120
Background color: 7
Hi-lite color: 23
Batch to execute:
Install functions: ENABLE
QUIK-INSTALL v2.0 - Copyright 1993 Michael L. Wester

Figure 14-1. *QUIK-INSTALL installation options*

Hack Facts
Install-Pro
Version 3.16
DB/Soft Publishing
3200 Truxel Road #199
Sacramento, CA 95833
Orders: 800-242-4775
CIS: 71355,470
132,086 bytes
Shareware: $40
IPRO320.ZIP

Install-Pro is a fine choice if you think that menu-driven programs are for the weak of mind or spirit, or if your situation calls for tighter control during program installations. Think of Install-Pro as being "for those tougher jobs," as the TV ads put it. Install-Pro is completely script-driven, giving you total control over what happens and when. Install-Pro takes a very detailed approach. Try this one also for programs that need some hardware checking in order to configure themselves appropriately to different systems. For example, Install-Pro does comprehensive environment detection, including minimum CPU, floating point processor, installed RAM, MS-DOS version, EMS, XMS, VCPI and DPMI.

Install-Pro can handle file splitting on large applications. You define the directory prompts and default target directories and also can set installation disk names (such as "Utilities Disk" or "Install Disk"). The program will check for sufficient disk space at any point or points in the installation, including optional portions. If a user is short of space, Install-Pro asks if they want to try to continue or abort the installation. All of this program's error handling is robust—and, as the docs put it, error reports "won't scare the dickens out of your users" because they are descriptive, not couched in "error 14 at *xxxx:yyyy*" terms.

Hack Facts
First Impression
Version 2.6
Harold Holmes
Lincoln Beach Software
P.O. Box 1554
Ballwin, MO 63022
314-227-2431
160,282 bytes
Developer license: $55
IMPRES26.ZIP

You might call First Impression the Mark VIII of shareware installation programs. This fine developer's tool lets you flip-flop between menus and scripts, in case you haven't yet formed an opinion on that age-old controversy or just feel there's a good place for both. It also gives you tighter control over the interface that your customers see during installation. That can be a real plus for applications with a distinctive "look and feel" that you would like to see reflected in your installation program. Figure 14-2 shows the First Impression setup options; note that the menu entries include what files to copy, what documents to print, specific DOS instructions, and other fine-tuning installation questions.

Oh, Yeah, Documentation

Quote

It takes a special person to be able to put into typed words many pages of useless or stupid programs. To get your feet wet at this technique, you may want to start off with a 10 or 20 page document on "How to Properly Turn On Your Computer." If you can handle that, next try "How to Properly Turn Off Your Computer."

—"Scoop," a neighborhood hacker

The docs are important if you want people to buy your programs. You may think that docs are reserved for people more anal retentive and compulsive than the typical hacker. "Oh, look, Joe has four comment lines for every line of C code and a 400-page user manual. And he has seventeen pencils on his desk lined up, all exactly the same length."

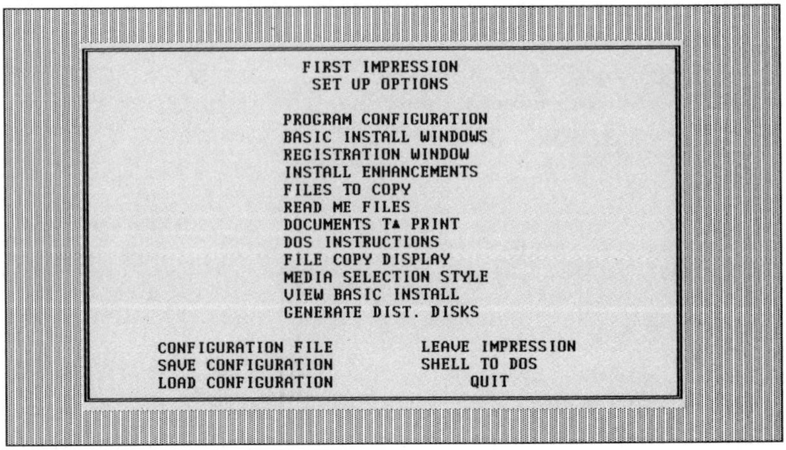
FIRST IMPRESSION
SET UP OPTIONS
PROGRAM CONFIGURATION
BASIC INSTALL WINDOWS
REGISTRATION WINDOW
INSTALL ENHANCEMENTS
FILES TO COPY
READ ME FILES
DOCUMENTS TO PRINT
DOS INSTRUCTIONS
FILE COPY DISPLAY
MEDIA SELECTION STYLE
VIEW BASIC INSTALL
GENERATE DIST. DISKS
CONFIGURATION FILE
SAVE CONFIGURATION
LOAD CONFIGURATION
LEAVE IMPRESSION
SHELL TO DOS
QUIT

Figure 14-2. *First Impression setup options*

But you only have to go that far if you're the type who wraps up the garbage neatly in gift paper before placing it carefully in the dumpster.

For the rest of us, docs are important but do not really have to be idiot-friendly. They just need to be accurate and complete, so reasonably bright people can use them. That's not as easy as it sounds.

Edit
Tip
Quote

Do not expose your LaserWriter to open fire or flame.
—from the drool-proof pages of the Apple LaserWriter manual

One of the primary benefits of documentation for a creator of shareware is that it doubles as marketing literature. Potential customers will unzip your program, search for a .DOC or a README, and try to determine just how useful it might be for them. A good doc persuades them to actually try the program, and that's Step 1 in a successful sale.

Another benefit of documentation is that it is much easier to maintain the code. You see, you will inevitably create one tool, sell it, go off and create forty or fifty more, and then forget how the first one worked. When it comes time to fix or enhance the original code, the documentation can serve as a gentle reminder of just what a program was (or purported to be) all about in the first place.

We bet you know at least one programmer who would strongly prefer to write code than manuals and other documents. If you have such a friend, here are some great tools to make the documentation chore a bit easier.

Hack Facts

SUPERMANual
Version 1.1
Auto-Jock SM
18 8th Street
Wheeling, WV 26003
304-232-1773
BBS: 609-383-9400
182,249 bytes
Shareware: $69
MANUAL11.ZIP

Since creating docs is such a mundane and unexciting chore, it would be nice to be able to annotate features in your code and have them automagically propagate into a document. Great dream, huh? But just a dream.

Then you woke up, and it turned out *not* to be just a dream. The SUPERMANual tool accomplishes just what you need. It may not leap tall buildings in a single bound, but it does automate user manual creation. (Which feat is more useful to *you*?)

The concept behind SUPERMANual is actually rather simple: you add comments to your source code in a structured fashion. Here's an example:

```
;$SUPERMAN$
;$CHAPTER$
;14
;$SUBCHAPTER$
;1
;$HEADING$
;Documentation Tools
;$TXT$
;This is an example of the annotations
;required for SUPERMANual to
;be able to generate the user manual properly.
;$END$
```

The first character(s) will vary depending on the source language of the code you are documenting. But the result is a manual generated from the actual source code. Do some cutting and pasting, add some commentary, and presto! A manual, based directly on the source, produced faster than you can say "double cheese with anchovies and pepperoni."

Hack Facts

SOURCE
Version 1.4
Rick Maddy
2727 Folsom Street, #104
Boulder, CO 80304
303-440-3682
CIS: 76460,1601
104,425 bytes
Shareware: $25
SOURCE14.ZIP

For a moment, let's expand the definition of "documentation" to include the actual source code. After all, well-written code has been called "self documenting." If you're using an editor like BOXER, it displays your code's keywords in different colors (that is, assuming you're taking advantage of the programs covered in Chapter 4). So why shouldn't your printer emphasize your code as well? If you agree, try the tool called SOURCE.

SOURCE supports highlighted printing of code in C, Pascal, FORTRAN, and Clipper. If that isn't enough, you can add your own. It has more than 40 print options to highlight comments, keywords, and blocks. Add page numbers, headers, banners, margins, tab stops, multiple columns, and line wrapping. SOURCE is fully user-definable, and supports most common printers. A good utility for working with source code files.

Looking Good

> *Remember: It is better to LOOK good than to FEEL good.*
> *—Billy Crystal (in his SNL Fernando Lamas character)*

You may find the whole idea behind tools such as Visual C, which emphasize point and click and a visual interface, annoying in the extreme. By making tasks easy, such tools have often also made them inflexible. However, that's no longer the case. Increased processing power and expanded libraries have made graphically oriented systems as fast and flexible as many users (including power users) may ever require. To the extent that such tools make a computing day go faster, they help a computer do what it's supposed to do—make people more, not less, productive. So people who deck their programs out in GUI clothing aren't necessarily cheating these days.

Of course, the best GUI clothing in DOS should combine the ease of the GUI interface with the advantages—chiefly speed and lack of intervening layers—of a DOS program. Achieving that goal is getting easier these days even in vanilla DOS, as batch file tools such as the Screen Wizard (see Chapter 10, "A Bag of Other Goodies") bring the flash and ease of pop-up windows to batch files. On the programming side, take a look at the potential of both DOS mode and VGA graphic mode screens to add zip to your product and enhance its appeal to users. You won't have to spend tens or hundreds of hours learning the ins and outs of graphical screen design; these programs have taken care of it for you.

> *Money is the root of all evil, and everybody needs roots.*
> *—from BLURBS, a quote-of-the-day program*

So check out the interface design offerings below. They'll save you much time. And there's an additional bonus: to attract those users who really *want* to reach for their wallets but have somehow gotten stalled, sometimes a bit of extra zip in the interface is all it takes to fire up their pay-for-the-program circuits.

Hack Facts

Screen Designer
Version 2.33
Michael Cocke
11 Cedar Road
Montville, NJ 07045
94,823 bytes
Shareware: $10
SD233.ZIP

Screen Designer acts like a paintbrush program for screens in DOS text mode, using two basic features to create zippy, character-based interfaces for your programs. The first feature lets you draw your screen directly, and the second lets you create source code in a variety of languages to reproduce that screen. As you draw the screen, you can toggle between entering characters and drawing lines and boxes. When you are satisfied with the interface, you then answer a series of questions on how you want the source code generated. Based on your answers, you end up generating code for C, BASIC, or Pascal programs. You can even extend it to create code for another favorite language if you like. Then drop the code into your program, and you're done.

The author says in the docs that he wrote Screen Designer to correct one of his own problems: "I tend to write truly horrible screen interfaces. This is because, like many programmers, I'm more concerned with the program than with its appearance. Screen Designer is designed to remedy those appalling interfaces." The result was a very nice, very convenient hack.

Hack Facts

Graphics User Interface Library
Version 1.01
Plain Design, Inc.
P.O. Box 135
Midland Park, NJ 07432
CIS: 73672,174
199,971 bytes
Shareware: $29
GUI.ZIP

Here's one for all you programmers with a bit more ambition in the interface department, who want to go beyond the ASCII character set. If your users might enjoy the elegance of bit-mapped graphics, here's a library to help you give it to them. Called GUI Library, it helps create buttons, scroll bars, and other familiar (and, these days, expected) VGA graphics mode effects. Once you've created the necessary VGA graphics elements, the program generates C code that you include in your programs.
The GUI program has pull-down menus

Order and simplification are the first steps toward the mastery of a subject.
—*Thomas Mann,* The Magic Mountain

and supports mouse operations. If you buy the source code for the Builder when you register, you can generate source for languages other than C.

The distribution file libraries are specifically designed for VGA 640 × 480 × 16 mode. It contains a full large model library for Borland C, Mix C and Microsoft C compilers. Full documentation and ordering information are provided on the DEMO.EXE Help screens.

Here is a sample scroll-down menu from the GUI Library demo program:

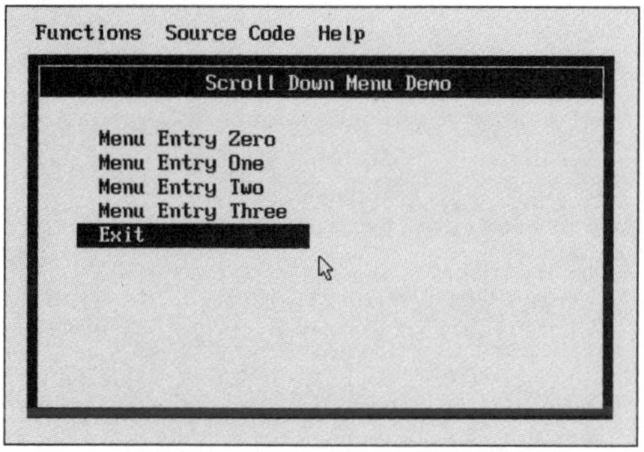
Functions
Source Code
Help
Scroll Down Menu Demo
Menu Entry Zero
Menu Entry One
Menu Entry Two
Menu Entry Three
Exit

Note the arrow cursor: even though the letters in the captured screen are in a standard VGA font, the cursor's a dead giveaway that the machine was working in graphic mode when the shot was taken.

Out of Control?

I'm so excited, and I just can't hide it! I'm about to lose control and I think I like it!
—*The Pointer Sisters*

With the possible exception of the situation that the Pointer Sisters sing about, it is usually better to be in control. This is especially true of computers, since, as every moviemaker knows, computers running amok can threaten the universe. In the programming world, control includes:

- Maintaining just one copy of a utility, even if it is used in several programs
- Saving a working version of a program while you program enhancements
- Preventing accidental changes to code

Here are some utilities to help you overcome the version control blues.

Hack Facts

Simple Version Control
James Shaw
9423 Fontainebleau Blvd.
#225
Miami, FL 33172
CIS: 72117,615
21,746 bytes
Free
VCONTROL.ZIP

You can achieve the minimal level of control by using the Simple Version Control software utility suite. It consists of just four small programs: PUT for updates, GET for read-only retrieval, LOCK for writeable retrieval, and VIEW to locate older versions. The utilities are hard-coded to use the ARJ compression utility (included on the CD-ROM and described in Chapter 5). Author James Shaw explains in the rather perfunctory docs that ARJ has all the functionality he needs; he just wanted something to automate the rather complex ARJ switches and a way to set the archive to Read-Only so he wouldn't accidentally change or erase it. Use these little utilities in a batch file to get the functionality that Shaw has found adequate for his projects. For simple control measures, this suite automates the task very nicely. It's also free—need we say more?

Hack Facts

Quick, Patch It
Version 1.3
Brad Huggins
P.O. Box 1102
Cordova TN 38018
CIS: 771044,1726
30,817 bytes
Shareware: $10
QPATCH13.ZIP

Brad Huggins' "Quick, Patch It" utility is a sort of quick-dry spackle for modified code. Huggins wrote it to help in a situation most programmers have encountered in one form or another more than once. Your new, wizard program goes into circulation or wide beta, and someone installs and tries it. The next day you get a call. It seems the installation went fine, though it took two hours and ate 45MB of hard disk space. But guess what—there's a bug! Any suggestions?

Such calls are easier to handle when they don't come in at 3:00 A.M., but whatever the time, assuming you can find and fix the bug, you'll need some way to install only the changed parts of the software. You don't want to ask your potential customers to spend another two hours watching the floppy light turn on and off.

Brad Higgins created this tool to make a "patch" disk with only the changes and additions made from one version to the next. Quick, Patch It requires you to copy your program to another directory before making your changes. When you are finished, Quick, Patch It compares the two directories to create the patch disk. It's a pain-free process that both you and your users will come to love.

Hack Facts

Shareware Tracker
Version 3.11
RMH Computer Services
P.O. Box 657
Beech Grove IN 46107-0657
317-782-9903
BBS: 317-784-2147
CIS: 73567,1547
RIME: ->5056
447,187 bytes
Shareware: $29
SWT311.ZIP

Project yourself now into a situation where you have a viable piece of software that other people actually want. This is what developers dream of. But you realize if you don't swim, you'll sink. To put it another way, things not developing...are dead. So you don't stop working on your successful program.

This leads to other problems. How will you track who has copies of what, so you can send updates? The "back of an envelope" approach won't cut it, especially for the IRS (which gets very interested when a successful new program makes its way into the market). Shareware Tracker by RMH Computer Services is a fine program that takes care of tracking and many more aspects of program management, all with a very professional user interface.

14

Tip

If you call The Roadhouse BBS for support with Shareware Tracker (use the number given in the Hack Facts box), sign on as RMH COMPUTERS, password SERVICES, to avoid all the first-time-user questions. While you're there, look for other nifty RMH programs to try.

it's best to start using the Shareware Tracker early in your development project, *before* you send your program out on its own. The program can help manage the entire development effort. It will keep track of your expenses and income, by program (what? you don't develop or market more than one program at a time?). It will track your submissions to dealers, BBSes, information services and the like. It will track your registered users. It will prepare merged mailings and print the labels. It's an entire office-automation system, sculpted specifically to help the small-office software programmer. This gem will keep a lot of potential chaos safely at bay.

Next Up

Tip

You can leave tips, advice on upgrading this book, or other messages for Craig Menefee at:

CompuServe: 73267,3243
American Online: CMenefee
Delphi: Craig Menefee
Internet: cmenefee@aol.com
or craigmenefee@delphi.com

This final chapter has wrapped up the text portion of our book. The appendices that follow contain procedures for accessing the CD-ROM and its contents. Start with the instructions in Appendix A. If you have trouble finding the file you seek, look in Appendix B for a chapter-by-chapter listing of the CD-ROM's contents. If there's anything not included that you'd find extremely useful, please let us know. Your input will help us upgrade the product in its next release.

Happy hacking!

011010 11000110 0011010 11001001 100010001

)11010 11000110 0011010 11001001 100010001

0011010 11001001 100010001

4 part

Appendices

A

Accessing the Goodies

To try the CD-ROM front-end software, follow the procedure in "Installing Programs the Easy Way" (on this page).

The files on the CD-ROM are organized according to the book chapter in which they are described. For example, the Qmodem Test Drive program described in Chapter 3 is on the CD-ROM in the directory \CHAP3, the Chapter 4 program Qedit Advanced is in \CHAP4, and so forth. To extract a specific file, the simplest approach is to use the "front-end" supplied with the CD-ROM. This software is very well-behaved and easy to use. It will not automatically plant any unwanted files on your hard disk, and will always let you choose where to extract a file.

Installing Programs the Easy Way

The easiest way to use the book's CD-ROM is to take advantage of the supplied front end program. It's absurdly easy to use, but here's a step-by-step anyway, just for quick review:

1. *Locate the subdirectory for the program you want:* Each program described in the book's text is stored in the equivalent directory on the CD-ROM. Programs in Chapter 3 are in \CHAP3, programs in Chapter 4 are in \CHAP4, and so on. The menu enhances this simple system by describing the contents of each subdirectory on the right side of the menu.

2. *Identify the filename:* Files on the CD-ROM are identified by distribution filename in the associated Hack Facts box or, where there is none, in the body of the text. Or you can look in Appendix B, "What's On the CD-ROM," where each filename is listed by chapter number, along with a brief description of what the program does.
3. *Log onto your CD-ROM drive:* The actual drive letter is determined when the CD-ROM drivers are loaded at boot time or from the command line. It will typically be the next letter up from your last hard drive or RAM drive.
4. *Enter the command* **GO**: GO.BAT is a one-line batch file that loads the program VIEW.EXE, which is actually the front-end program itself. Both GO.BAT and VIEW.EXE are located in the root directory of the CD-ROM. Hackers, feel free to use the command **VIEW** instead of **GO**. (Hey, GO.BAT is just there because two letters are easier to enter than four.)
5. *Select a subdirectory:* The light bar will highlight a subdirectory in the range of \CHAP3, where the first program was described in the book, through \CHAP14, the final chapter. Use the cursor keys to highlight the directory you want. When the appropriate chapter subdirectory is highlighted, press ENTER. The screen will change to show a selection of distribution filenames stored in that subdirectory.
6. *Select a file:* Move the cursor down to the desired file, and press ENTER.
7. *Specify a destination:* The front end will display a default destination drive and directory for the selected file. Change this default value if desired, then press ENTER.
8. At this point the program will extract member files from the selected distribution program into the drive/directory you specified in Step 7. (In the case of a self-extracting file, it will be copied to the target drive/directory rather than extracted.) If the destination directory doesn't yet exist, the program will create it. Once the files have been extracted or copied, the front-end will log to that directory and then exit to the DOS prompt. At this point you can refer to any README or DOC files for instructions on using or installing the program.

Tip

If your program was self-extracting (a file ending with an .EXE extension), type in the filename and press ENTER to finish the extraction process. Some of the distribution files have "nested" archive files inside. Use UNZIP or PKUNZIP to extract any nested ZIP files, or PKUNPAK to extract any nested ARC files, and then check the README or DOC files for further instructions.

Accessing the Files Directly

To use the files on the CD-ROM without benefit of the supplied front end, start by putting some archive-unpacking software somewhere on your hard disk—preferably somewhere on the Path, or at least pointed to by a batch file. Here's an easy way to get what you need:

1. Log onto the CD-ROM drive
2. Enter the command **CD \UTILS**
3. Copy the programs UNZIP.EXE and PKUNPAK.EXE to a utility directory that is included in your PATH= statement (for example, C:\UTIL)

You can now issue a command of the form **CD \CHAP***n* (where *n* represents the number of a chapter) followed by **DIR** to locate the file you need. Here's a bit more on how the CD-ROM files are stored.

ZIP Files

These files have all been compressed using PKZIP version 2.04G. To decompress them directly, first copy the archive file to the directory where you plan to use the program or the files it contains. Then use UNZIP (see below) to decompress the files in the archive.

Using UNZIP.EXE

You'll find UNZIP.EXE in the \UTILS directory of the CD-ROM, ready to use. Copy it to a directory on your hard drive, preferably one that is on your path, so you won't have to read it from the CD-ROM every time you need it. (CD-ROMs are slow.) Then uncompress the ZIP file using a command of the form

UNZIP *[Drive:\Dir\Filename]*

where *Drive:* is the drive letter of your CD-ROM drive, *Dir* is the directory (*Chap3*, for example) on the CD-ROM where the target ZIP file is located, and *Filename* is the name of the ZIP file.

Self-Extracting (SFX) Files

Self-extracting or SFX files and programs have an .EXE extension. To unpack these files directly, first create and log into the subdirectory where you plan to use them. Then simply enter the full pathname of the target SFX distribution file, in this form:

Drive:\Dir\Filename

Making Sense of IZXTQLTL.ZIP

The DOS 8-plus-3 file naming conventions lead to some downright weird filenames. It's one of several things the Mac crowd hates about DOS. The limits of that 11-character filename limit get quite vexing in collections of cryptically named archive files. When you go prowling the CD-ROM for a specific program, here are some tips to make the hunt easier.

The name of a program's archive file will almost always be derived from the program itself, but the name will only occasionally be identical. The Buffit screen recall utility may be in BUFFIT.ZIP, for example, but the Qmodem telecomm program is in QM452TD.ZIP (for "Qmodem v. 4.52 Test Drive")—a much less obvious name.

If the name of the file you need doesn't jump off the screen at you, try scanning the file listings in Appendix B. They're organized alphabetically by chapter, which should make it easier to narrow the search. If you still don't make a connection, check the Hack Facts boxes or program descriptions in the text of this book. There, you'll find the actual distribution filename for each program included on the CD-ROM.

B

What's on the CD-ROM

The table in this appendix has names and brief descriptions for all the files and programs on the CD-ROM included with this book. When looking for a file, it's probably easiest to use the installation software on the CD-ROM (see Appendix A, "Accessing the Goodies"). You can also check the corresponding CD-ROM directory for a program's ZIP or EXE file and copy it directly to the hard drive directory where you want to install the program. All files that are not self-extracting are ZIP files created by PKZIP 2.04G.

Program Files Included on the CD-Rom

Note

The following list begins with Chapter 3, where the first of the book's CD-ROM programs are described.

Chapter 3: Walking the Wires

COMMO	ZIP	{COMMO}: telecommunications; macro-operated, flexible.
DRWY222	ZIP	Doorway: remote access for telecommunications, BBS programs.
DSZ	ZIP	Zmodem by Omen Technology: fast, reliable file transfers.
DSZBG	ZIP	Background and information docs for Zmodem, DSZ, Ymodem, etc.
DSZEXE	ZIP	.EXE version of DSZ.COM; minor differences.
DSZNEW	ZIP	Information specific to the 2-94 edition of DSZ.
HS121	ZIP	HS/Link: fast, reliable, two-way file transfer.
JT	ZIP	JaxTalk: gnat-sized comm program; a functional novelty.
LYNC30	EXE	Lync: telecommunications; small memory needs, great for limited iron.
QM452TD	ZIP	Qmodem Test Drive: telecommunications; full-featured, powerful.
TH331	ZIP	TinyHost BBS: a minimal but very capable host program.
THP111	ZIP	TinyHost Plus: TinyHost enhanced with automatic file transfers, more stats, etc.
TINYTERM	ZIP	TinyTerm: telecommunications; small, capable, great for laptops, etc.

Chapter 4: Programmer Friendly

ASAVITV3	ZIP	Automatic file saver: TSR program for use with editors, etc.
BFP214A	ZIP	Back and Forth Professional: task switcher, fully enabled trial version.
BFP214B	ZIP	Help and support files for Back and Forth Professional.
BH_NGS	ZIP	Cbrief macro guides (Norton Guides format).
BOXER60A	ZIP	Boxer: text editor; powerful, many features (colorize keywords, etc.).
NEWKEY54	ZIP	NewKey: keyboard macro program; many powerful features.

QEDIT3	ZIP	Qedit: text editor; longtime programmers' favorite—a shareware classic.
RB14	ZIP	Rainbow: lets you colorize keywords in any text editor.
TDE32A	ZIP	Thomson-Davis Editor: powerful, PD, with full source code.
VDE165B	ZIP	A pure ANSI version of the VDE text editor, for less than 100% IBM-compatibles.
VDE172	ZIP	VDE: text editor; small, fast, with near-word-processor power.
WCED18C	ZIP	Command editor; aliasing plus UNIX-like command completion.

Chapter 5: Data Compression and Encryption

ARJ241	EXE	File compressor; super-reliable and flexible.
CHK4COMP	ZIP	File management utility; checks for compressed executables.
ENCRYPT	ZIP	Encrypts files; turns user password into long encryption key.
LHA213	EXE	File compressor; free, from "Yoshi" of Japan; excellent.
LZESHELL	ZIP	English-language shell for LZEXE91.
LZEXE91	ZIP	Executable file compressor; free, from France.
MAKEREAD	COM	Turns text files up to 60K into scrollable COM files.
PK204G	EXE	PKZIP: Katz file compression utilities; the industry standard.
PKL115	EXE	PKLite: executable file compressor from Phil Katz.
SHEZ97	ZIP	Shell EZ for compressed files: a power user's front end.
TINY39	ZIP	TINYPROG: an executable file compressor for developers.
UNLZEXE5	ZIP	Expands LZEXE-compressed executables; supported by LZESHELL.
ZC210	ZIP	ZipComment: comment manager for ZIP files; minimalist, simple, fast, free.
ZOO210	EXE	ZOO: file compressor; great cross-platform flexibility.

Chapter 6: Disk-O Magic

3DRVS260	ZIP	3_Drives: lets you mix and match 3-4 drives or controller types.
AUTOR11	ZIP	AutoRestore: manages restoring of Stowaway'd files.
BRINF126	ZIP	BackInfo/RestInfo hard disk rescue utility.
DEVLOD18	COM	Devload: loads device drivers (e.g., CD-ROM) from command line.
DQWIK110	ZIP	DiskQwik: doubles many IDE controller data transfer rates.
DRVPAD	ZIP	Drive padder; reserves drive letter block for SCSI device use.
DUGIDE10	ZIP	IDE drive snooper; reports IDE disk characteristics.
EDDY7C	ZIP	Eddy: directory editor; manages files, dates, attributes, more.
FIXMBR21	ZIP	FixMBR: hard drive integrity/recovery management.
HDTST535	ZIP	HDTest: hard disk tester; a powerful shareware classic.
MEATHOOK	ZIP	Meathook: sidesteps SHARE violations on networks, in Windows.
PALERT24	ZIP	Palert: monitors available memory and disk space, EL reporting.
PARTED2F	ZIP	PartEd: partition table editor.
PREBACK	ZIP	Preback: backup reminder; reminds, even forces, regular backups.
PTQNUTIL	ZIP	Patriquin Utilities: the complete set in one ZIP file.
SHOWF251	ZIP	ShowFAT: maps drive's FAT in ASCII characters; FAT snooper.
SPKT451S	ZIP	Speedkit: Hyperdisk cache with screen, keyboard, and other utilities.
STOW220	ZIP	Stowaway: stores unused programs and files off the main drive.
ZIPZP715	ZIP	ZipZap: direct file/sector disk editor.

Chapter 7: Don't Forget Your Memory!

ASQ130	ZIP	ASQ: tutorial and system diagnostic/ snooper utility.
DMC35	ZIP	DMC: memory controller for TSRs and devices; best of its breed.
DOSM21	ZIP	DOSMAX: fine control over upper memory blocks.
FAKEHI	ZIP	Fakes HIMEM.SYS 4.0 driver for SMARTDRV.EXE on limited iron.
FL150	ZIP	FastLoad: read programs and data, from EMS/XMS, not disk.
HI-RAM	ZIP	HiRam: high memory manager; the original shareware release.
LGROOM	ZIP	LegRoom: task-switcher that uses minimum memory resources.
MAM1_09	ZIP	MAM (Memory Allocation Manager): superior mapping, flexible.
MEMKT202	ZIP	Memory Management Kit: optimizes 8088/80286 system; includes HRAM.
MSCAN	ZIP	MEMSCAN: scans and reports memory usage during program execution.
SRDSK205	ZIP	SRDISK: a dynamically resizable XMS/EMS RAM disk driver.
TLB-V230	ZIP	The Last Byte: fancy, downward compatible memory management.
TLBA230	ZIP	The Last Byte Advanced: utilities for the main TLB program.
TSRCOM35	ZIP	The classic TSR management utilities (Mark, Release, and more).

Chapter 8: Ports of Call

COMCHK18	ZIP	CommChek: captures serial data for analysis and troubleshooting.
COMSET	ZIP	Non-TSR; makes COM 3&4 recognizable; changes port addresses.
COMST12	ZIP	COMSET: Installs COM3-4 in DOS BIOS area; enables access.

COMTAP21	ZIP	comTAP: serial comm line monitor, analyzer, and debugger.
CTSSPU13	ZIP	CTS Serial Port Utilities; snooper, monitor, and more.
CYBDRV11	ZIP	Cybercom: for Windows jumpers, a decent 16550 driver.
EASYNET	ZIP	EasyNet: connects two computers with null modem cables.
IOMON2	ZIP	IO Monitor: a comm port monitor with full source.
MODEMD52	ZIP	Modem Doctor: the ultimate modem diagnostic snooper utility.

Chapter 9: Taming the Wild Printer

AC12MUSC	ZIP	AccuMusic: a utility for printing sheet music.
CP42	ZIP	CodPr: formats and prints source code; useful and readable.
DJCLRFL	ZIP	DeskJet Color Cartridge Refill: refills your color cartridges.
DL110	ZIP	DownLoad: Downloads non-native fonts to a Laserjet/compatible printers.
DMP205	ZIP	DMP: a superior print spooler; can redirect to other resources.
DOCSM326	ZIP	DocSmash: saves paper; prints ASCII files 4+ to a page.
DSKVLP10	ZIP	DiskEnvelope: prints cutout jackets, with file lists, for 5 1/4" disks.
JPRT11	ZIP	Utility for printing Japanese characters.
KNOWBARS	ZIP	KnowBars: utility for printing TSR bar codes.
LPTMON10	ZIP	LPTMON: monitors activity on parallel ports.
NENSC113	ZIP	Nenscript: ASCII-to-PostScript format converter.
NJNLQ143	ZIP	NJNLQ: produces near-letter-quality output from 9-pin printers.
NPRN10	ZIP	NewPrint: file formatter and printing utility.

Chapter 10: A Bag of Other Goodies

2ALL_210	ZIP	2ALL: converts archived files from one format to another.
4DOS5A	ZIP	4DOS: a powerful, flexible COMMAND.COM replacement.
4DOS5B	ZIP	A complete computing environment for all 21 types of DOS.
4DOSBU	ZIP	Batch file and other 4DOS support utilities.
4DOSINF	ZIP	4DOS information file; evaluation aid.
AUTORD2	ZIP	AutoRead: a speedy file reader; includes automatic indexing and a lookup system.
BACKSOON	ZIP	A screen saver that accepts and displays messages from passers by.
BATMNU23	ZIP	BATMENU: adds terrific screen control and menus to batch files.
BUFFIT	ZIP	Buffit: a backscroller that captures scrolling text-mode screens.
CLIKIT	ZIP	Command Line Interface Toolkit: a suite of command line utilities.
DIRX	ZIP	A shell for detecting compressed executable files.
DMKIT	ZIP	DOS driver code for all major sound cards; quite flexible.
FAC171	ZIP	Find Area Code: fast, flexible, fuzzy text database searches.
FFF45	ZIP	Fast File Finder: fast and powerful; also a file manager.
GET25	ZIP	GET 2.5: environment and errorlevel batch services, complete with manual.
GET26U	ZIP	GET 2.6: GET upgrade. (Use the GET 2.5 manual.)
GRAB65	ZIP	Grab Plus: classic envelope addresser.
GRFWRK70	ZIP	Graphics Workshop: views, converts, edits, and prints graphics.
JRGN300	ZIP	The Jargon File: a comprehensive guide to Hackish culture.
KSONIC	EXE	KaleidoSonic: multimedia screen show; a DMKIT driver application.
NG_CLON	ZIP	A TSR hypertext reader for Norton Guides databases.

B

NG_DOS	ZIP	DHNG: a DOS Help database in Norton Guides format.
PCAT3B	ZIP	PC Catalog: keeps track of files and comments; includes many other options.
PCC21C	ZIP	Personal C Compiler: non-ANSI DeSmet C, fully functional.
PDMI30	ZIP	Pull Down Modem Information: a great modem troubleshooting tool.
PIGLATIN	ZIP	An AI language filter; translates text into Ig-pay Atin-lay.
POCK40	ZIP	PocketD, a small, powerful, colorized directory list utility and directory manager.
PWRBAT	ZIP	PowerBatch compiler: supports DOS, 4DOS, and NDOS command, and more.
RCALC	ZIP	A non-TSR calculator for programmer's using dec/hex/bin/oct expressions.
ROLLBACK	ZIP	Rollback: a screen backscroll utility; can handle graphics.
RV251	ZIP	RView: a fast archive viewer; redates, sorts, and more.
RVS	ZIP	RViewShell: a small, fast, archive management shell; windowed.
SCRSAVER	ZIP	Screen Saver: executes any specified DOS program.
SHROOM24	ZIP	SHROOM (SHellROOM): swaps application memory before shelling.
SKEY40	ZIP	Stackey: a powerful keyboard stuffer and batch file enhancer.
SKREST	ZIP	Support files for STACKEY; includes FILEKEY, a session automator.
ST101	ZIP	Screen Thief: a powerful, flexible screen capture program.
SW-46	ZIP	Screen Wizard: colorful screen control utility and batch file enhancer.
SWSAMP	ZIP	Examples of Screen Wizard batch file screens and automations.
TB323	ZIP	TurboBat: makes batch files into executible COM files.
TEE	ZIP	TEE: records program output; pipes to disk or console; includes source code.

Chapter 11: We Interrupt This Program

DOSREF33	ZIP	DISREF: a reference guide to DOS functions.
INTER39A	ZIP	Interrupt List: a reference guide to Interrupts.(File 1 Of 3.)
INTER39B	ZIP	(File 2.)
INTER39C	ZIP	(File 3.)
INTVUE15	ZIP	Intervue: a viewing program for INTERxx Lists.

Chapter 12: Video Wizardry

DETMODE	ZIP	C++ code for detecting video type.
DIR_RVID	ZIP	Restores part of screen with direct video.
DIR_SVID	ZIP	Saves part of screen with direct video.
DIR_WRIT	ZIP	Writes characters directly to video RAM.
FPCLIB36	ZIP	FlashPac C library: Directs video functions for fast screen I/O.
GETFREQ	ZIP	Determines video frequency of your monitor.
PHIRES	ZIP	Lets you use Hi-Res video modes (C).
PLSMA3	ZIP	Plasma display, with C source code.
PSK	ZIP	Programmer's Survival Kit: lots of routines.
SMOOTH	ARC	Assembly source for smooth scroller.
SV	ZIP	Set Video: includes Pascal source.
SVGKT4	ZIP	Super VGA/VESA test routines.
TAVID12	ZIP	Turbo Assembler video routines.
TAVIDEO	ZIP	Turbo C video routines.
TIFF_11B	ZIP	Tools for displaying TIFF images with VESA.
UVBE43	ZIP	A 32-bit universal VESA driver.
VESA32	ZIP	A 32-bit universal VESA driver.
VESAKB	ZIP	C++ source code for handling VESA monitors.
VESAMO	ZIP	C++ source for changing VESA modes.
VFAQ1	ZIP	A list of video manufacturers.
VIDID	ZIP	An assembler function for determining video type.
VIDTYP17	ZIP	Sets environment variable to video type.
VMODE2	ASM	Assembly code for changing video modes.
XLIB06	ZIP	X-mode graphics code (C).

Chapter 13: Down in the Bits

A86LIB3	ZIP	A86 Library: routines for use with the A86 assembler.
A86V370	ZIP	A86 macro assembler; includes source code, batch files, and library files.
ASMFLOW3	ZIP	AMSFLOW: tracks progress in ASM files; generates flow charts.
ASMFORM	ZIP	AMSFORM: formats ASM language files to readable code listings.
ASMLIB	ZIP	ASM-linkable subroutines, plus a nifty E16 editor.
ASMWIZ	ZIP	ASM small program subroutines; support for multiple assemblers.
C-UTIL	ZIP	Fast, UNIX-like utilities for DOS programmers, with source code.
CONCUR_C	ZIP	Context-switching ("concurrent") C programming module.
CPARSE	ZIP	CParse: command line parsing routines (source code).
CXREF3A	ZIP	C xref: tracks C modules and outputs, including global variables, etc.
D86V370	ZIP	D86: symbolic debugger: a companion debugger for A86 (or other assemblers).
DISATR11	ZIP	DISASTER: an interactive disassembler.
FUZZGEN	ZIP	Fuzzy logic search code generator and CASE tool.
MC141	ZIP	Micro-C compiler: fast and simple, with great documentation.
MD8610#1	ZIP	Masterful Disassember: for executables and machine instructions. The MD screen works much like a text editor; resulting code is labled and commented. (File 1 of 3.)
MD8610#2	ZIP	(File 2.)
MD8610#3	ZIP	(File 3.)
PPT100	ZIP	PPT: tracks and changes variables in different C modules.
SMALLC22	ZIP	C-language compiler; includes Small Assembler; fast.
SOSENG	ZIP	SOS-ENGINE: a debugger that tracks file input and output.

TSRCOLEC	ZIP	Several public domain TSR programs with code.
VISIONS2	ZIP	Visions: a C programmer's text-windowing library package.

Chapter 14: Hacker Graduation

AVTS	ZIP	ARIS Version Tracking System: low-cost version; a control/configuration management system.
GUI	ZIP	GUI library and tool kit for creating graphics-mode interfaces.
IMPRES26	ZIP	First Impression: menu- or script-driven installation program.
IPRO320	ZIP	Install-Pro: super customizable installation program.
MANUAL11	ZIP	SUPERMANual: automatically creates user manuals from code.
QINST2	ZIP	QUIK-INSTALL: creates customized, simple program installations.
QPATCH13	ZIP	Quick, Patch It: reinstalls only what's changed or updated.
SD233	ZIP	Screen Designer: a paintbrush-style program for DOS text mode.
SOURCE14	ZIP	SOURCE: a source code printing utility with keyword highlighting.
SWT311	ZIP	Shareware Tracker: an office system for shareware authors.
VCONTROL	ZIP	Simple Version Control: provides automatic backup of code revisions.

Index

0101001 1010011 011010 1010111 1010011 011010

A

B

C

D

I

J

K

L

M

N

O

P

T

U

X

Y

Z

About the CD-ROM

Disc Contents:

All of the programs listed in this book can be found on this CD-ROM. They are all DOS programs. The CD is organized in directories that correspond to the chapters in the book. Appendix B in the book lists all the files, in alphabetical order by chapter, with brief descriptions.

There is an install program on the CD that will move and unzip files of your choice to your choice of directories on your hard disk. To use this program, simply go into your CD drive and type **GO** at the prompt. A directory of the chapters will appear. From these you simply select the file you want to move, the destination and follow the menus. The file will be unzipped in the directory you select.

System Requirements:

Only a CD-ROM drive is required, though you should check to make sure you have plenty of space on your hard disk.

Using the CD:

To open the files we recommend that you use the program described above, which is located in the root directory of the CD. The programs are provided on the CD for your convenience; they include both free software and shareware. We have tested the programs and have concluded that they perform their function well. However, because they are shareware, we do not offer technical support for the individual programs, nor can we vouch for their robustness. Each shareware program includes a screen informing you of registration fees and technical support policies. You can also locate the shareware developers for support by looking in the Hack Facts boxes throughout the book. Remember to read the README files. Remember also to register any shareware on the CD that you decide to use.

For more instructions on the use of the CD, see Appendix A, "Accessing the Goodies." If you find any problems with the CD media or with the file structure on your CD, call Osborne **McGraw-Hill** at 800-227-0900.

WARNING: BEFORE OPENING THE DISC PACKAGE, CAREFULLY READ THE TERMS AND CONDITIONS OF THE CD-ROM WARRANTY ON THE FOLLOWING PAGE.

Limited Warranty:

Osborne **McGraw-Hill** warrants the physical compact disc enclosed herein to be free of defects in materials and workmanship for a period of sixty days from the purchase date. If Osborne **McGraw-Hill** receives written notification within the warranty period of defects in materials or workmanship, and such notification is determined by Osborne **McGraw-Hill** to be correct, Osborne **McGraw-Hill** will replace the defective disc.

The entire and exclusive liability and remedy for breach of this Limited Warranty shall be limited to replacement of defective disc and shall not include or extend to any claim for or right to cover any other damages, including but not limited to, loss of profit, data, or use of the software, or special, incidental, or consequential damages or other similar claims, even if Osborne **McGraw-Hill** has been specifically advised of the possibility of such damages. In no event will Osborne **McGraw-Hill**'s liability for any damages to you or any other person ever exceed the lower of the suggested list price or actual price paid for the license to use the software, regardless of any form of the claim.

OSBORNE, A DIVISION OF McGRAW-HILL, INC., SPECIFICALLY DISCLAIMS ALL OTHER WARRANTIES, EXPRESS OR IMPLIED, INCLUDING, BUT NOT LIMITED TO, ANY IMPLIED WARRANTY OF MERCHANTABILITY OR FITNESS FOR A PARTICULAR PURPOSE. Specifically, Osborne **McGraw-Hill** makes no representation or warranty that the software is fit for any particular purpose, and any implied warranty of merchantability is limited to the sixty-day duration of the Limited Warranty covering the physical disc only (and not the software), and is otherwise expressly and specifically disclaimed.

This limited warranty gives you specific legal rights; you may have others, which may vary from state to state. Some states do not allow the exclusion of incidental or consequential damages, or the limitation on how long an implied warranty lasts, so some of the above may not apply to you.